LEICA R4 REFLEX MANUAL

by Theo Kisselbach

English edition by Brian Tompkins, A.R.P.S.

HOVE FOTO BOOKS

FIRST EDITION
First Printing   October 1981 German
First Printing   October 1981 English

ISBN 0-906447-12-7

Published by
HOVE FOTO BOOKS
34, Church Road,
Hove, East Sussex,
United Kingdom.

U.K. Distribution
ARGUS BOOKS

Argus Books Ltd.,
Argus House,
14, St. James Road,
Watford,
Hertfordshire,
United Kingdom.

Printed by Design & Print, Shoreham-by-Sea, West Sussex, United Kingdom.

CONTENTS

EDITOR'S NOTE

For as long as I can remember the name Theo Kisselbach has been synonymous with the Leica camera. I still have on my bookshelf the 1967 edition of the 'Leica Book'. The well thumbed pages of this manual remind me that as an impoverished schoolboy it served to generate an interest in the Leica camera that has remained with me ever since.

In the production of this manual in its English edition special thanks are due particularly to Janet Taylor, B.A. (Oxon.) for her time spent on translating the original manuscript. Also an enormous debt is owed to Ann Tompkins, B.A. Hons., R. Dip., A.D.B.(Ed.) and to Sandy Robins, L.C. for their many hours spent in the production of this manual.

B.T.

ACKNOWLEDGEMENTS

The Publishers would like to thank Ernst Leitz, Wetzlar for permission to use their registered trade marks such as "Leica", "Summicron", "Elmar" etc.

FOREWORD

In my hands I have a miracle of modern technology, the Leica R4. After some fifty years experience of using the Leica camera, at last with the advent of modern technical advancement it has been possible to produce a camera which is able to undertake any photographic assignment with the minimum of fuss and the maximum amount of efficiency. All photographic problems are at once resolved, or at least the means to solve them are at hand. The aim of this book is to enable the R4 user to extend his photographic experience and how this latest product of Leitz can help in the achievement of this.

The camera's automatic functions react immediately to changing circumstances, thus enabling the photographer to concentrate on the subject and make the exposure at precisely the right moment. The problem of exposure under constantly varying lighting conditions has been completely eliminated. The slightest change in the intensity of light will be immediately and automatically compensated for. The Leica R4 is the basis of an extensive universal photographic system. A range of superbly designed lenses are incorporated within this system. These lenses range from an all embracing wide angle of 15mm to a distance bridging 800mm. This enables all photographic assignments to be undertaken. Also contained within this system are a range of accessories including motor drive, power winders, micro and macro photography accessories which together provide a photographic system capable of undertaking a wide range of assignments.

The speed of operation and reliability of the photographic system is not only recognised by the enthusiastic amateur but is relied upon by the hard working professional. The Leica R4 is a photographic tool, a camera which will allow the photographer to develop and expand his photographic horizons and because of the systems versatility will never impose restrictions on the photographer's development. As an analogy a violin could be used. Put a Stradivarius into the hands of a competent amateur and the resulting music will be acceptable. Put the same instrument into the hands of a great virtuoso and the instrument's capability and the player's ability will combine to produce music which is splendid. This is also true of the Leica R4. By means of its automatic functions it can provide the beginner with a camera which will ensure that every negative or transparency is perfectly exposed. Put it into the hands of the gifted photographer and it will allow him the freedom, the control, to produce the masterpiece.

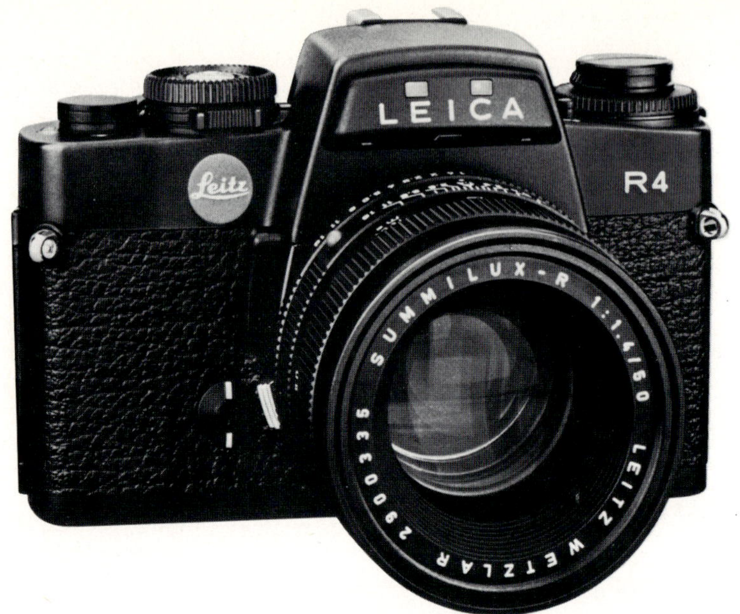

Leica R4: Black Chrome.

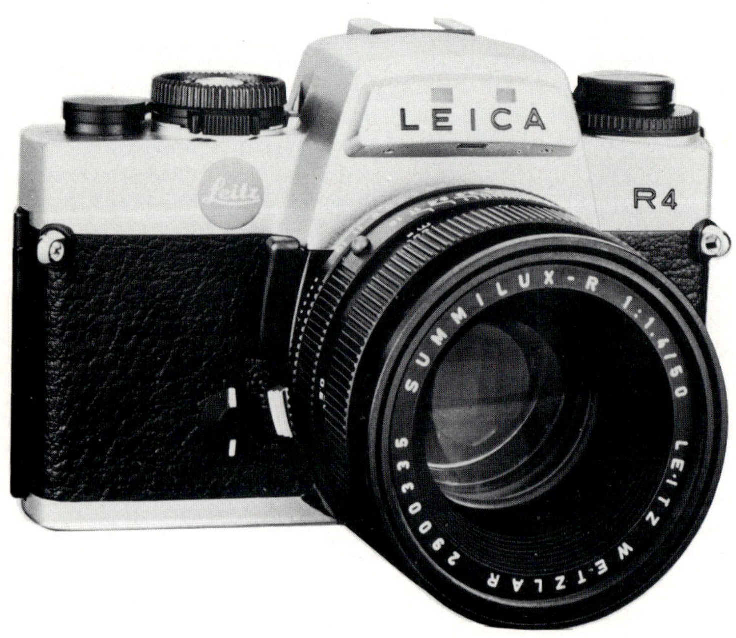

Leica R4: Silver Chrome.

PREFACE

Any reader of a manual on a new photographic product would expect the book to contain precise operating information and the uses and applications that the camera can be used for. However, it should be born in mind that any reader of a textbook concerning a new car, whilst being able to describe precisely the operating functions would never be able to instil in the reader the art of driving. This can only be achieved one way, that is by practice. This is also true of a photographic manual. The reader having once mastered the mechanical operations of the camera can only improve his photographic skills by practice. Although not wasted, time spent reading photographic books can never replace time spent practising the photographic art. Because of its mechanical and optical efficiency the new Leica R4 must be the choice of a discerning photographer. It will allow the newcomer to acquire and master basic skills and from there develop them. Or it will allow the experienced amateur or professional to polish those skills which have already been acquired. At whatever level the Leica R4 will enable the photographer to advance. Obviously in an ideal world I would prefer it if I could chat with you on an informal basis, person to person, however this is not possible and the media of the written word becomes the only practical solution. However I would remind the reader that to obtain the maximum benefit from a book he should read it in a critical fashion, be guided by it but adapt the ideas and suggestions to suit his particular requirements. In this way he will obtain the maximum benefit from the book. However one thing that I would stress above all others and that is in spite of the danger of repeating myself. It is no fallacy that practice makes perfect. Constant practice will induce familiarity with the Leica R4 and its associated system so that alongside the automatic features of the camera will be the automatic response of the photographer. Operational sequences should be established to suit the individual and once these have been established then no photographic opportunity will be missed because of hesitancy on the part of the user. The camera is always ready to respond, practice will ensure that the photographer is too. All metering modes should be used during this practice and please do not forget that it is also important to practice with the camera set to manual operation.

Despite the advances in photographic technology it remains the photographer's perogative to select and choose his subject. The basic process of photography is often linked to the human process of seeing. The lens of the camera works in exactly the same way as the lens in the human eye. The auto-diaphragm is represented by the iris. The sensitive emulsion by the retina behind the eye. However there are basic yet fundamental differences. The human process of seeing is automatically and constantly monitored by brain functions. The brain will compensate for subject movement so that the object in view remains stationary. Within small limitations the focal length of the human eye can change. Automatic compensations are made for changes in scale and perspective.

Scale and the relative proportional scale of one subject to another is of paramount importance and one which should never be neglected by the aware photographer, practice using the available lenses whilst viewing the same

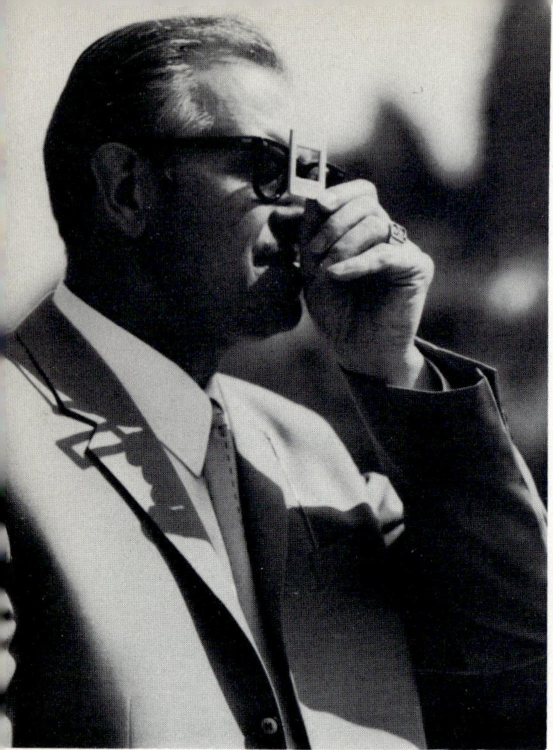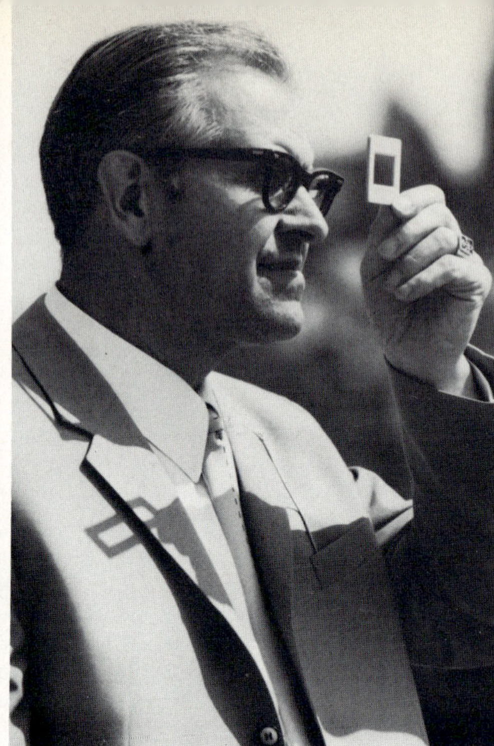

Using the empty slide holder to aid picture composition.

subject, balancing the scale of foreground against the scale of background, in an attempt to achieve a well balanced picture. The dynamic effects of dominant foreground achieved with the ultra wide angle, the compressive capabilities of the long focal lengths, all have their place and the seeing photographer will utilise the individual characteristics of different focal length lenses to achieve his desired effect. One point which I feel requires clarification is that the use of different focal length lenses on the same subject taken from the same viewpoint will not alter the perspective of the subject, it will merely alter the scale. The use of different focal length lenses for the beginner or indeed sometimes for the experienced photographer can be bewildering. However I can suggest a simple device which will be found most useful and will allow the user to judge accurately the focal length of the lens required for each subject. Obtain a standard 5 x 5 slide transparency. Holding this slide at 50mm in front of one eye with the other closed will enable the viewer to look through the 24 x 36mm aperture. The view obtained will closely approximate the angle of view of the camera's standard 50mm lens, reducing the distance between the eye and the viewer will demonstrate the view of the wide angle lens, increasing the distance will correspondingly demonstrate the angle of view of lenses which are longer than standard. The aware photographer should make a practice of carrying this small device at all times even when not engaged in the pursuit of his photographic interests.

It is an aid with distinct advantages and will enable the photographer to develop a seeing eye. The distance at which the viewer is held relates to the focal length of the lens. Balance and composition can be easily judged. It will often be found that the most effective composition is achieved with lenses having longer focal lengths than the standard 50mm, long lenses enable the user to omit extraneous details from his subjects. It will be found by practice that it is the omission of extraneous details which makes the picture. Photograph and concentrate on the actual subject. Avoid the beginners mistake of trying to photograph everything with one exposure. Having read the above the photographic beginner will obviously question the need for lenses of wider than standard focal length. After all if the object of photography is to concentrate and breakdown subjects to the bare essentials why have lenses which encompass a staggering angle of view of 180°. It is because lenses of these focal length are particularly important to photographers engaged in architectural and technical fields. Also the aware landscape and pictorial photographer finds them particularly suitable. Lenses of extremely short focal length are difficult to use effectively but once mastered can achieve results impossible other than by their use. Aside from their pictorial use the photographer will realise that the possession of lenses of differing focal lengths is extremely important to the user of the 24 x 36mm miniature format. To achieve exhibition prints every square millimeter of the negative is important. The subject must fill the frame in order to achieve this the appropriate focal length lens should be used. In my many years of photographic experience I have encountered people who, apart from practising photographers have expressed an interest and would like to know how the camera mechanics and electronics function. There are people who have a keen interest in highly technical subjects. For instance optics and optical glass manufacture. In fact subjects of a highly complex nature which are not essentially important and do not enable the photographer to take better pictures. It is of more importance that the photographer has a sound grasp of essential functions of the camera in an operating sense. The ability to control the effects of these functions is of more importance than knowing how these functions are effected. It is not the object of this book to deal with these highly technical subjects and I have tried to keep them to a minimum. On the following pages you will find a description of the Leica R4, handling and operational tips. The terms are those used in the Leitz introduction brochure as it would not be sensible to use terms differing from those used previously. Leitz have produced excellent brochures and instruction leaflets and I have considered whether I could refer in some instances to these publications, but unfortunately this would lead to certain difficulties in practice if the appropriate publications were not available to the reader. In fact it is often a practical advantage to read several publications, whilst they may be describing the same operation, they will invariably describe it in a slightly different manner, thus enabling the reader to obtain a total grasp. Please remember in the section dealing with the handling of the Leica R4 we must understand that the mental processes must be interpreted into a physical response and that this can only be achieved by constant practice until this complicated function of physical and mental response becomes absolutely instinctive.

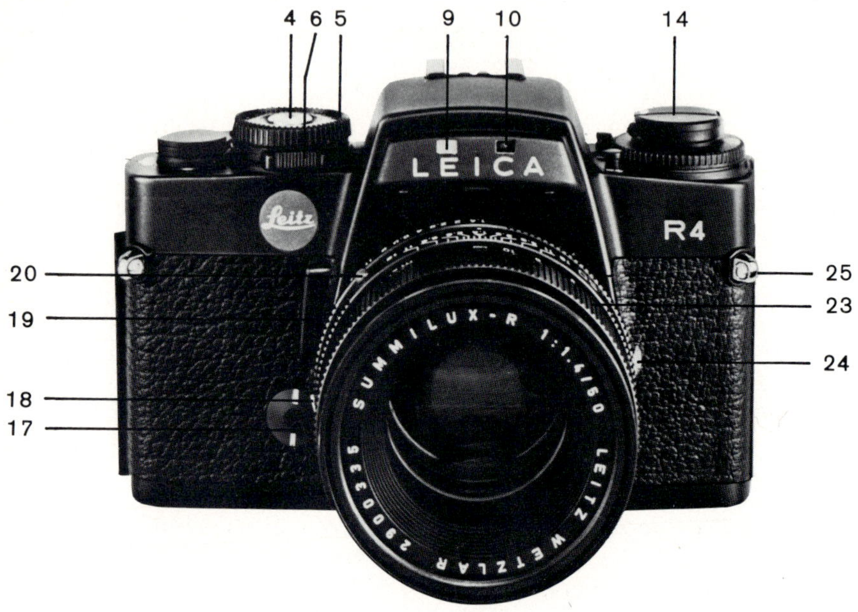

1. Film counter.	17. Self timer.
2. Film transport indicator.	18. Lens locking release.
3. Rapid film transport lever.	19. Depth of field preview lever.
4. Shutter release and cable release thread.	20. Lens locating button.
	21. Diaphragm setting ring.
5. Shutter speeds.	22. Depth of field scales, fixed ring.
6. Programme selector.	23. Focusing ring.
7. Indicator for programme setting.	24. Flash contact.
8. Accessory shoe with flash contacts.	25. Carrying strap lugs.
	26. Film identification window.
9. Illuminator for aperture setting display.	27. Viewfinder blind control.
	28. Viewfinder.
10. Self timer indicating LED.	29. Battery compartment cover.
11. Film speed setting lock.	30. Tripod socket.
12. Light diode for battery tester.	31. Rewind button.
13. Film speed setting lock.	32. Contacts for motor winder or drive unit.
14. Rewind handle.	
15. Film speed setting rin.	33. Motor drive and winder drive connection.
16. Exposure override.	

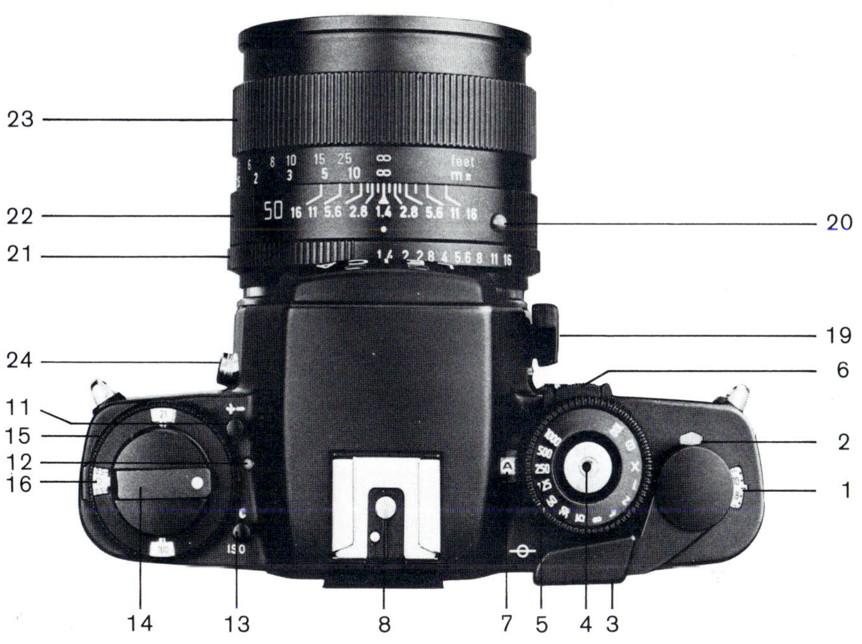

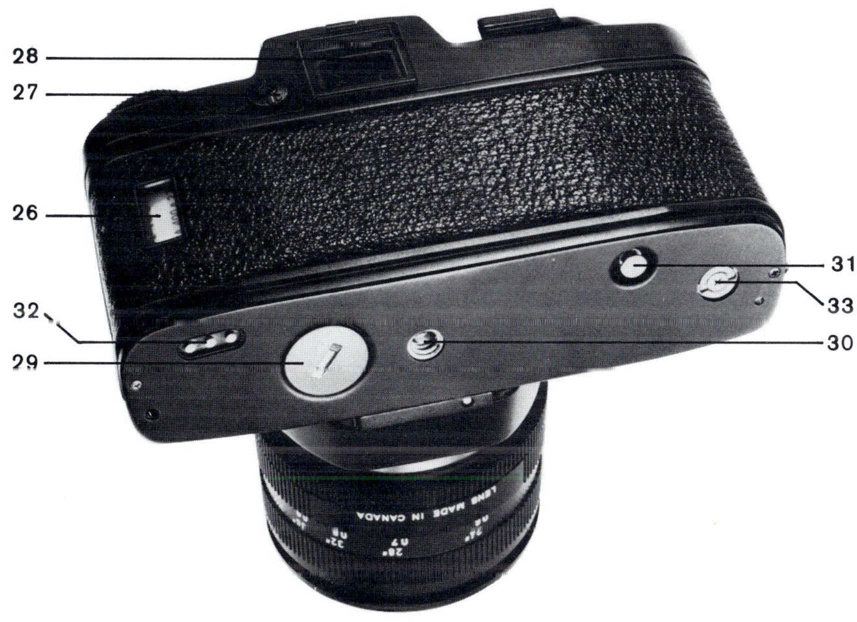

THE CAMERA

INSERTING AND TESTING BATTERIES

Cameras with electronic shutter and .exposure control will obviously only function correctly providing that the batteries contain sufficient energy. On the Leica R4 two silver oxide batteries of 1.55 volts are used. They are placed in the battery compartment located in the camera base plate. It is of the utmost importance that these batteries are clean, the battery compartment is readily locked or unlocked with the aid of a small coin. Insert the batteries in accordance with the symbols provided. Batteries only have a limited life, in order to check their performance press the test button (13) on the top left hand side of the camera, operate the test knob for approximately five seconds, note the intensity of light produced by the LEDs, if this intensity varies or fluctuates during the five seconds it indicates the imminent exhaustion of the batteries and that they should be replaced immediately. Batteries can also fail because of oxidisation, if this occurs they should be removed and cleaned, together with the appropriate contacts. If on subsequent reinsertion the battery tester still indicates substandard performance then of course replacement is necessary. Expended batteries should be immediately removed from the camera, even if replacements are not to hand, this action of course renders the automatic features of the camera inoperative. However photographs can still be taken using the mechanical facilities provided, 1/100th of a second and B exposure times. The life of a standard battery, given that they are stored at normal temperatures and subject to normal usage is given as two to three years by the manufacturer, higher storage temperatures and heavy usage will obviously shorten these times considerably, it is therefore important that fresh batteries are always carried, in order to facilitate this procedure small cases are available which attach to the camera carrying strap thus providing a convenient method of ensuring a readily available supply without inconvenience. Suitable batteries of the same capacity and performance are also used in hearing aids and watches. The brand names of the various producers providing a suitable product is contained in the following list:

Manufacturer	For cameras	For hearing-aids	For watches
EVER READY	—	S76E	—
MALLORY	MS 76 H	MS 76 H	10 L 14
MAXELL	SR 44 F	—	—
NATIONAL	G 13	G 13	—
RAY-O-VAC	RS 76 G	RS 76 G	—
UCAR	EXP 76	S-76 E	Nr.357
VARTA	V 76 PX	V 76 HS	Nr.541

When using the Leica R4 in conjunction with the motor or film winder, the power is provided in a different manner. The batteries contained within the camera base plate become non functional and the automatic electronic functions of the camera are powered from the battery pack contained within the motor or power winder. Test this power supply switch on the exposure

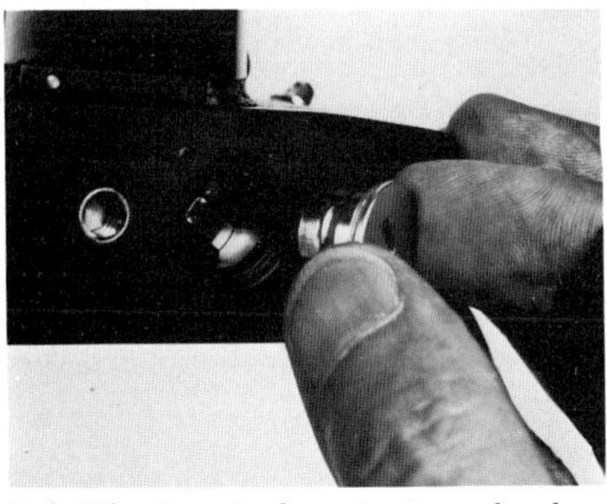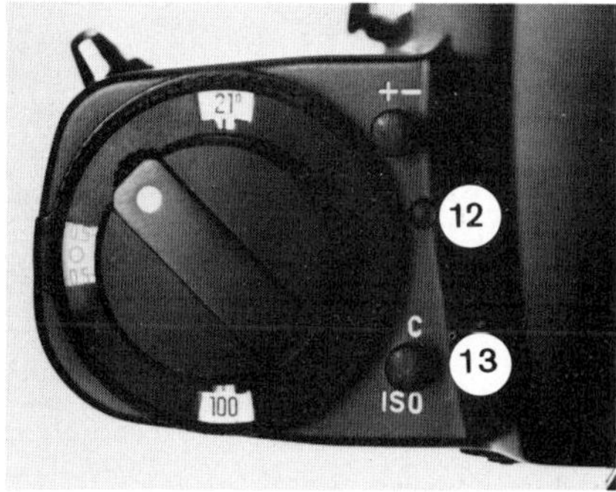

Left: When inserting batteries ensure that the polarity is correct. Right: When testing the batteries operate the test button for approximately 5 seconds.

meter system by lightly pressing down the shutter release or by pressing the locking button on the programme selector (6).

GENERAL TIPS

Batteries from different manufacturers and those in different states of discharge should never be used together, the answer is to carry a fresh reserve. New reserve batteries should be kept at home. To maintain them properly they should be stored in their original containers in the vegetable compartment of a refrigerator, this prolongs their shelf life. Never throw used batteries into a fire, it is possible that they will explode. Also note that the batteries are not rechargeable.

INSERTING THE LENS

Leica R4 lenses are interchanged without regard to the lens setting. Grip the lens by the fixed ring (22) holding the lens in the right hand align the red dot with the bayonet lock release catch, insert the lens in this position and turn in a clockwise direction, a distinct click indicates that the lens is securely located.

REMOVING THE LENS

Grip the lens by the fixed ring (22) depress the bayonet locking catch located on the camera (18) turn the lens anticlockwise and remove. It is always advisable to interchange lenses in the shade or at least avoiding the direct rays of the sun.

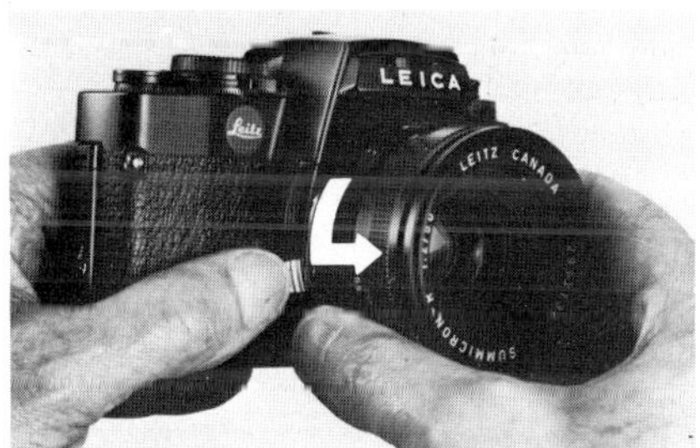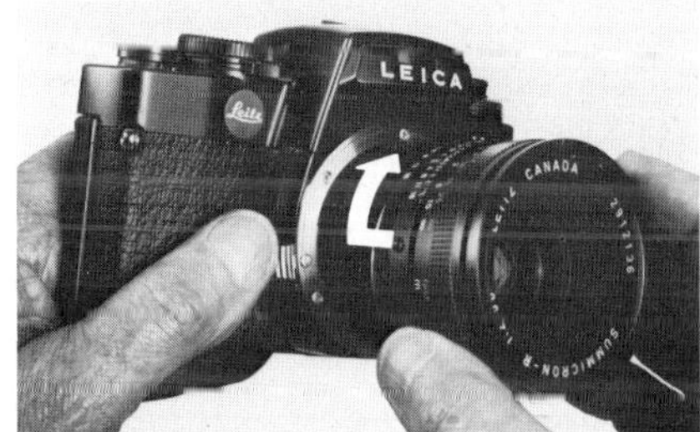

Removing and inserting the lens.

FILM LOADING

The film loading sequence is extremely simple and quickly mastered, but from bitter experience I would advise that this operation is never carried out other than by the photographer. Of all the problems that can arise from carrying out this operation incorrectly the jamming of the film transport mechanism is the most dangerous. Practice loading and unloading with dummy film. Carry out this operation in accordance with the instructions. Once mastered this operation will become totally automatic and films will be correctly loaded even in the most hurried situations. To check if the camera is loaded the rewind knob should be rotated, if no film is present in the camera the photographer will be readily aware by the lack of friction. The Leica R4 is also provided with an inspection window through which the cassette can be observed. This window is also used for determining which type of film is loaded. Only film cartridges employing standard type spools can be used, the all metal cassettes provided by Leitz for earlier cameras cannot be used. Never leave films lying about in full sunlight. It should be made a standard procedure that on inserting a film the appropriate setting (15) on the film speed dial is adjusted to suit.

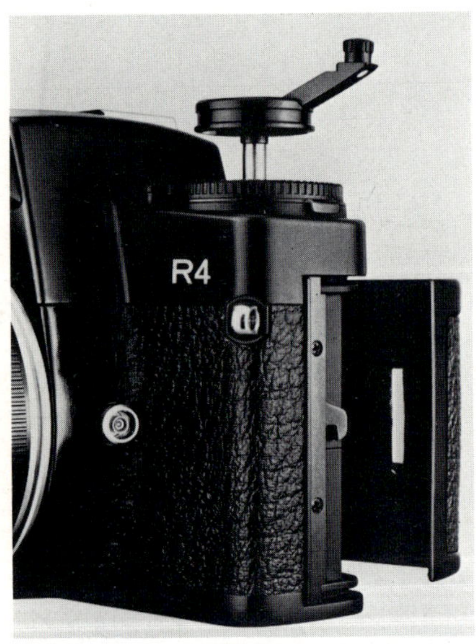

To open the camera back pull up the rewind knob and the back will spring open. This will also return the picture counter to the 'S' (start) position. If you now wind the shutter on and release it it will ensure that the take up spool is always in the same position for loading.

Draw one to two centimetres of film from the film cartridge. Then grasp the end of the film, emulsion away from you, between the thumb and index fingers. Slide the end of the film into one of the slots in the wind on spool. Ensure that the film perforations engage with the teeth of the film transport mechanism.

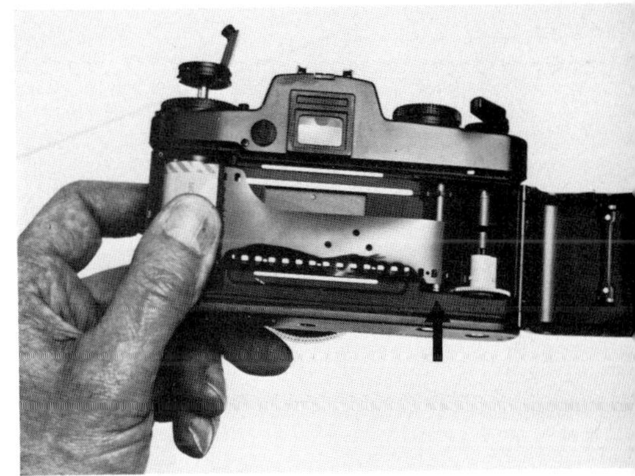

Place the film cartridge into the empty chamber. Now push in the rewind knob ensuring that it engages with the cartridge. Now whilst the camera back is still open transport the film with the rapid advance lever, ensure that the film is being wound onto the take up spool and that it is being correctly held by the parallel film guides.

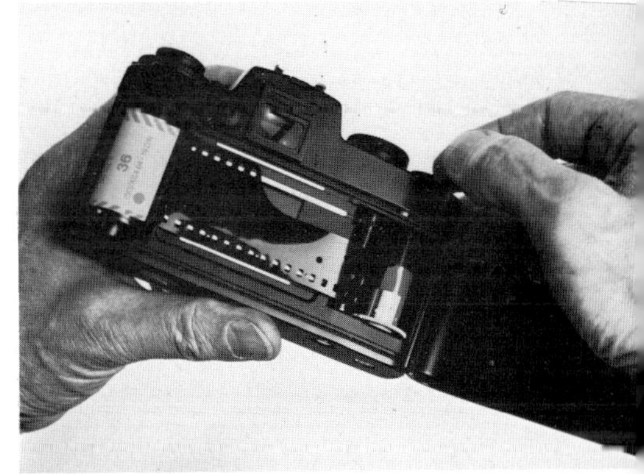

Now snap the camera shut, the rewind knob should now be turned in the direction of the arrow until a slight resistance is felt. Release the shutter and wind on. When carrying out this operation check that the rewind knob rotates, this will indicate beyond all doubt that the film is being correctly wound on. Carry out this operation once more, the camera is now ready for use.

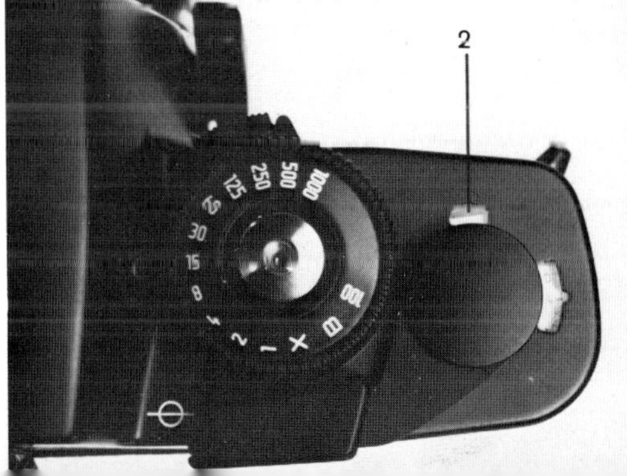

It is possible to see that the film is being properly transported by observing the small indicator window located at the side of the wind on lever. This window indicates the progression of film by the gradual advancement of a coloured indicator.

SETTING THE FILM SPEED

To set the automatic exposure system for the sensitivity of the film press the locking button (13) at the same time rotate the setting ring (15) until the desired film speed is displayed in the viewing windows. The adjustment range is from ISO 12/12 (ASA12) to ISO 3200/36 (ASA 3200). The now internationally accepted rating of film in ASA is very simple. The rating is structured proportionally. For example a 100ASA emulsion is exactly twice the speed of a film rated at 50ASA avoiding the earlier complication of film speed where for example with the DIN system the marked difference of 3° plus or minus would indicate a film being half or twice as sensitive.

INSERTING THE FILM

Pull up the rewind crank (14) to open the camera back. After some spring force has been overcome the camera back opens automatically and the film counter returns to (S) start. It should be noted that this operation is identical when using the Data back DB Leica R4. Wind the shutter with the rapid transport lever and release it. Pick up the film cartridge with the emulsion side pointing towards you, push the end of the film obliquely from above into one of the slots of the take up spool. Ensure that the end of the film is fully gripped by one lug and protrudes under the next, pull up the rewind crank and insert the film cartridge into the chamber. Now push in the rewind crank. The edge of the film must be parallel to the film guide and the sprockets of the transport drum must engage in the perforation holes when the rapid transport lever is operated. Wind on once so that it will be taut in the film guide and the cartridge mouth is correctly located. To close the camera merely snap the back shut. Release the shutter, transport the film through one frame and again release the shutter. The camera is now ready for use. The film counter (1) indicates the figure 1, the various film lengths currently available, i.e. 20, 24, and 36 are marked in red. The correct loading and transport of the film is indicated by a red signal (2) in front of the transport lever. It progressively advances towards the front edge of the window with each exposure.

REWINDING AND UNLOADING FILM

When the film has been exposed the rapid transport lever can no longer be operated. It is important that this lever should not be forced in order to obtain one more exposure, the only result of this will be a film torn out of the cartridge with disastrous effect. Before the film is removed it must be rewound

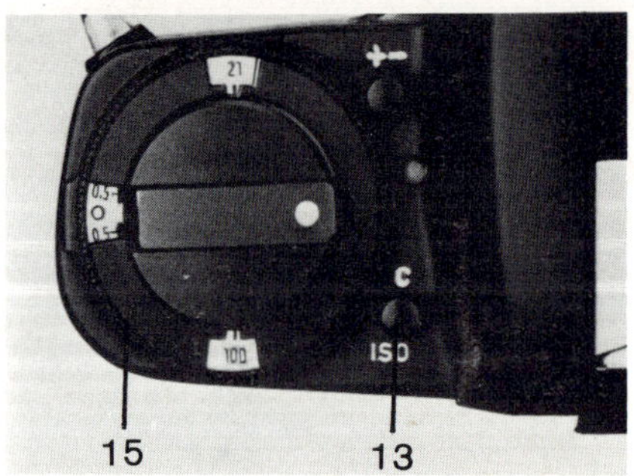

Film Sensitivity Settings.

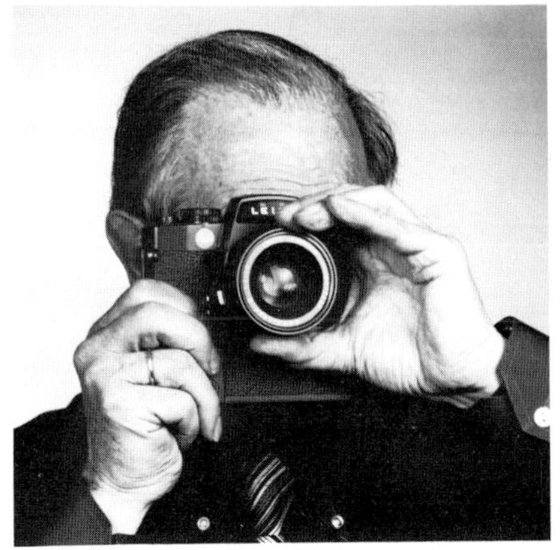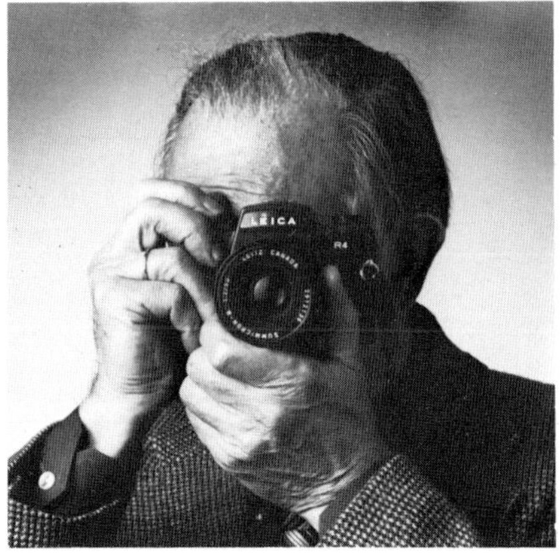

Left: The incorrect method of rotating the focusing ring in the horizontal camera position. Right: The correct method, ensuring the camera is supported.

into its cartridge, to achieve this press the rewind release button (31) which is located on the bottom of the camera. Pull out the rewind lever crank and rotate it clockwise in the direction of the arrow until the film is pulled out of the take up spool. Rewind until a slight resistance is felt. It is my advice that once this resistance is felt stop rewinding. If this is done then on removing the cartridge from the camera the leader will still protrude from the cartridge mouth, thus helping subsequent operations in the darkroom. Open the camera body by pulling up the rewind crank and take out the film cartridge.

HOLDING THE CAMERA

The manner in which the camera is held contributes significantly towards the success of the photographer. More photographs are ruined by camera shake than is commonly accepted. The Leica R4 is held in the right hand as illustrated above. The thumb and index finger of the left hand operate the focusing ring of the lens and supports the camera at the point of gravity. In this manner all controls fall readily to hand. When making an exposure the camera should be firmly held using the forehead and the nose as additional support. The right hand index finger should gently squeeze the shutter release in order to obviate camera shake. The rapid wind film lever is operated by the thumb of the right hand. There are two positions for holding the camera in the vertical position. The standard one is that the Leica R4 is held in such a position that the rapid wind lever is on top (see page 18) Here also the lens rests in the left hand and focusing is carried out in the normal fashion. The forehead should be used to aid camera steadiness. In using the camera in either the horizontal or vertical position it is important that it is held accurately. Straight horizons should not slope and truly vertical lines should not lean over. The second vertical position in which the camera is turned so that the rapid wind mechanism is underneath (picture page 18 right), enables the photographer to use the left eye. The shutter release is then operated by the tip of the right thumb, with the index finger providing a balancing or steadying effect on the camera. The Leica R4 user will find that the camera is more readily usable when the camera strap is employed.

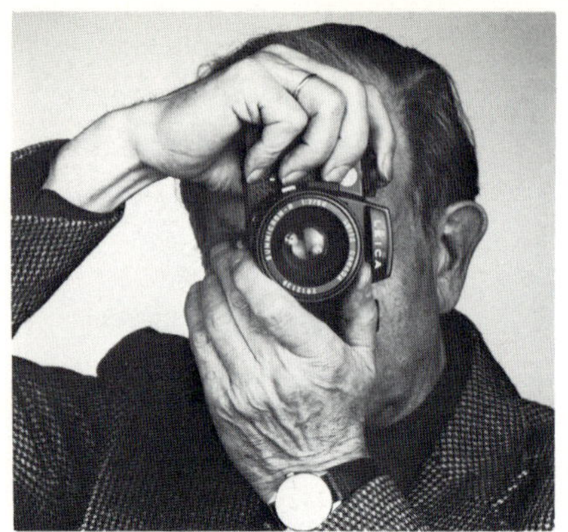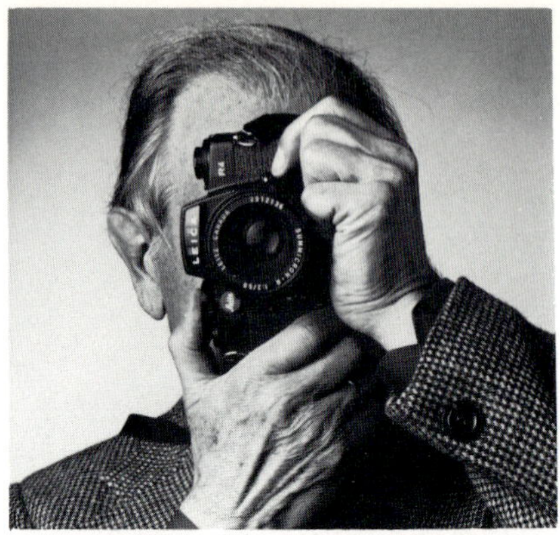

Left: Correct methods of holding the camera in the vertical position.

Ever ready cases whilst providing excellent protection have always been a misnomer. For the transportation of the photographic outfit the range of combination cases produced by Leitz are to be highly recommended. The shutter release knob is provided with a screw thread in order that a standard cable release can be used. When making an exposure the following sequence of operations are initiated. The mirror swings up and out of the light path. The automatic diaphragm stops down to the selected value. The light measuring system swings upwards. The shutter is released. The automatic diaphragm returns to the fully open position and the mirror swings back to the viewing position together with the metering system mirror. These operations are carried out with extreme rapidity thus ensuring that the viewfinder screen is blank for the minimum amount of time, thus allowing the photographer an almost continuous view of the subject.

THE VIEWFINDER

All the adjustable functions can be seen within the large brilliantly clear viewfinder. Thus allowing the photographer complete control of the indicated automatic functions. Changes in focal length, viewpoint, lighting, can be instantly seen. The Leica R4 is a single lens reflex camera. Interposed between the lens and the film plane there is a sprung mirror set at an angle of 45° this mirror reflects the light path passing through the lens at an angle of 90° upwards onto a focusing screen. The ground glass screen is observed by means of a pentaprism which enables the image formed on the viewing screen to be observed from an angle of 90° by means of an ocular system. This pentaprism reverses the inverted image, thus enabling the photographer to view the subject the right way round and in fully corrected form. The viewfinder image provides the photographer with the facility of observing 92% of the image formed by the lens. Thus allowing for minimal taking errors. Although of course the viewed area will correspond exactly to the area of a commercially mounted camera slide. L.E.D. displays (Light Emitting Diodes) show all operational functions which correspond with the selected programming.

18

CORRECTION LENSES

The standard viewfinder is provided with a lens of –1 dioptre, correct for normal sight. In order to check whether this correction is suitable for the individual the black engraved ring located in the centre of the screen should be critically examined. This ring should appear perfectly sharp. If not then an eyesight correction lens is indicated, the appropriate prescription should be obtained from an optician. The lenses are available in the following strengths + and –0.5, 1.0, 1.5, 2.0, 3.0 Dioptre (spherical). However it should be noted that the viewfinder is perfectly usable for those who normally wear spectacles.

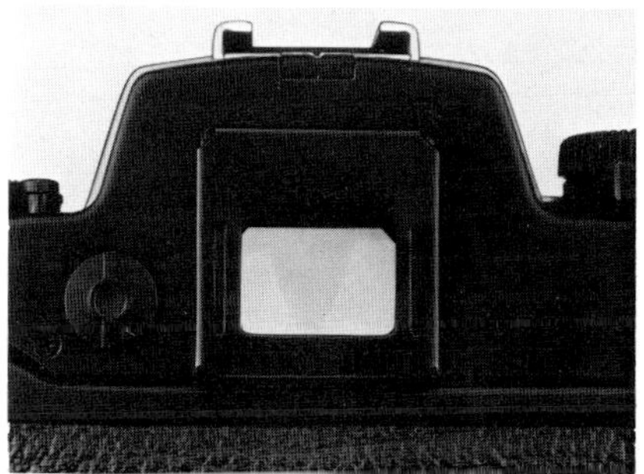
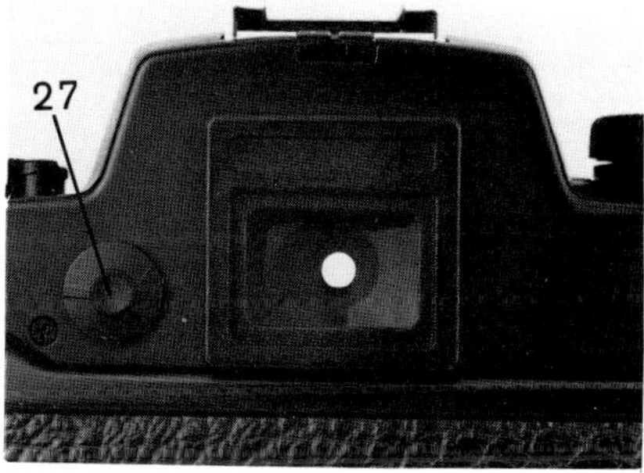

Left: Correction lenses. Right: Shutter blind.

VIEWFINDER BLIND

The Silicon photodiode of the metering system is located in the bottom of the camera where usually it is protected from stray light. However in certain extreme cases, i.e. using the camera mounted on a tripod in the studio when stray light can be reflected through the viewfinder and adverseley effect the metering. To obviate this the Leica R4 is supplied with a viewfinder blind. A switch (27) is located to the left of the eyepiece window. To operate the blind turn the switch in an anticlockwise direction.

FOCUSING

The Leica R4 is supplied with a standard focusing screen which is ideal for most general purposes, replacement No 14303. The centre of this screen is provided with a three millimetre split image circle, incorrect focus is indicated by the displacement of the subject, this displacement being most noticeable if the subject contains straight lines. Around this circle is another one of seven millimetres diameter, this area is provided with rectangular prisms, it is used for subjects which do not contain easily discerned lines or features. The out of focus subject is seen to shimmer and becomes clear and steady once correct focus is obtained. The outer area of the screen consists of matt triangular prisms producing a ground glass effect. This area is of particular importance when using longer focal length lenses A useful tip particularly when photographing in the closer ranges is to roughly focus the subject and make final adjustment by slightly altering the subject distance by moving the camera slightly backwards and forwards.

With wide angle lenses, focusing is often difficult owing to the small scale of the subject, here the following procedure is recommended. At distances over two metres the distance is estimated by eye and the focus set accordingly. The microprism field will become difficult to discern when using lenses of extreme focal length or at limited maximum aperture.

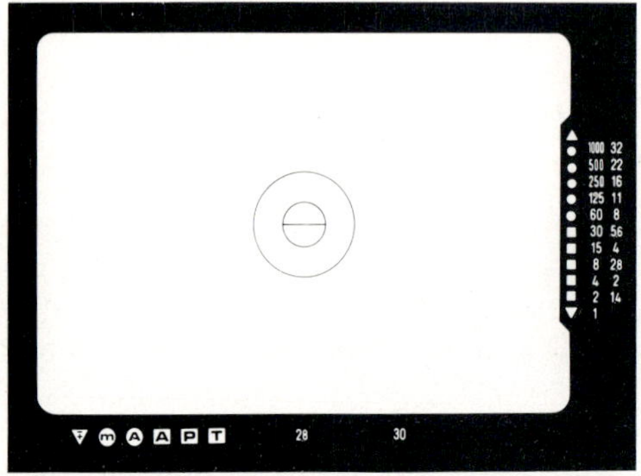

The viewfinder display

INTERCHANGEABLE FOCUSING SCREENS

For particular applications the Leica R4 system contains, including the standard, five focusing screens. They are supplied individually in a case containing tweezers and a dusting brush. The Matt screen order No 14304 is recommended for use with longer lenses and for closeups. It is less bright than the standard because it spreads the light more evenly thus enabling the planes of sharp focus to be more easily discerned. The microprism screen order No 14305 corresponds to the standard with the exception that it has no split image facility. The number four screen is supplied with a fully matt surface engraved with grid lines and is very suitable for architectural and technical applications. At the centre of the screen are two indicators set precisely ten millimeters apart facilitating the scaling of the subject. Screen number five is a clear screen order number 14307. This completely transparent screen is provided with an engraved cross line and a circle denoting the selective metering field. This focusing screen is supplied for use in the fields of photomicography and astronomical photography. Focusing is by means of an aerial image to aid this a cross is denoted in the centre of the metering area.

INTERCHANGING SCREENS

Changing screens should only be undertaken with the tweezers supplied, on no account should they be handled otherwise. A blower brush can be used to remove small particles of dust. Should the focusing screen become badly soiled then it should be cleaned in an ultra sonic bath such as those used by opticians. Screens are made from synthetic materials and should never be cleaned with cloths. To change screens hold the tweezers between the thumb and the index finger, press to open the tweezers. Carefully position them against the focusing screen at an angle of 30° then release the pressure of the thumb, this will allow the tweezers to grip.

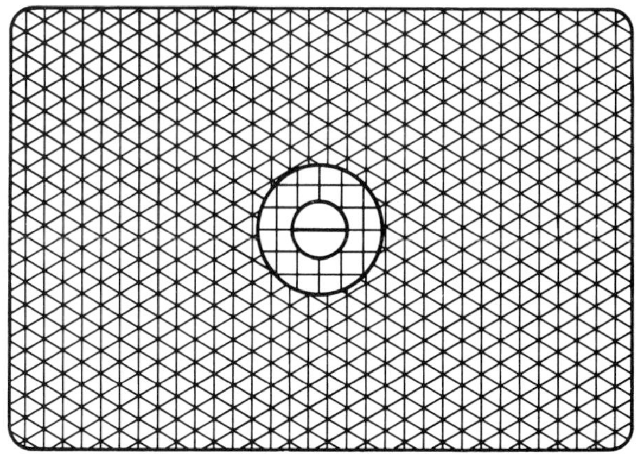

The Leica R4 is supplied with the standard No 1 screen.

The full matt screen is intended for use in close up photography and when long focal length lenses are being used (2).

The Microprism screen No 3 is similar to the standard screen but does not have the split image facility.

For architectural and technical photography the Full Matt screen No 4 is to be recommended.

The clear screen No 5 produces an exceptionally bright picture with the finest details resolved. It is designed primarily for scientific usage.

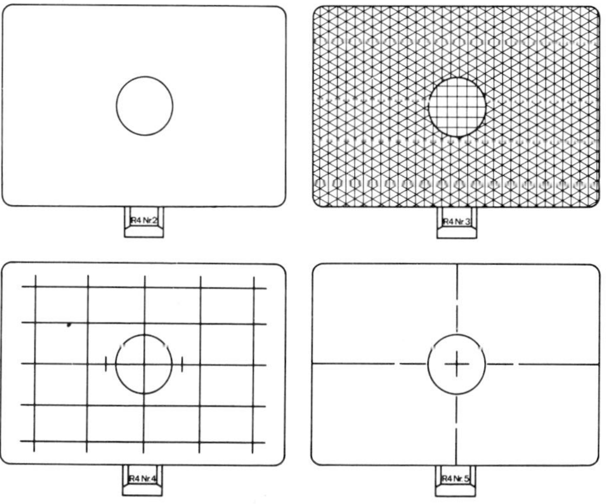

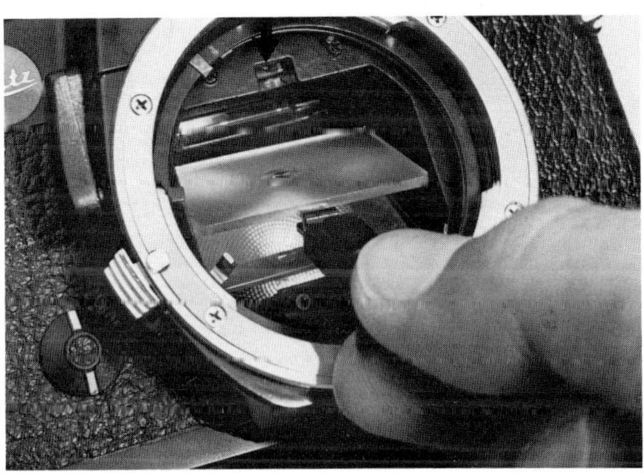

All focusing screens hould be changed strictly in accordance with the instructions and using the tweezers provided.

BASIC EXPOSURE INFORMATION

With the traditional hand held exposure meter there are two different methods of measuring light, one method is to measure the light that is reflected from the subject, the other is to measure the light which is falling onto the subject. However with a built in metering system it is the former which is used. In order to achieve exposure evaluation which is acceptable at both high and low levels of light intensity a 'norm' must be established. A grey card possessing a reflective value of 18% is used in order that the meter can be calibrated to a known point of reference. In practice many subjects contain areas of widely differing reflective value, but providing that these variations remain within the accepted latitude of the photographic emulsion both highlight and shadow detail will be resolved. In this respect even reversal colour film will withstand exposure differences of + or – 1/2 a stop, but a medium speed black and white emulsion correctly processed is capable of handling a latitude of some seven or eight stops. In order to assess the general overall exposure suitable for the average subject the integrated method is the most suitable. With this method the various contrasts of the subject are averaged out and a mean exposure arrived at. This method is very convenient and for some 80% of subjects perfectly acceptable. However for subjects containing a greater than normal range of contrast the integrated method becomes less reliable. In order to overcome this problem the Leica R4 is provided with a second metering system, the 'Selective light', this enables the photographer to measure the reflected light from a small area of the subject. In order to clarify the two metering methods I feel that an example would be useful . . . The photographer wishes to photograph a 'solo' performer at the theatre, the artist is lit by spotlights. With integrated metering the overall exposure will take into consideration the total field of view, in extreme circumstances this could mean that 95% of the picture is completely black and the remaining 5% containing the actual subject only represents a fraction of the measured area. Therefore for this type of subject the selective metering should be selected. Frame the important part of the subject within the metered area as indicated by the seven millimetre circle and expose accordingly. If the subject is to be off centre in the frame use the memory lock to retain the correct exposure, compose, frame and shoot.

A further example is shown. The triangular shaped blocks are the same shade of grey on the left and right hand sides, the three pictures show how different illumination of the right hand side alters the contrast. Two identical light sources at a distance of 50cm illuminate both sides. The nut casts a weak shadow to both sides both shows no plasticity. The grey colour on left and right sides produces an identical value on the meter, the light is equal. Centre. The illumination source for the right side has been moved one metre providing 1/2 of the light intensity. Clear shadows and a plastic image has resulted. Bottom. The lamp on the right side was moved to 2 metres providing insufficient illumination. However we can still measure the difference of the exposure and take necessary measures for a difference in contrast of a factor of 1:16. Using the integrated system the entire quantity of light is measured

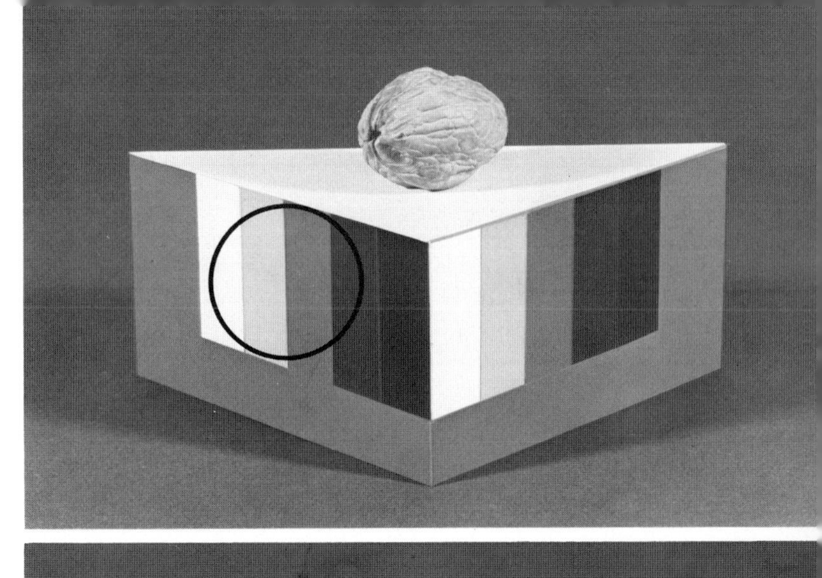

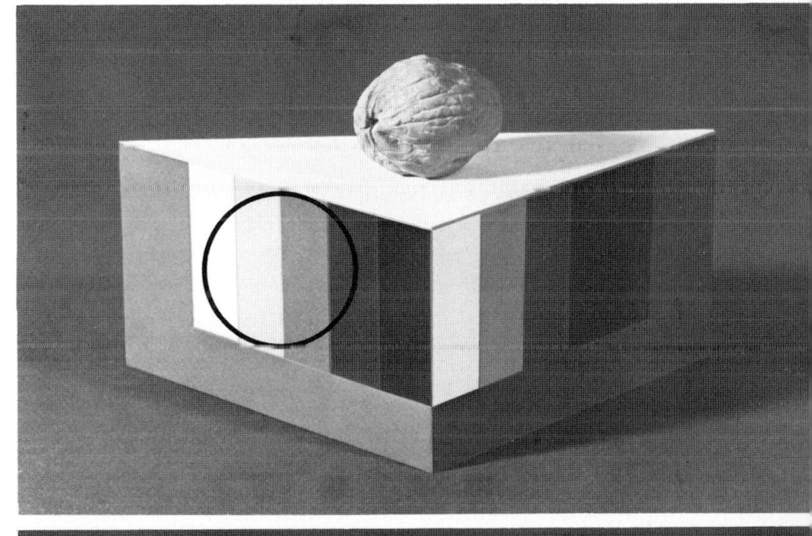

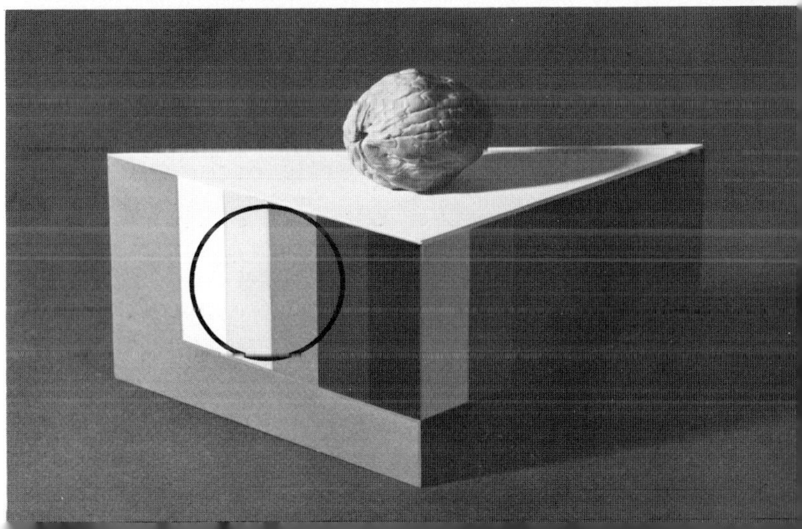

and deviations are less than one would expect from the differences in illumination between the upper and lower pictures. With selective metering we can measure the bright and dark sides and choose the exposure time. In this case the same exposure time was chosen for all three illustrations because the difference in the decrease in the light on the right side was to be shown clearly. The light was measured on the left hand side at a spot denoted by the circle.

In normal black and white photography there are obviously situations where the reproduction of a scale of grey (see lower right hand picture) is desired. This can be easily achieved on the negative by lengthening the exposure time, reproducing this in the final print is more difficult. If the gradation capabilities of a soft grade photographic paper are utilised then the tones of grey on the left and right will be balanced out. Differences in reflective value between black and white are about 130. The difference in exposure alters the relationship between the white on the left and the black on the right in the middle picture to 1:120 and in the lower picture 1-480. Since only the relationship of 1:30 can be covered in the control picture then an exposure should be made for the important parts of the subject, selective metering makes this possible. The exposure of colour reversal film is somewhat different, a higher range than 1:30 can be reproduced with projection, but because of the rigidly controlled process of reversal film the bright sections caused by excessive exposure are devoid of detail. There is no sense in overexposing to achieve detail in the shadows because then the highlights would lack detail. Even when there is a high contrast of illumination expose according to the left scale of grey as shown by the circular markings. The reliability of the selective metering system is also shown in the following example (see page opposite). The same subject is used four times, the only difference being that the background is changed, the exposure time remains identical in each case because the varying brightness of the background plays no part in the metering function and is not included. As before the spot marked by the circle is used for metering. With integrated metering the differing brightness of background have a marked influence, particularly with the white background which gives an indicated short exposure time.

Integrated exposure is the best method in most cases where the subject does not contain a vast range of contrast and the light and dark areas are evenly spread. Apart from subjects containing a normal contrast range there are subjects in which the subject contains a very few tones and a low contrast range, for example the normal snow scene. These subjects often contain no objects of medium brightness under full sunshine. In the mountains the reflection from snow is so bright that the indicator on the exposure meter will often go past the limits. In order to compensate for this patches of open shadow should be used to judge exposure. If there are no suitable objects from which to obtain a reading then the correct exposure can be obtained by metering at close distance the light reflected from the palm of the hand with the light shining directly on it. In order to to able to take a photograph with only an instants warning it is best to have the integrated metering mode selected on the programme selector and then with the manual over ride select a one stop over exposure.

24

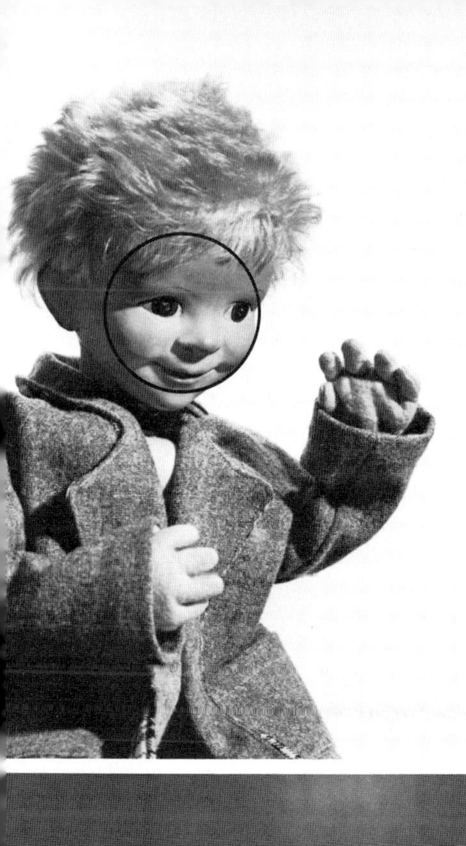
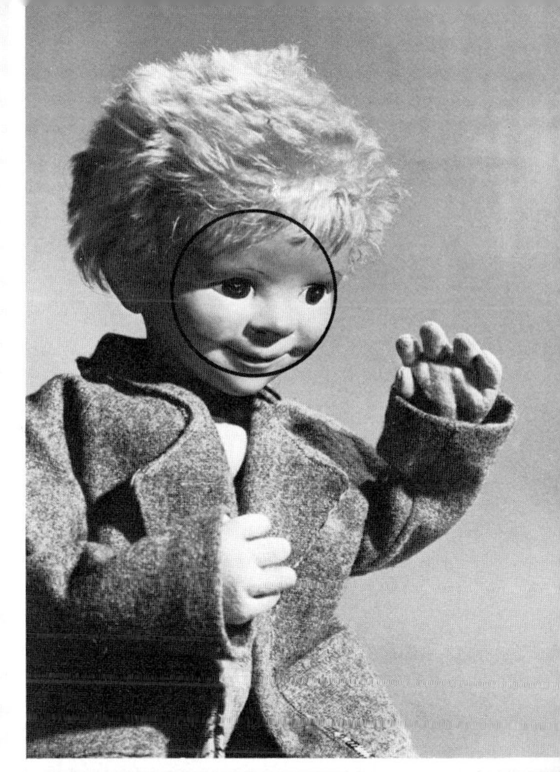
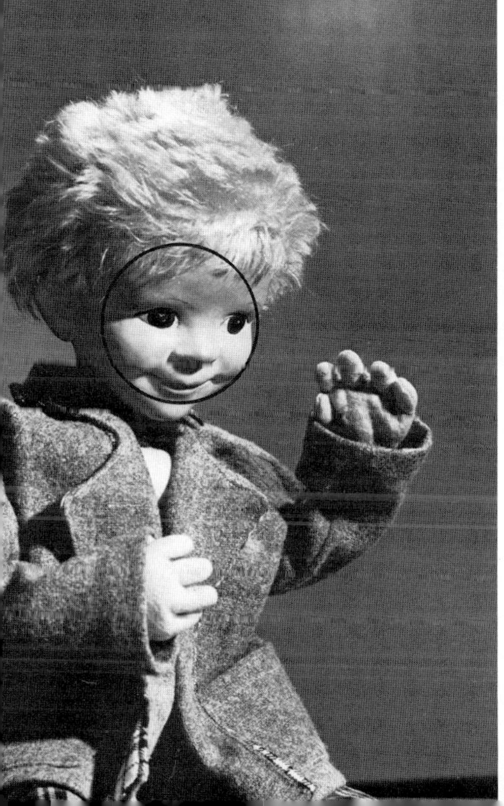
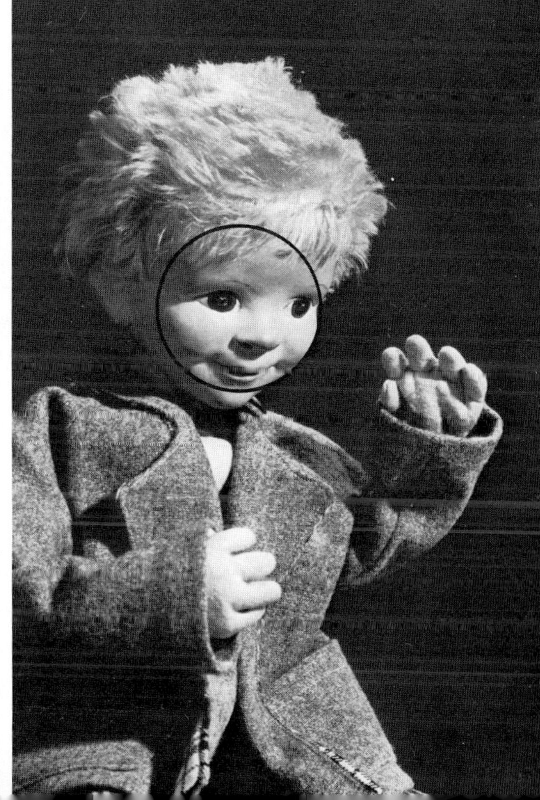

Photographing a room through a window is extremely difficult because the range of brightness contained in the subject often exceeds the latitude of the photographic emulsion. Although the human eye can cope with this problem with no difficulty this type of subject is fraught with photographic difficulties, the exposure range being outside the normal resolving capabilities of an emulsion. If, for instance, the subject to be photographed indicates an exposure of 1 second at f/8 then it could easily be that the landscape outside the window would be indicating an exposure of $1/250$th at the same aperture. The photographer the must decide on the relative importance of the individual subjects. If the subjects within the room are of the prime importance then obviously the landscape is going to receive a considerable amount of over exposure. If a middle value is chosen it will still be obvious that the subjects contained within the room will be under exposed and the external subjects over exposed. While some degree of compensation can be achieved at the printing stage it is fairly obvious that some form of artificial lighting should be used to bring up the interior intensity of the light to a closer value to that outside.

While sophisticated automatic metering systems can now guarantee the photographer an almost 100% exposure success rate it must be realised that under certain conditions the photographer has to control and monitor the automatic metering functions. It must be remembered that often the most successful photographs are those taken under extremely difficult lighting conditions. The experienced photographer will use the camera's automatic functions as an aid to enable him to tackle difficult photographic assignments but he will use it as a tool which combined with his own photographic experience will enable success to be achieved. The beginner must gain this experience. He will not be able to decide in many instances which mode of exposure metering should be used. Therefore I would suggest that the full capabilities of the Leica R4 system are used and careful notes made in order that reference can be made and photographic progress and experience gained. Note the following: a colour reversal film as previously mentioned has very small latitude of exposure one stop over exposure produces a print which is too light, one stop under exposure will produce a print that is too dark. If the subject content contains a large contrast range do not expose for the shadow otherwise the highlights will become burnt out. A black and white negative film will only become slightly more dense when subjected to a degree of over exposure. However with the same degree of under exposure the middle tones will suffer adversely. When photographing an important subject it is advised that two or three exposures are made thus bracketing the exposure range.

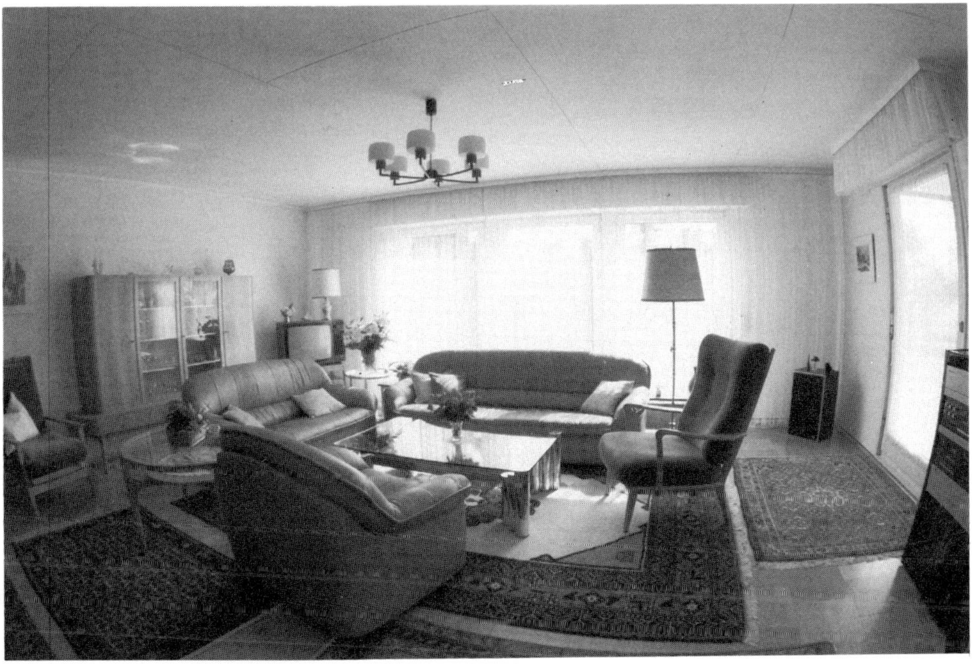

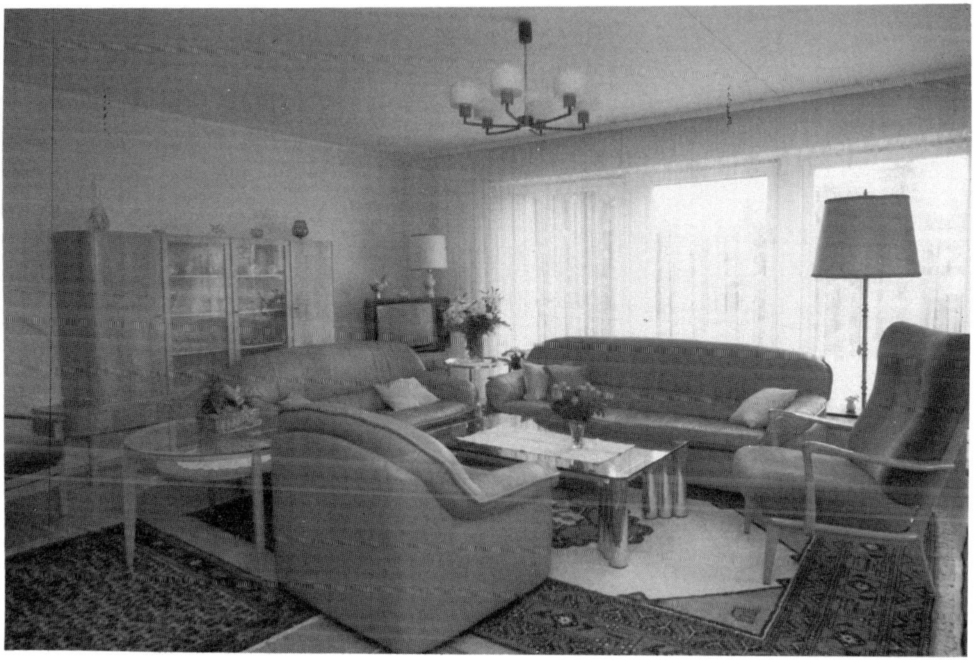

EXPOSURE METERING MODES

The exposure system on the Leica R4 is one of the most technically advanced in its field. It is only switched on when needed, to fulfil its function and only then is any energy used. If the shutter release is slightly depressed or the programme selector lock (6) is depressed the L.E.D.'s will commence functioning. The exposure meter functions are carried out through the lens normally with the lens set at full aperture regardless of the aperture pre-selected by the photographer, thus providing the brightest possible viewing conditions. In order to provide the facility for controlling and monitoring the automatic functions the viewfinder is also equipped with various readouts. It is advisable to practise with a camera when it is not loaded with film, it is not the object of this particular exercise to decide on which of the metering functions to use but merely to aquaint ourselves with the mechanical operation. By depressing the programme selector lock (6) the programme selector can be adjusted in the viewfinder (7) next to the shutter speed selector. The selected programme is indicated. Now pick up the camera, put it to the eye and look through the viewfinder. It will then be noted that the metering mode selected is now indicated at the bottom left hand edge of the viewfinder screen. When read from left to right it will be noted that the symbols are placed in the following order:-

Selective metering: (M) manual.   shutter speed and lens apertures are controlled manually in this mode with selective metering.

(A) aperture.   automatic shutter speed control with selective metering. Shutter speed selected automatically to suit pre-determined aperture setting.

[P] automatic programme.   the camera automatically and continuously sets the shutter speed and lens aperture.

[T] time.   automatic aperture control. Aperture selected automatically to suit pre-selected shutter speed.

Integrated metering: [A] aperture.   automatic shutter speed control using large field integrated metering.

It is important to note that in the [P] and [T] modes the lens must be set to its minimum aperture failure to do this means that the full aperture scale is not available to the automatic function.

Note that all programme functions are designated in English. There are five programmes designated with two symbols and four letters. The circle denotes that the mode is using the selective spot metering system and the square symbol denotes the integrated system. As previously described there are two different methods of exposure evaluation which are necessary in order to achieve correctly exposed negatives over a large photographic range. With the integrated metering system the mean average exposure will be established, with a selective metering mode only the subject contained within the 7mm circle will be assessed.

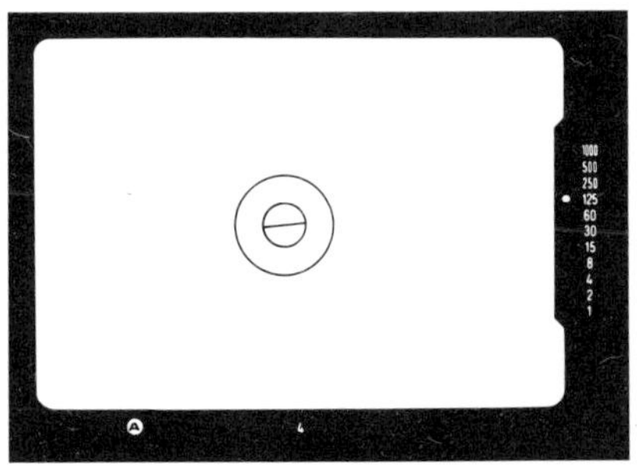
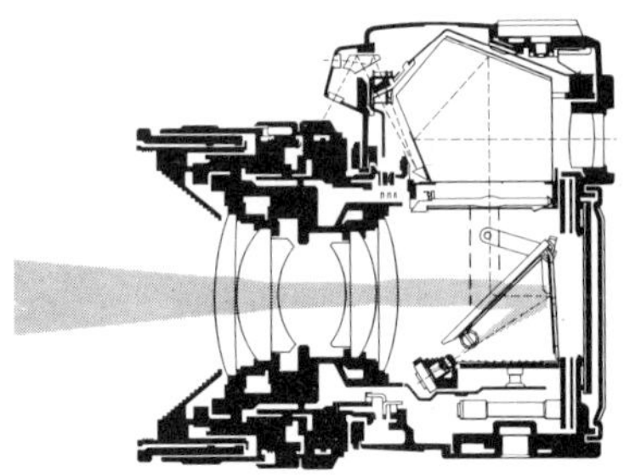

Selective Metering: If the main subject of our photograph is of a contrast widely different from the overall brightness of our picture the integrated system is not suitable as it will give an average exposure for the entire view. Therefore in these conditions the selective metering mode should be used.

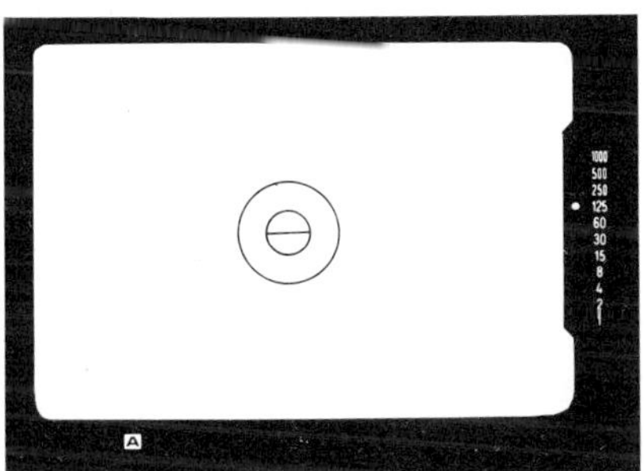
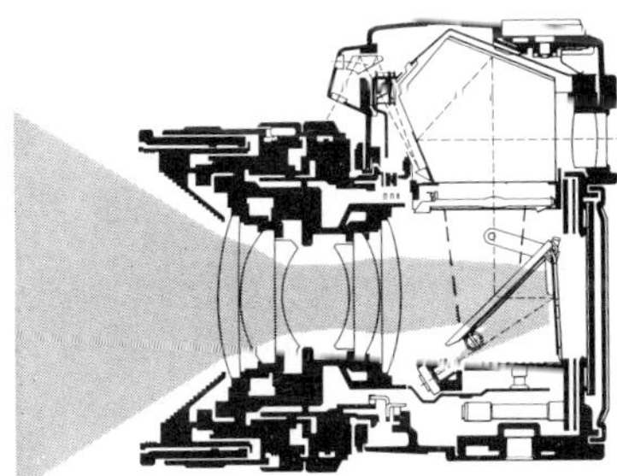

Integral Metering: This is the correct metering mode for use with subjects containing an overall level brightness range. For meter calibration the central part of the viewfinder is selected as with experience it is shown that it is this area which usually contains the main features of the subject.

Exposure through the lens: Part of the light being passed through the lens of the camera is transmitted to the silicon photo diode installed in the bottom of the camera, through a semi transparent mirror. The special Fresnel reflector used to direct the light contains no less than 1345 micro reflectors. With the Leica R4 two different metering facilities are provided, selective and integrated.

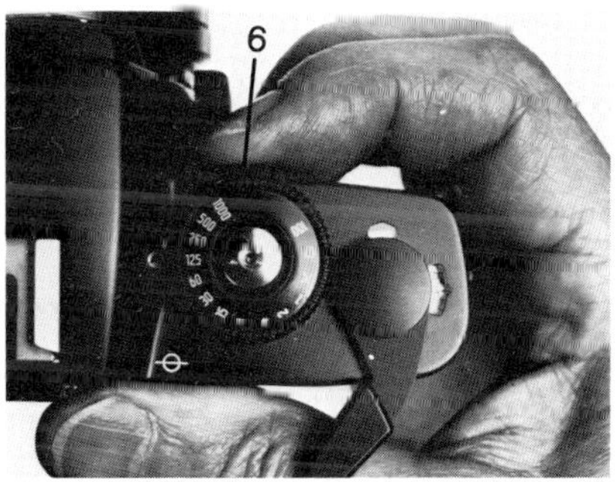

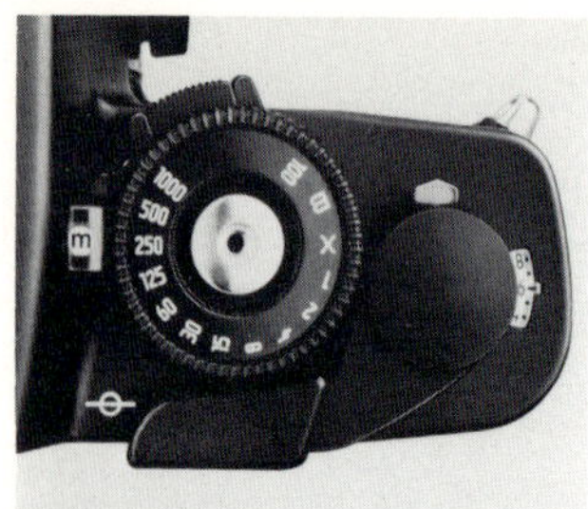

(M) MANUAL ADJUSTMENT WITH SELECTIVE METERING

On difficult subjects it is often useful to turn off the camera's automatic facilities. The shutter speed and aperture controls are adjusted manually. Although this method is slow it increases the photographer's experience.

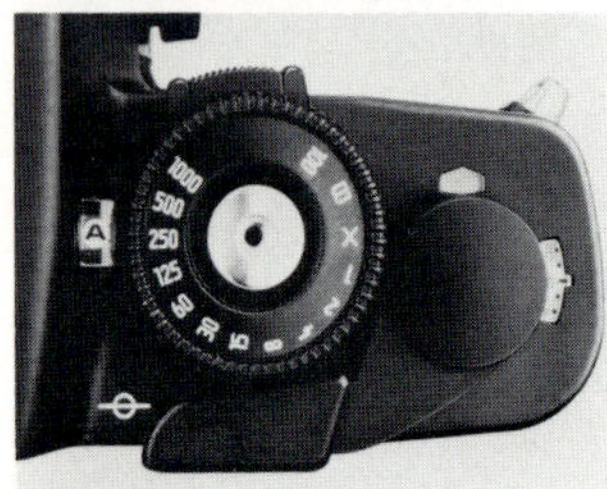

(A) AUTOMATIC SHUTTER SPEED CONTROL WITH SELECTIVE MEASUREMENT

The aperture is predetermined and the automatic metering facility will adjust the shutter speed to correspond. This is the mode to use when maximum depth of field is required.

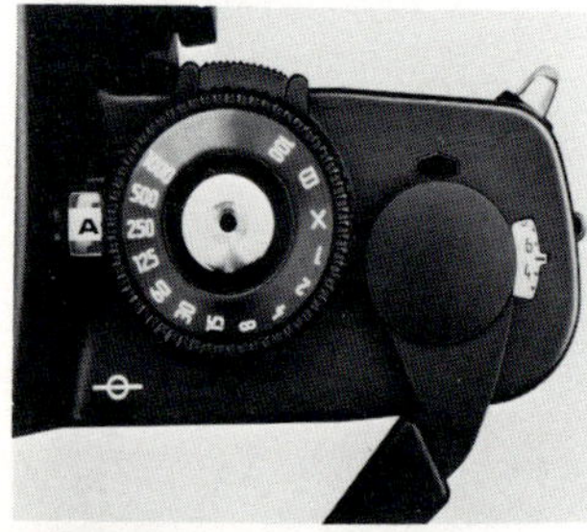

A AUTOMATIC SHUTTER SPEED CONTROL WITH INTEGRATED METERING

The aperture is predetermined by the photographer and the automatic metering facility set in the integrated metering mode adjusts the shutter speed to correspond.

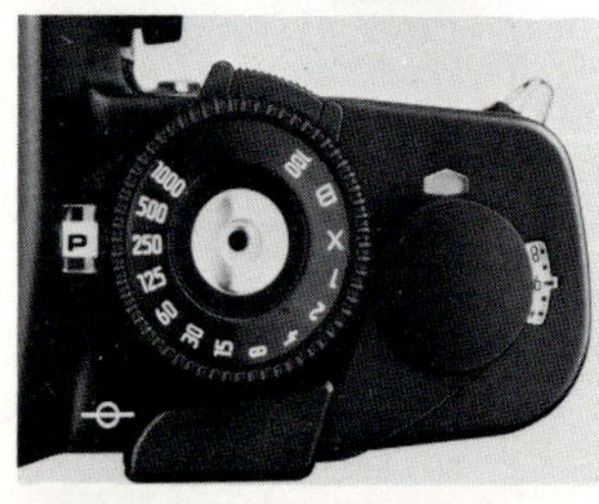

P AUTOMATIC PROGRAMMING WITH INTEGRATED METERING

In this mode it is important to ensure that the lens being used is set to its minimum aperture in order that the full range of aperture settings are available to the metering system. The camera automatically and continuously sets the shutter speed and lens aperture in relation to each other. The shutter speed ring may be set to any value between $1/100$th to 1 sec. but not at X,100 or B.

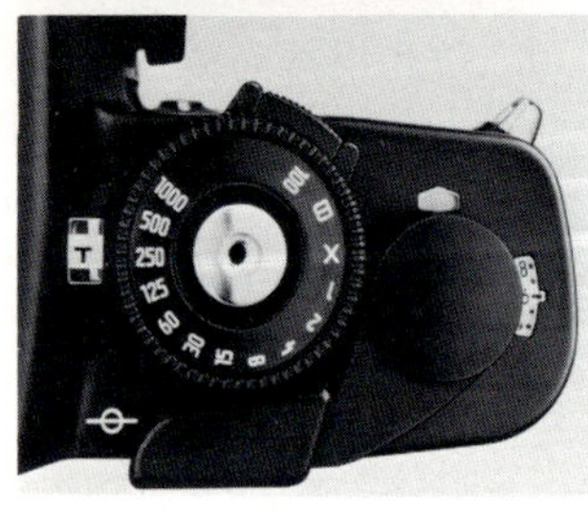

T AUTOMATIC APERTURE CONTROL WITH INTEGRATED METERING

To use pre-select the desired shutter speed and set the lens to its minimum aperture. This mode is used when it is essential that the highest possible camera speed is used and that the aperture is automatically controlled to relate to this.

(M) MANUAL ADJUSTMENT WITH SELECTIVE METERING

Shutter speeds and apertures are set manually. 1. Select the appropriate exposure time, view the subject, adjust the lens diaphragm until the shutter speed displayed in the viewfinder frame by a red L.E.D. corresponds to the selected exposure time. 2. Adjust the lens to the required aperture then transfer the indicated shutter speed in the viewfinder to the shutter speed control ring. Intermediate shutter speeds cannot be selected.

(A) AUTOMATIC SHUTTER SPEED CONTROL WITH SELECTED METERING

Pre-select the desired lens aperture. The shutter speed ring can be set to any value but not at X,100 or B. When the metering system is used in the selective mode there is a memory storage facility. A reading can be stored when the slack is taken off the release button. The programme L.E.D. is extinguished and the camera can be panned until the desired composition is achieved. The release button is now pressed and a predetermined exposure given. The exposure can be stored for about 30 seconds. The L.E.D. display of the shutter speed remains functional and indicates any changes in the lighting conditions, however the original exposure is retained. The measured value is unlocked if the finger is removed from the release button.

[A] AUTOMATIC SHUTTER SPEED CONTROL WITH INTEGRATED METERING

This mode is used in the same manner as the previous mode but for subjects that do not contain excessive contrasts. This mode is perhaps the most useful and will be found adequate for some 80% of subjects.

[P] AUTOMATIC PROGRAMMING WITH INTEGRATED METERING

This is the best programme for easy photography. Not only the novice but the experienced photographer will find that this metering mode is the most convenient when it is a requirement that the camera is always prepared for the unexpected. The exposure time selected by the programme is displayed on the right hand side of the viewfinder by light emitting diodes.

[T] AUTOMATIC APERTURE PRIORITY WITH INTEGRATED METERING

When very fast shutter speeds are required, for instance in sports photography this metering mode is the most important. The aperture control is automatically selected to relate to the predetermined shutter speed.

SHUTTER SPEED CONTROL RING

The figures from 1000 to 1 ($^1/_{1000}$th of a second to 1 second) and X are shown in white, B and 100 in red. Click stops are provided for each value and the required shutter speed is set opposite the programme selector indicating window. X indicates $^1/_{100}$th of a second for use with electronic flash synchronisation, B provides for exposures longer than one second when using the camera in its manual mode. $^1/_{100}$ indicates $^1/_{100}$th of a second and is used with the camera in its mechanical mode i.e. in the event of battery failure. B can also be used. When the shutter ring is set on X, B or 100 even if the batteries are functioning there is no metering indication, the upper triangular L.E.D.'s in the view finder are then illuminated.

VIEWFINDER DISPLAYS

Programme $\boxed{\text{M}}$ with selective exposure. Metering is not automatic it operates in the same manner as a built in non-coupled exposure meter. Shutter speed and aperture controls are manually adjusted, the shutter speeds 1 second to $^1/_{1000}$th are electronically controlled. Intermediate values cannot be selected, however they can be adjusted to correspond with an engraved shutter speed by means of adjusting the lens aperture. When the camera is switched on the exposure meter indicates the selected shutter speeds by red L.E.D.'s but these are not automatically set. Either by adjusting the shutter speed control or the lens aperture control the exposure can be obtained which corresponds to the exposure indicated. The automatic modes in circles or squares indicate automatic metering, however the two modes are different.

The Ⓐ within a circle indicates automatic metering with selective measurement. The $\boxed{\text{A}}$ in a square indicates integrated metering. Since it is often experienced that the important subject which requires accurate exposure is not contained within the centre of the viewfinder programme Ⓐ alone incorporates a measured value storage facility. The exposure meter covers only the 7mm circle engraved in the viewfinder therefore the camera is pointed so that the subject is contained within this circle and an exposure reading obtained. This value can be stored when the slack is taken off the release button (4). The programme L.E.D. is extinguished in this release button position. The camera can be panned until the desired composition is achieved. The release button is now pressed and the exposure made. The shutter speed can be stored for approximately 30 seconds. The L.E.D. display of the shutter speed remains functional and indicates any change in the lighting conditions, however the stored exposure is the one that the camera will use. Removing pressure from the shutter release instantly unlocks the memory's storage programme.

$\boxed{\text{A}}$ contained within a rectangle provides automatic exposure using the large field integrated method. This mode is the most suitable for general photography of most subjects. Both programmes have the following details in common. The shutter speed is pre-selected at any speed except X, 100 or B, the selected programme can be seen to the left at the bottom of the viewfinder. Shutter speeds are visible on the right hand side of the viewfinder and the appropriate shutter speed is indicated by a red L.E.D. When the camera is

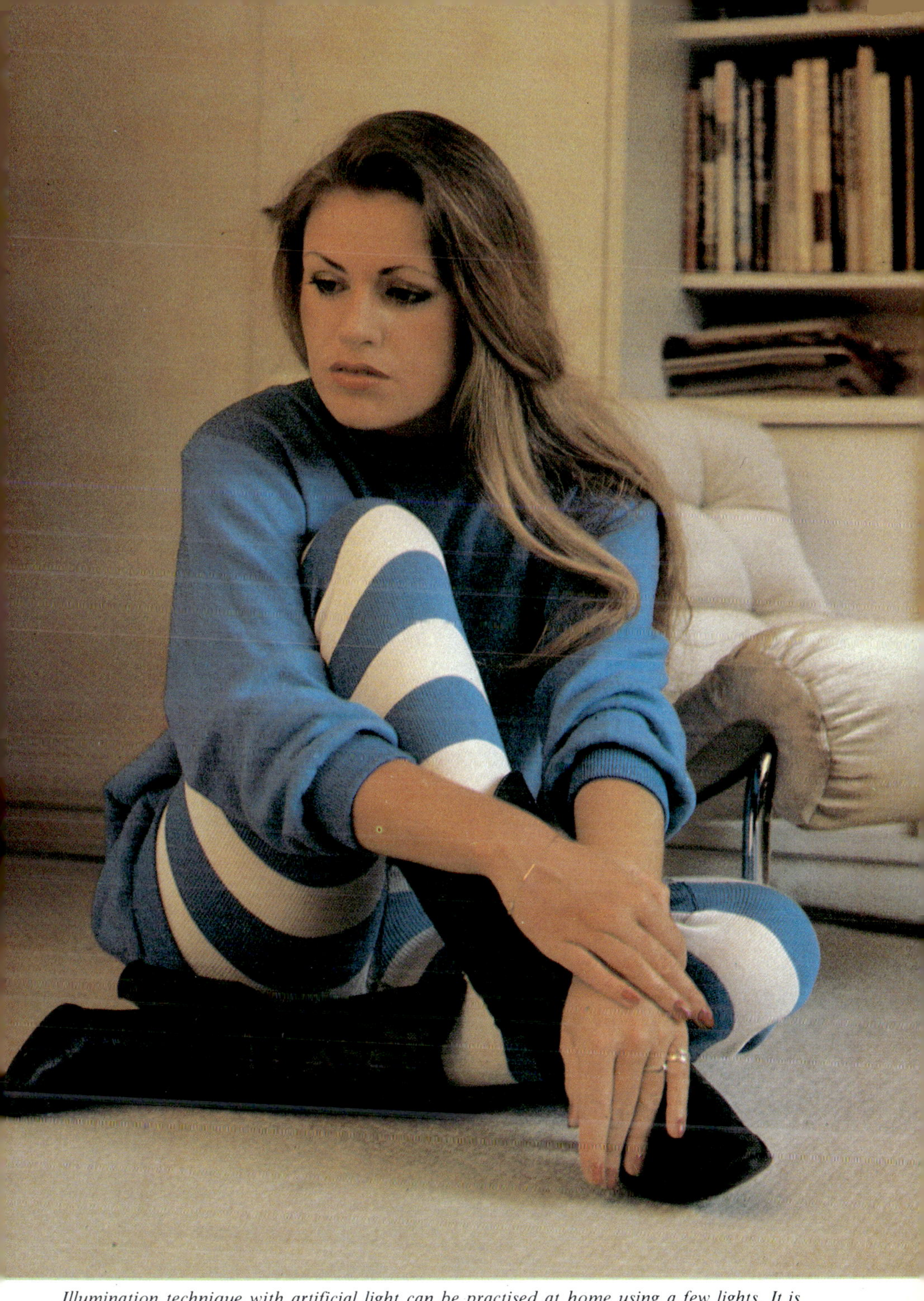

Illumination technique with artificial light can be practised at home using a few lights. It is important that the lights stand in a well determined relationship to each other, therefore they should not be too powerful in most cases 200 watts is sufficient. Photograph: Inge Springmann.

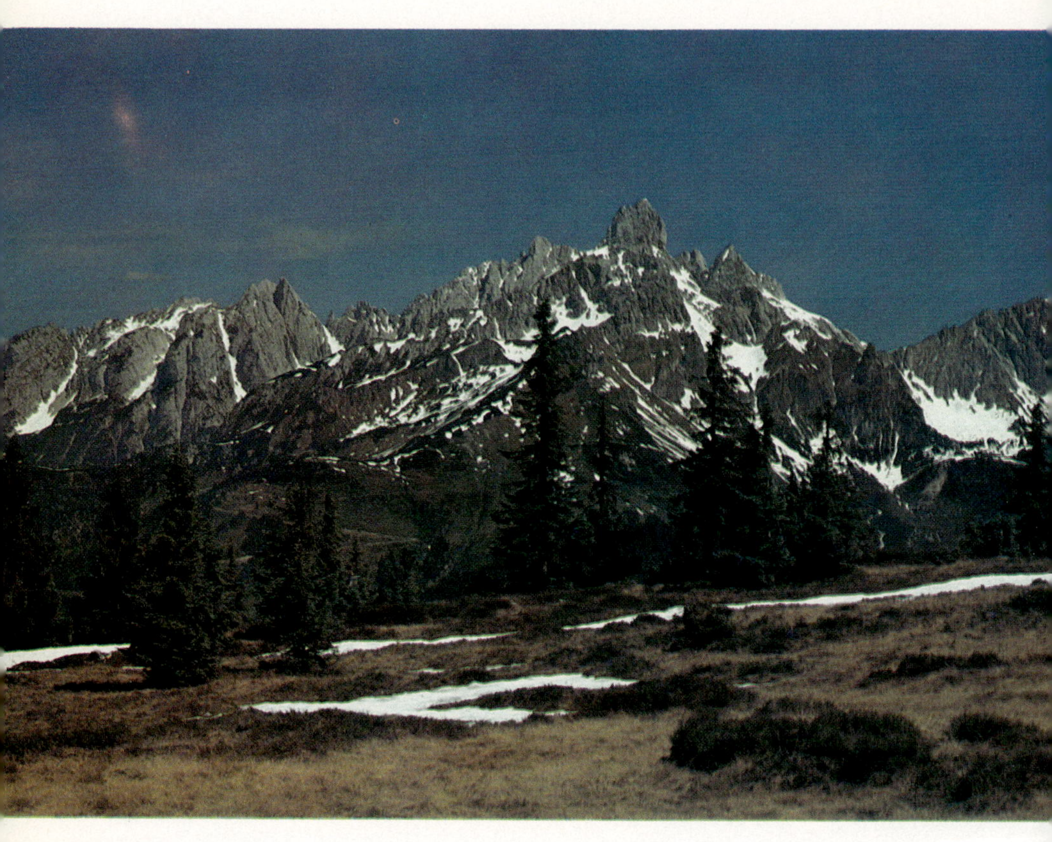

"Bischofsmutz" taken with Elmarit-R 60mm f/2.8.

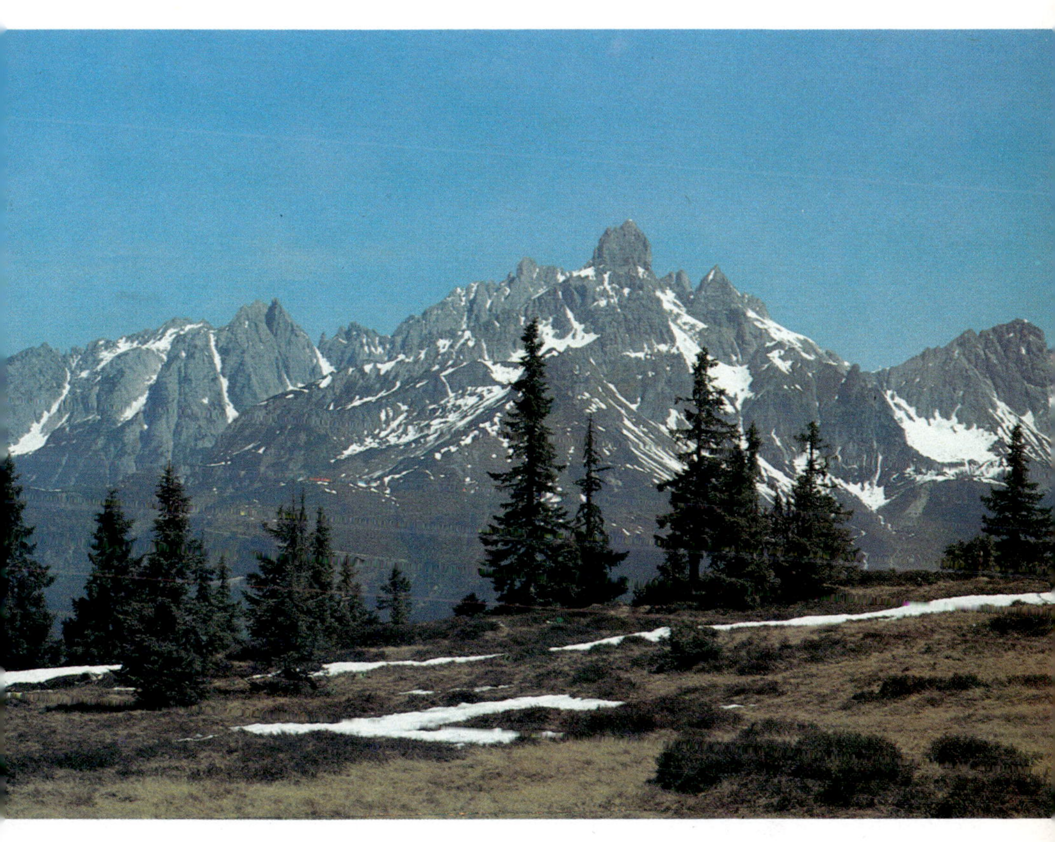

"Bischofsmutz" taken with Leitz circular polarising filter.

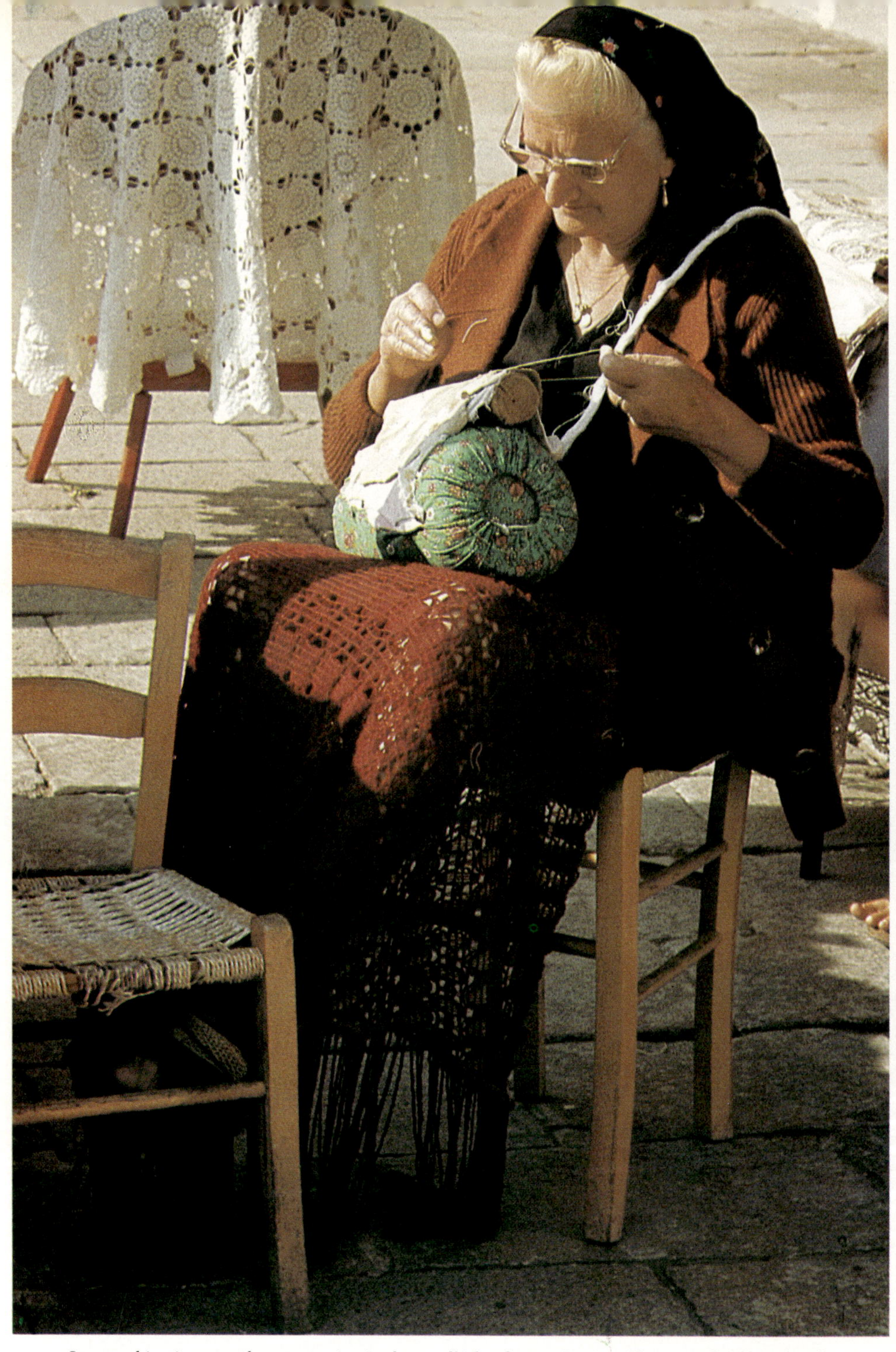

Lace making is a popular occupation in the small islands near Venice. Photographs show details. White hair shows well against a dark background. A longer focal length, 90 or 135mm is an advantage.

switched on with intermediary values two L.E.D.'s are illuminated and the shutter speed is electronically controlled to give an intermediate speed. Shorter or longer exposure times are achieved by controlling the lens apertures. The rectangular shaped L.E.D.'s displayed against shutter speeds of $1/30$th of a second and longer indicate that care must be taken during exposure in order to prevent camera shake. Under extremely bright conditions a red triangular L.E.D. at the top of the scale will indicate that a smaller lens aperture should be used. A triangular shaped L.E.D. at the bottom of the scale signifies that an exposure of one second or longer is required.

The automatic programme $\boxed{P}$ is of particular importance to the non technically minded photographer or the inexperienced. With this programme both shutter speed and lens aperture are automatically selected and controlled in such a way that even the most experienced photographer would not be able to select a more correct exposure. Note: in order to use the whole range of apertures correctly the lens diaphragm should be set to its minimum aperture. The shutter speed control should not be set to X, B or 100, other than this any shutter speed can be selected. The programme is visible in the viewfinder at the bottom left, next to it the diaphragm is indicated. The programme display flashes if the lens is not fully stopped down. The abbreviated shutter speed range is visible in the viewfinder on the right hand side, the longer times are covered over in order to draw attention to the danger of camera shake.

Programme $\boxed{T}$. The desired shutter speed is predetermined, this mode is of most use when photographing subjects such as sports. The programme is indicated to the bottom left hand side of the viewfinder. Next to it the apertures are shown and on the far right the exposure time. If the lens should not be completely stopped down then the programme display flashes and no red L.E.D.'s are visible in the viewfinder. The diaphragm scale on the right side of the viewfinder is indicated in white. If the subject should require an intermediate shutter speed two L.E.D.'s will indicate that there is nothing to worry about since the shutter speed will be exactly set to the required time. The electronically controlled shutter speeds from 1 second to $1/1000$th can be set to any fraction of a second, e.g. $1/370$th. If aperture settings of $f/8$ or smaller are used the red L.E.D.'s are visible. Apertures from $f/5.6$ and larger are indicated by square L.E.D.'s thus indicating to the photographer larger or smaller depth of field. In bright lighting conditions or weak light, selected exposure times outside the scale of indicated exposures is shown by a triangular L.E.D. which can usually be adjusted by altering the aperture control.

The programmes $\boxed{P}$ and $\boxed{T}$ require automatic diaphragm Leica-R. Lenses and accessories without automatic diaphragms are not suitable for use with these metering modes. The Elmarit 180mm up to lens no. 2939700 and the Telyt 250mm up to no. 3050600 can only be used on automatic timing with integrated metering.

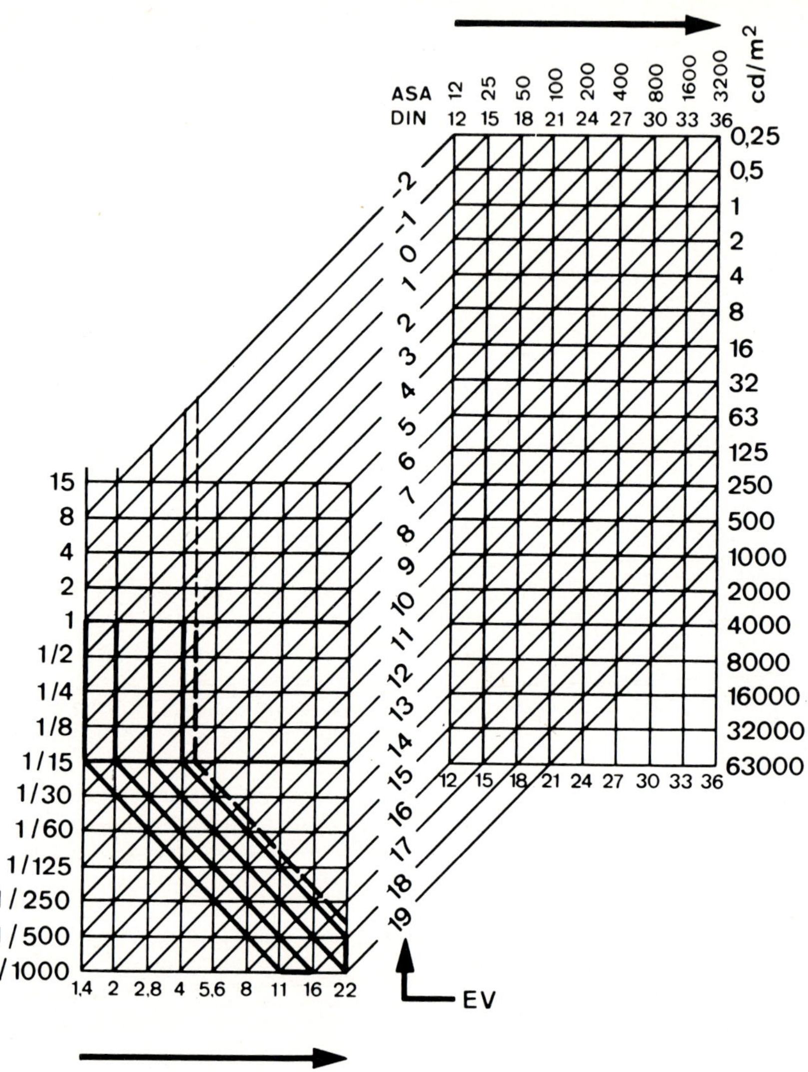

WORKING DIAGRAM OF THE EXPOSURE METER

This working diagram gives an overall picture of what information can be produced from an automatic exposure meter. The limit values, that is the measuring range, is also visible. To begin with the lines appear to be confusing but become more clear when the system is understood. All positions both vertically and horizontally alter their intensity in the proportion 1:2, that is they either double or halve according to the direction. If diagonal lines are followed then the intensity remains the same. Apart from the familiar apertures and shutter speed times which are on the left of the scale. The film sensitivity is from 12 to 36 DIN (12 to 3,200 A.S.A.) and the lighting intensity (C.D. per square metre = Candella per square metre) together with the exposure values are produced in one diagram. They are connected by diagonal lines. The film sensitivity is also taken into account. Here is an example. We have a light intensity of 2,000 C.D./m² which equals bright sunlight, film sensitivity 21 DIN. As is usual with diagrams look for the intersection of the information from the light intensity and the film sensitivity by laying a right angle (corner of a post card) on it in such a way that we have the intersection. Then we look downwards along the edge of the card crossing over the exposure value for 14 until aperture f/11 is shown on the third vertical in the block on the left (aperture and shutter speeds). If we lay the right angle on it again we can read off ¹/₁₂₅th of a second horizontally. The resultant exposure being ¹/₁₂₅th of a second at f/11. The measuring range of the exposure meter with the integrated method covers brightness varying from 0.5 C.D./m² or in practical values with a film of 100 A.S.A. an aperture of f/1.4 at 1 second up to f/22 at ¹/₁₀₀th of a second. With selective metering the values begin at 1 C.D./m² up to 63,000 C.D./m² with a film of the same rating. It is technically possible to obtain automatically controlled exposures of longer times but in practice there is no point because with exposure times greatly in excess of 1 second reciprocity will become a factor, a factor which is not determinable with an automatic exposure facility. Those who have to work using longer exposure times should have the corresponding data sheets for individual films sent to them by the film manufacturers.

STOP DOWN METERING MODE

A few lenses, the P.C. Curtagon and extreme telephoto's and some accessories do not have an automatic diaphragm. Metering is carried out at the working aperture. When the automatic metering is used a prerequisite is that the lenses must be Leica triple cammed. Only metering programmes Ⓐ and A are suitable. Exposure correction with the selective exposure meter is rarely necessary. The very small measuring field makes it a simple task to meter a small portion of the subject, therefore it is questionable. Where the corrections are necessary with photographs of high contrast, i.e. for snow and beach scenes one would under expose without any correction because of the high reflective contrast of the subject, for subjects such as these a degree of over exposure is required. In the case of the snow scene + 1 would be sufficient. However a very bright beach scene may require a factor of +2. Very dark subjects would be too light without a correction and a degree of under exposure would be required. To adjust the manual override the catch (11) is pressed and the scale (16) is set to the desired value with the lever next to it. Half values are adjustable up to a factor of +/−2. When the camera is set to override a symbol containing I or is seen in the bottom left hand of the viewfinder which flashes intermittently when an exposure correction has been selected, to remind the photographer.

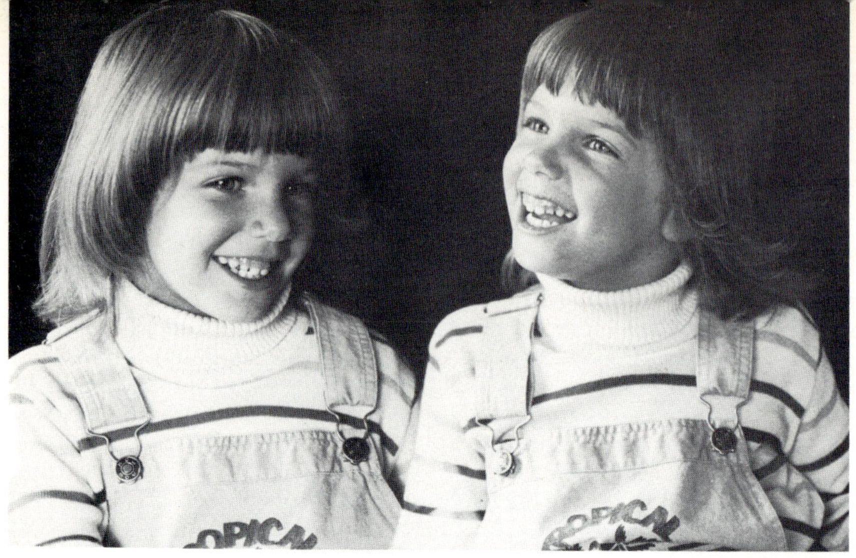

Double exposures of people are particularly successful when photographed against a black background. It is only required that the area used in the first exposure is not encroached upon. Black velvet reflects less light than most other materials, however black velour paper provides an acceptable substitute.

DELAYED ACTION

The automatic electronically controlled delayed action (1) has a running time of approximately 8 seconds. Set the delay time by the knob (17) clockwise through 30°. The self timer sequence commences when the camera is switched on by a slight touch of the release button or by pressure of the locking button of the programme selector. An L.E.D. (10) flashes and approximately 2 seconds before the exposure is made this becomes constant. The function, which can only be selected when the camera is wound on and can be disengaged by merely turning the knob back to its neutral position, i.e. 30° anticlockwise.

MULTIPLE EXPOSURES

With the Leica R4 the facility for making deliberate double or multiple exposures is provided. This is useful when making up title slides or multiple image photographs seen in advertising. It can even be used to give the impression of an X-ray photograph illustrating the internal mechanism of a piece of machinery. Multiple exposures of a subject are very simple providing the background is dark and unobtrusive. Sophisticated combinations can be made using models to produce an impression of an animated sequence. To undertake these more complex tasks it is suggested that the photographer should experiment with combinations of exposure and composition as the overlap of the subject will become increasingly complex. To avoid disappointment it is necessary to take each sequence several times.

Multiple exposures can be made very simply with the Leica R4. After the first exposure the rewind button (31) located at the base of the camera is depressed and the film wind lever is operated, thus cocking the shutter with the film transport mechanism disengaged. The frame can be exposed again and if more exposures are required the procedure is merely repeated.

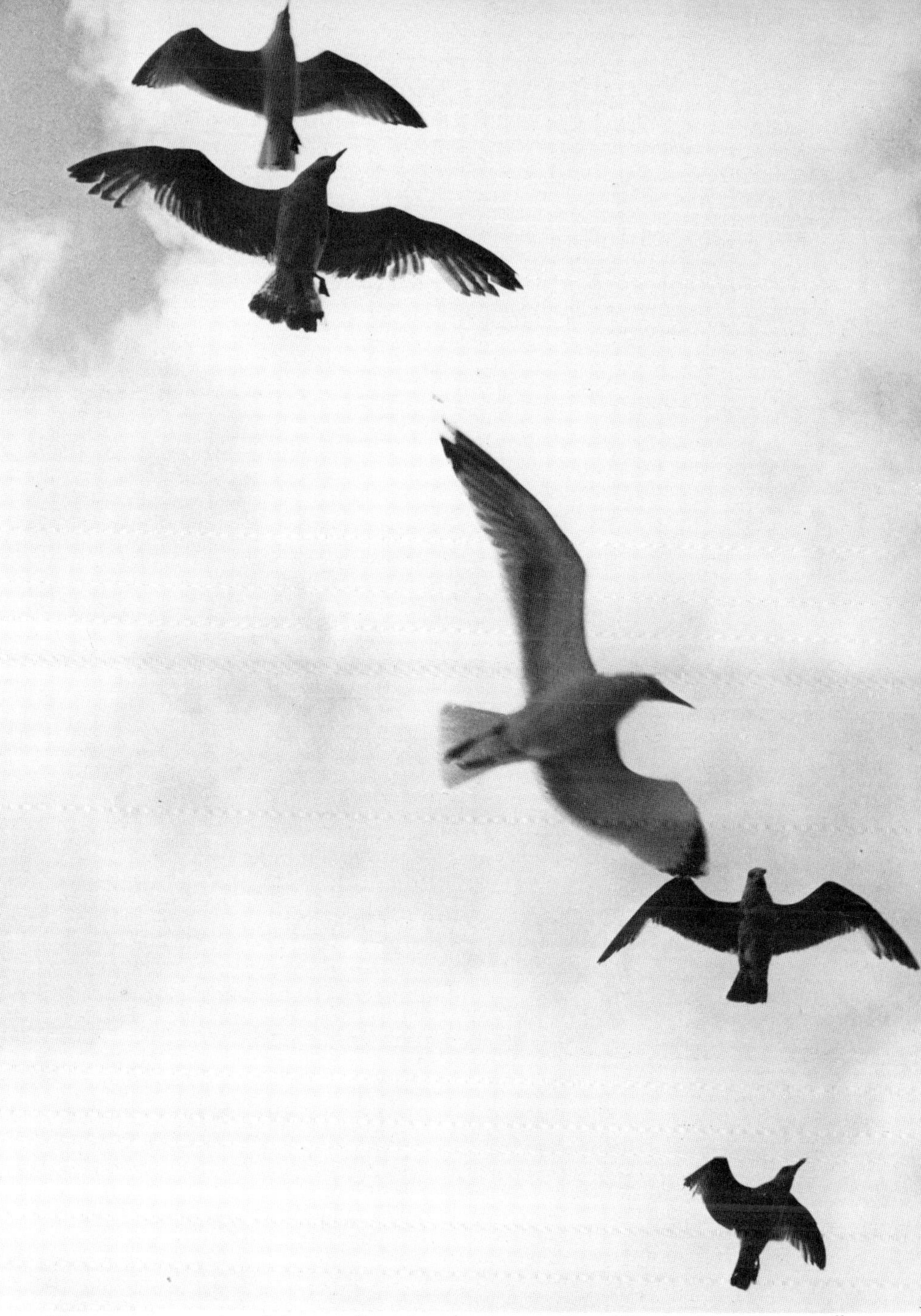

The exposure metering of the seagulls against the sky provides a difficult subject. The overall brightness of the sky has the most effect on the meter. Therefore to ensure that the detail is retained for the birds an exposure override correction of +1 should be used.

FLASH SYNCHRONISATION

The focal plane shutter of the Leica R4 allows flash synchronisation to be used at $1/100$th of a second (marked with X on the shutter speed control ring) longer exposure times are also usable ($1/60$th to 1 second plus B). All normal electronic flash guns fitted with standard coaxial leads are usable. The contact (24) for plugging in the flash lead (X contact) is located on the front of the camera at the left hand side. Electronic flash equipment with hot shoe connections are located in the camera accessory shoe which is provided with the appropriate contacts. Expendable bulb flash guns are also connected either by means of the standard flash socket (24) or by means of the hot shoe facility. The following table gives the recommended exposure times for expendable flash bulbs:-

FLASHBULBS	M2	1-1/60 s, B
	AG 1, AG 3, GE 5, 25, M3, M5, PF1 FP 5, PF 60, XM 1	1-1/30 s, B
	FP 26, PF 6, PF 45, PF 100, XM 6	1-1/15 s, B

The shutter speeds and aperture combinations appropriate to the guide number can be adjusted with the camera in the manual mode by setting the shutter ring to X. The fact that the flash gun has recycled is indicated by a flashing triangular L.E.D. located on the right hand side of the viewfinder. This flash equipment is provided by several manufacturers (Braun 370 B.V.C., Braun 4.10, Mecablitz 45 C.T.5, Mecablitz 60 C.T.2, Vivitar 285). This automatic facility is provided regardless of which metering mode the camera is set on. With aperture priority and programme modes the aperture is no longer set automatically by the camera's metering, therefore the aperture must be set manually to the appropriate stop when using flash equipment, according to the guide number and distance from the subject. If it is no longer set to flash readiness or if the flash equipment is switched off the Leica R4 automatically readjusts itself to the selected programme. If the batteries fail you can still utilise the flash facility if the shutter speed control is set to $1/100$th or **B**.

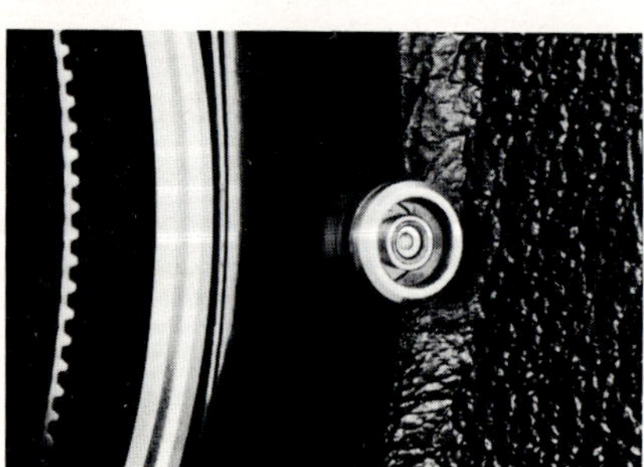
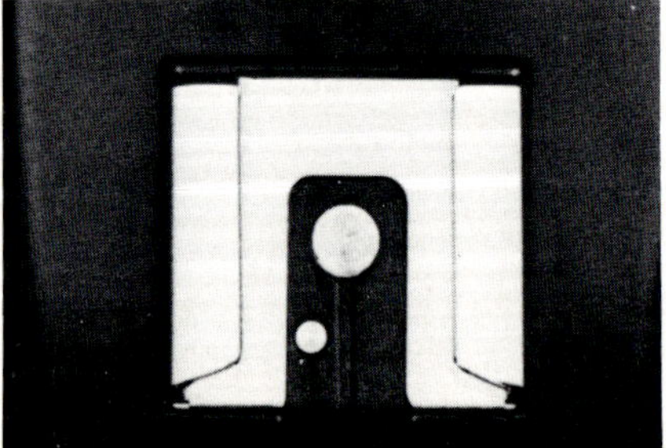

THE MOTOR WINDER R4

All Leica R4 cameras can be used in conjunction with the Leica R4 motor winder unit. The film transport and shutter setting are taken over by the motor unit, increasing the speed of operation. This enables the photographer to be completely free to concentrate on the subject and to make exposures in rapid succession. It is often found in photography, particularly in subjects such as portraiture that it is the second exposure which is the successful one. The subject, not realising the camera's rapid operational function will relax immediately the first exposure is made. The power winder facility will enable the alert photographer to immediately take the second and probably more successful photograph in rapid succession. The motor drive and the power winder differ in the speed with which successive photographs can be taken. The motor winder allows two exposures per second and with the motor drive this speed is increased to four frames per second, although it also has provision for reducing this speed to two frames per second and indeed to single shots. Both units can be switched to allow multiple exposures to be made. However this switch does not automatically reset itself. The camera is provided with an acoustic signal to indicate the multiple exposure selection, when the shutter release is depressed to its switching position or when the programme selector is used. The motor units are powered by means of six alkaline manganese batteries in the case of the motor winder, or ten with the motor drive. Rechargeable nickle-cadmium batteries may also be used.

When the camera is to be stored with the motor attached it is advisable to remove the battery pack as it is not unknown for the batteries to oxidise and cause damage to contacts if subjected to long storage periods. In extremely cold conditions the output of the batteries is reduced. In these conditions it is advisable to keep a spare battery pack in the pocket. It is also possible to obtain a battery extension lead which enables the battery pack to remain in the pocket and provide power externally to the motor. Obviously the readiness of the motor depends on the condition of the batteries. Even when purchasing new batteries ensure that they are in fresh condition and are not leaking. Standard batteries are not rechargeable, this is possible only with the nickel-cadmium type.

With nickel-cadmium batteries it is advisable to recharge them after periods of storage. To recharge them follow the manufacturers directions. When the motor is attached the total energy supply, including that required for metering is taken over by the motor battery pack, thus saving the standard camera batteries. There is an adapter for external supply (note that a different lead is used for the motor winder and the motor drive) however the motor accessories, handgrip, cable release and remote control apparatus are used in common with both the motor winder and the motor drive.

Which motor the individual photographer uses will depend on personal preference and requirements. I personally use the R4 winder. It is very quiet and its capacity to take two frames a second is perfectly adequate for my requirements. On a film with 36 exposures the advantages for me are that I can concentrate on the subject without being restricted or interrupted by the necessity of winding on the film manually.

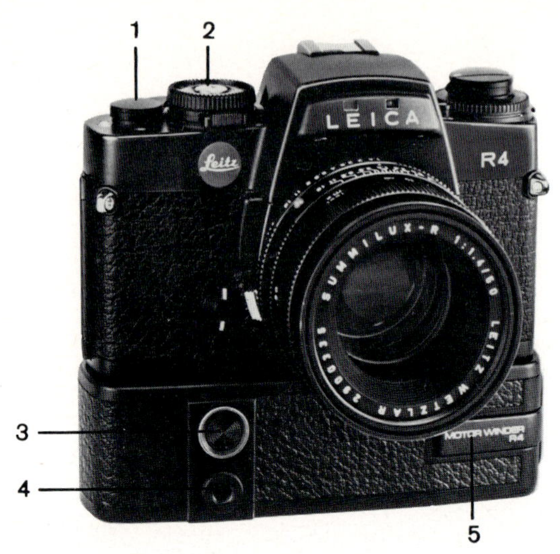
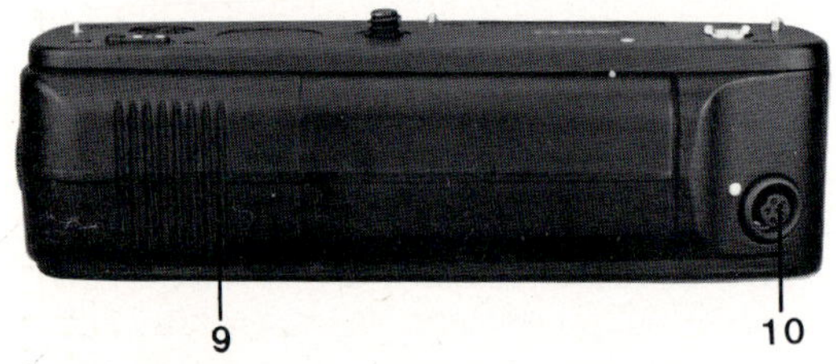

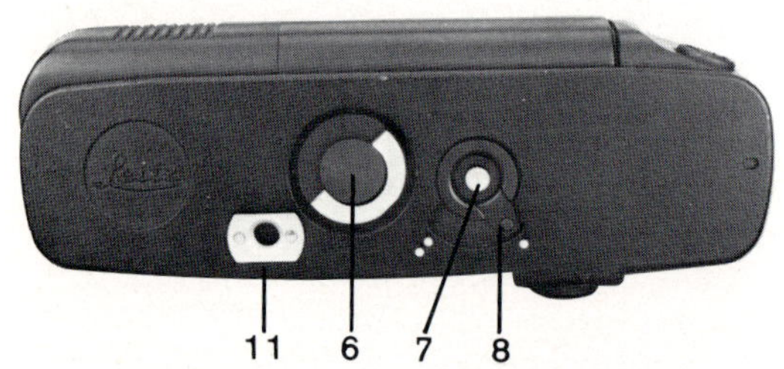

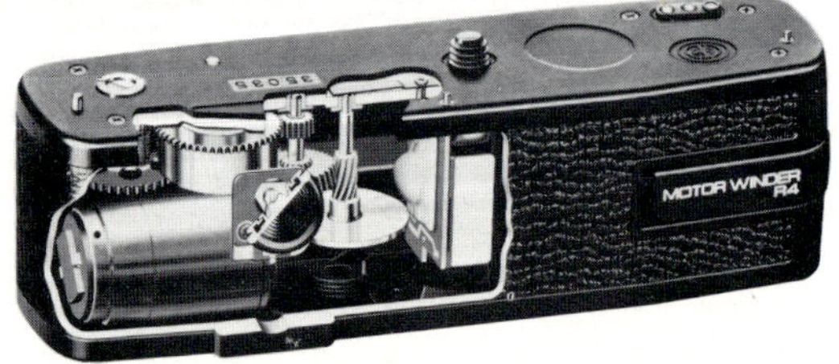

The mechanism of the motor winder is particularly quiet in operation. This is contributed to by the use of a specially developed rubber used in the drive train.

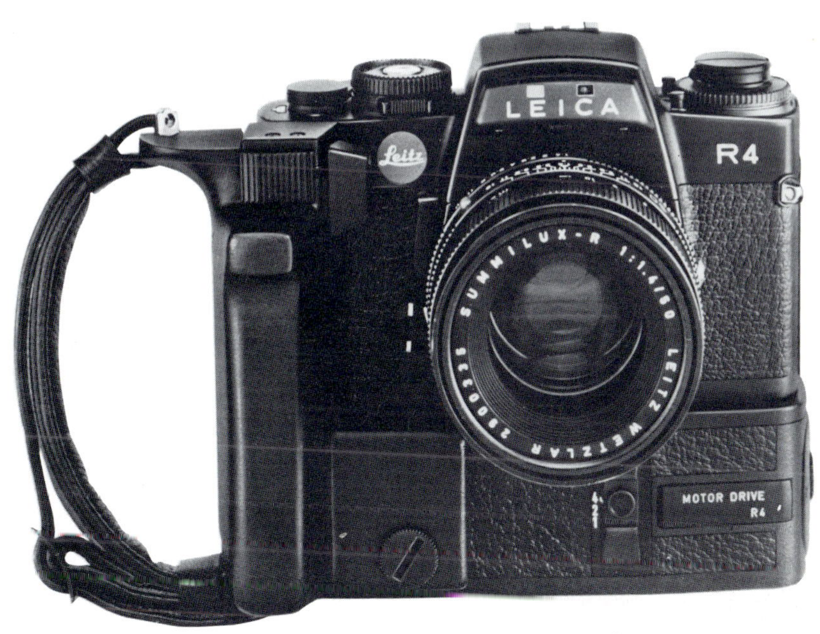

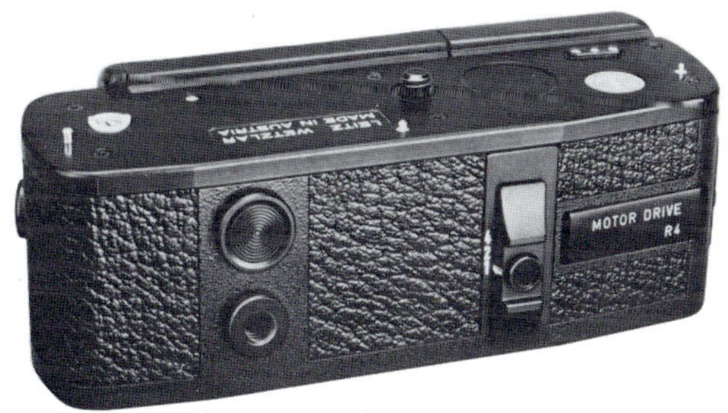

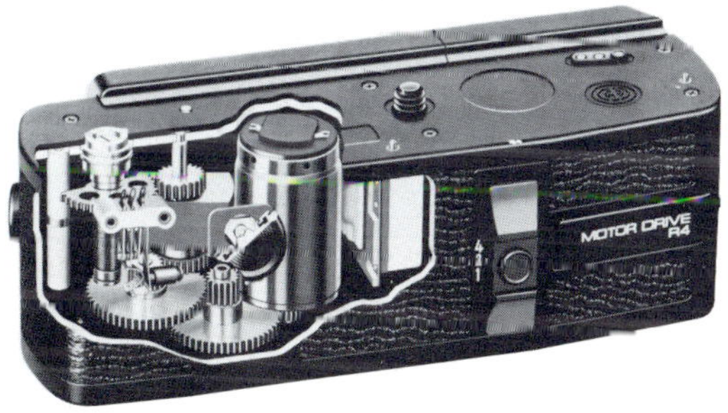

The motor drive of the Leica R4 enables the photographer to adjust the taking rate from 2 to 4 frames per second. Single shots with the motor drive acting as a winder unit. In other respects the operation of the motor drive unit is the same as the motor winder unit.

ATTACHING THE R4 MOTOR WINDER
(The same applies to the motor drive)

The motor winder can be attached or removed from the Leica R4 regardless of whether the camera is loaded or not. First of all remove the protective cover and the contact protector on the upper side of the winder. Wind on the film (2) but leave the rapid transport lever in the off-set position, thus preventing the winder from being switched on inadvertently whilst being attached to the camera. To attach the winder first insert the guiding peg on the winder into the slot provided in the camera casing and then orientate the winder so that the contacts line up. Turning the screw will securely lock the two units (6). Push the rapid wind lever into the rest position, the combination of Leica R4 and motor winder is now ready for use.

INSERTING THE BATTERIES

The battery housing (9) can be taken out when the unlocking button (5) is released. For safety reasons it is provided with a double lock. The capacity of the batteries is 1.5 volt each. Alkaline batteries (leak proof) are to be recommended and the size is R6. Long life nickel-cadmium batteries of the same capacity may also be used if preferred.

Loosen the screw on the edge of the battery compartment by means of a coin until it is released and can be removed from the motor unit. Insert the batteries strictly in accordance with the diagrams supplied with the actual component. Push the casing together and screw it back. Finally push the battery casing into the winder or motor unit until an audible click informs that it is securely in position.

The power supply on the Leica R4 is provided automatically when the motor winder or motor drive is attached to the camera, the camera's internal is automatically switched off.

If the batteries' output reduces by a certain value the motor function is automatically switched off, the electronic camera function i.e. metering and shutter operations will however continue to function as long as there is sufficient supply.

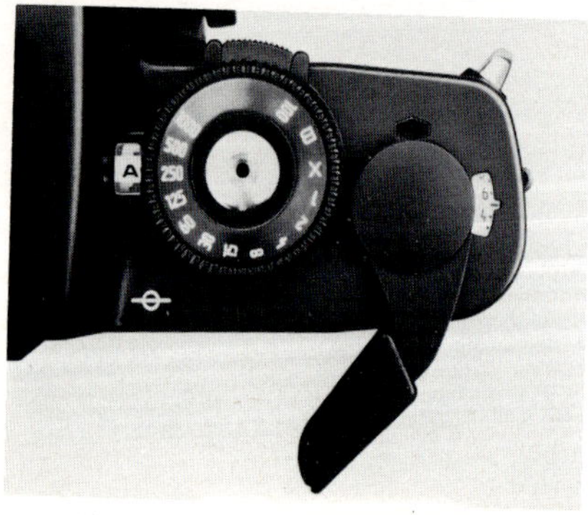

When the lever of the Leica R4 is turned outwards the motor winder will not function. In this position the shutter will not release. When the camera is being loaded it is recommended that the lever is put into this position.

Remove spent batteries as soon as possible. When changing the batteries always put in new ones or freshly recharged nickel-cadmium type, never mix batteries of varying ages and stages of expenditure. Batteries supplied from different manufacturers should never be intermixed. I always keep fresh batteries as previously stated in the vegetable compartment of my refrigerator. **Important!** With the motor unit attached the battery tester described in the instructions is no longer applicable. This function is now carried out by pressing down the button on the programme selector. A battery test for the motor function is not connected with this.

UNLOADING AND LOADING THE CAMERA WITH THE MOTOR ATTACHED

The advance lever should be swung out into the readiness position when inserting a film with the winder switched off. The film is then loaded in the normal manner and once completed the rapid film winder should be returned to the neutral position. After 36 exposures according to the film counter the winder automatically switches off. To remove the film the button for releasing the rewind (7) on the underside of the winder is pressed. Then the film is rewound and taken out of the camera in the usual manner. When the film winder is motorised only 36 exposure film should be used.

TAKING TIME EXPOSURE PICTURES

When time exposures are taken the shutter speed dial should be used on the setting B. Time exposures of any length can be made and the camera's release button must be used. Long time exposures are possible with the winder if they have been indicated and selected by the metering mode. Even with a motor or winder attached the film can still be transported manually. To do this the rapid wind lever must be pushed into the stand off position before the photograph is taken.

TAKING A SERIES OF PICTURES

By pressing down on the release button on the winder (3) exposure after exposure follows, as long as there is sufficient film in the camera and pressure is maintained. When the camera is operating on shutter speeds of $1/60$th of a second and shorter about two pictures per second are exposed. All settings can be used except for B as explained above.

ELECTRICAL RELEASE

Various releases are available and can be attached to the connecting socket (10) on the winder according to requirements. Either series or individual photographs can be taken in this manner. When double exposures are required with the winder the selector switch (8) remains in its normal position. The button for freeing the rewind spool must be pressed before the first photograph is taken. The first exposure is made by using the camera release button. When the camera is set the button (7) automatically resets itself for the second exposure.

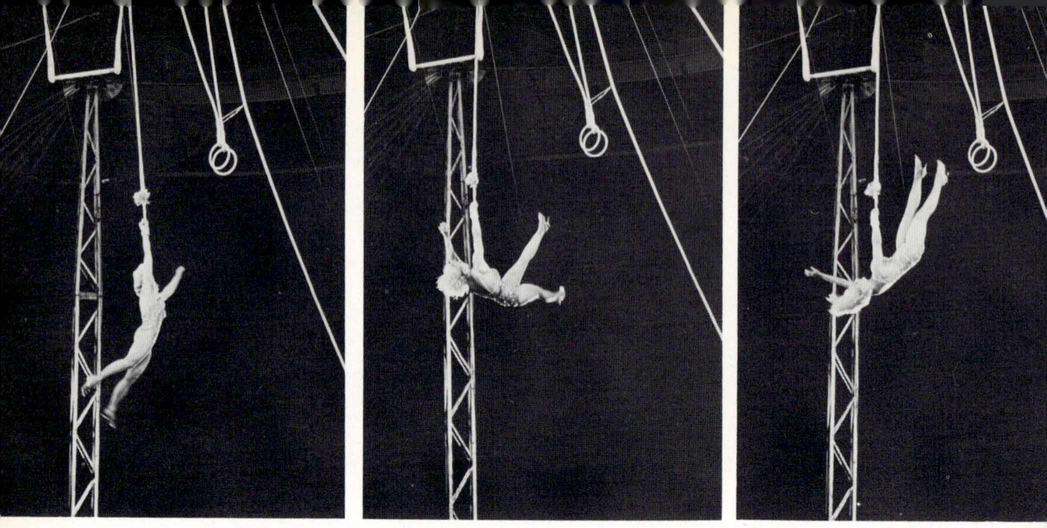

The main advantage of the Motor winder is that it enables the camera to be always ready for t
next photograph. Since it immediately winds on it is possible to release again without pausing.
ability to photograph at two frames per second is only of secondary interest it is in the high spe

MULTIPLE EXPOSURES WITH THE WINDER

To take multiple exposures the selector switch (8) is put into the correct position and remains there until the desired number of exposures has been made. When in this position an acoustic signal is given out when the camera's electronic systems are switched on by pressing down the release button or programme selector lock. When the multiple exposure sequence has been completed the selector switch (8) must be returned to the normal position.

ACCESSORIES FOR THE R4 MOTOR WINDER AND MOTOR DRIVE UNITS

THE R4 HANDGRIP

The R4 hand grip is for use in rapid action hand held photography. This hand grip enables the Leica R4 complete with a power winder to be held more steadily. The leather hand grip is adjustable to suit individual requirements.

Before fitting the hand grip the camera carrying strap should be removed for subsequent reattachment to the camera, after the hand grip has been installed. The hand grip can be screwed into the appropriate threaded socket on the motor winder by means of a coin. In order to avoid unintentional exposures whilst carrying out this operation the release button on the hand grip can be locked. Individual exposures are possible if the camera release button is used. For a series of pictures the release located within the hand grip is used.

THE R4 TRIPOD ADAPTER

This tripod adaptor with a ¼" threaded socket allowing the Leica R4 complete with motor drive or motor wind unit (or the camera alone) to be securely attached to a tripod.

48

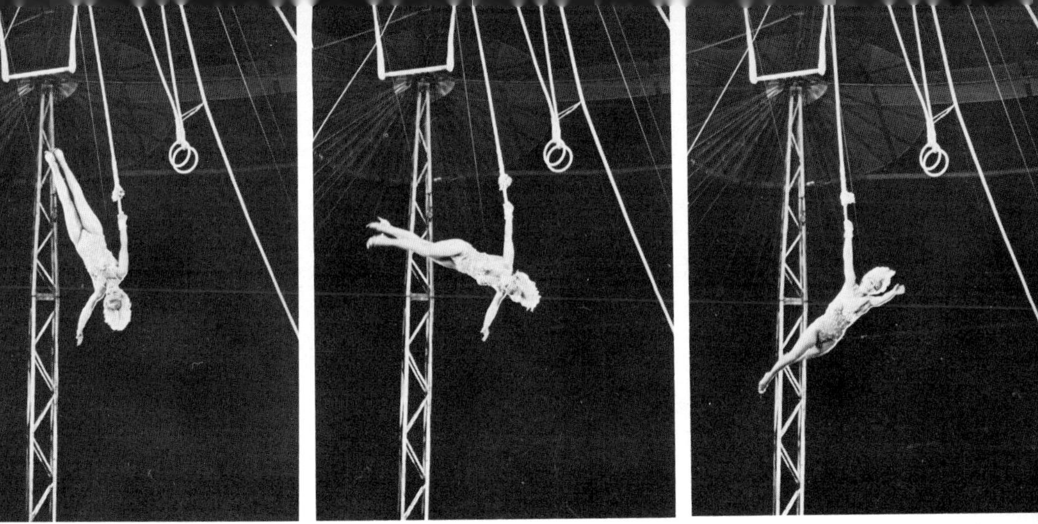

...ge of four frames per second that the motor drive proves its worth. Interesting series of photographs such as this series taken at the Krone circus. Elmarit-R f2.8 90mm.

CABLE RELEASE

This cable release is provided in two types, 30cm long for use with the universal hand grip and shoulder support, and 5m long for electronic remote release. By making use of several extension cables which are provided in lengths of 25 metres this distance can be increased.

THE ELECTRONIC CONTROL LEICA R4

This small and handy device is designed for the remote operation of the camera. It is provided with a digital display readout of the number of exposures. It can also be set so that a series of photographs are taken at pre-determined intervals. These intervals can be adjusted over a range of two frames per second to intervals of 10 minutes between successive exposures. The control device is supplied with an extension cable 2.5 metres in length which is attached to the remote device and which is plugged in to the five pin connecting socket located on the front of the winder. By utilising additional extension cables the distance can be extended up to approximately 100 metres.

BATTERY CASING (reference MWR order no. 14280)

This accessory is for the MR motor winder only. A second battery pack kept always loaded with fresh or recharged batteries is the easiest way to ensure rapid replacement of power during a photographic session. It will be found that when photographing under conditions of extreme cold having two packs will enable the photographer to keep one in his pocket and one in the camera.

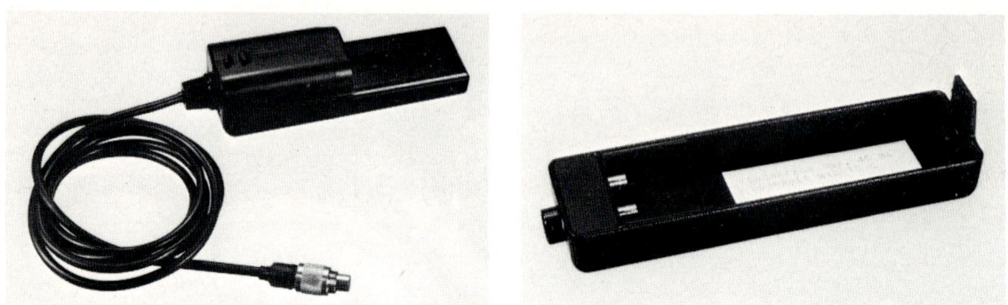

Left: External power supply MW-R. Right: Battery storage housing MW-R.

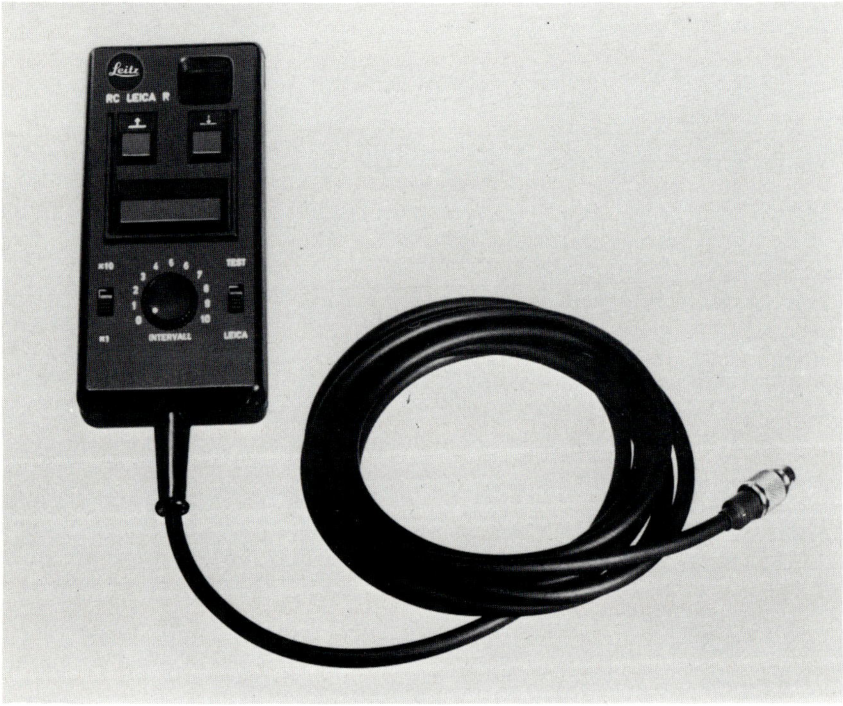

Electronic remote control device R.

The two packs should be frequently interchanged so that the batteries do not suffer from the effects of the cold. The power supply can be carried in the pocket and connected by means of an extension lead (order no. 14278) which is plugged into the winder in place of the normal battery casing. Special storage batteries and power supply units up to a maximum of 8.5 volts can also be attached to this adapter. When a second battery power supply is used with the Leica R4 motor drive the order number is 14322 and the adapter for the external supply MDR is 14323.

Faults	Cause	Remedy
1. The motor winder does not operate.	The available film has been exposed.	Rewind film and remove.
	The manual rapid film winder is not in the rest position.	Push the lever back to rest position.
	Camera has been incorrectly fitted to motor.	Remove motor and fit correctly.
	Spent batteries.	Remove and replace batteries.
2. The motor winder is sluggish.	Spent batteries.	Remove and replace batteries
3. The shutter release jammed.	Camera is incorrectly fitted to motor.	Remove motor and fit correctly.
4. There is an audible warning signal when the release is touched.	Selector switch for multiple exposure is switched on	Move switch to normal position.
5. Camera does not operate.	Incorrectly inserted batteries.	Remove batteries and replace according to indicated markings.
6. Film cartridge jams.	Incorrect film loading.	Replace film.

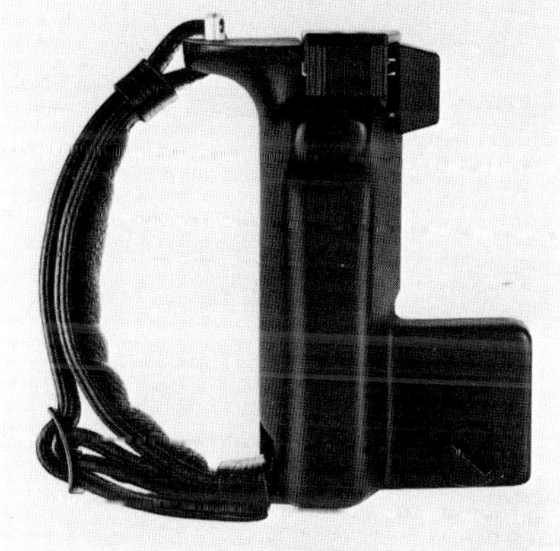
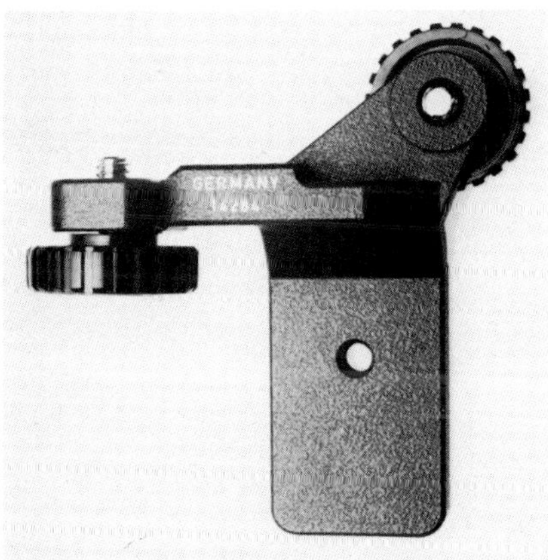

Hand grip and tripod adaptor for the Motor Winder R4.

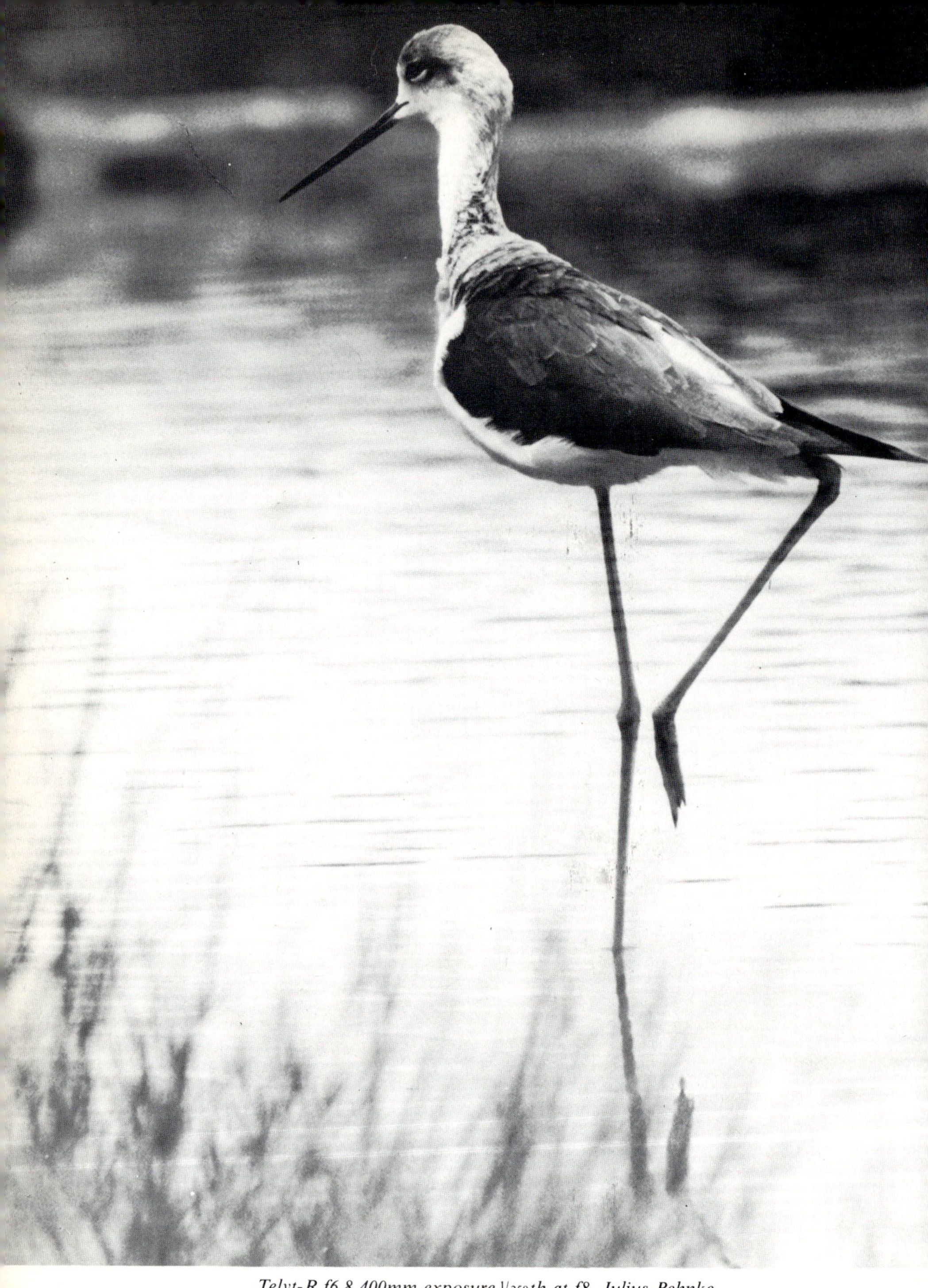

Telyt-R f6.8 400mm exposure ¹/₂₅₀th at f8. Julius Behnke.

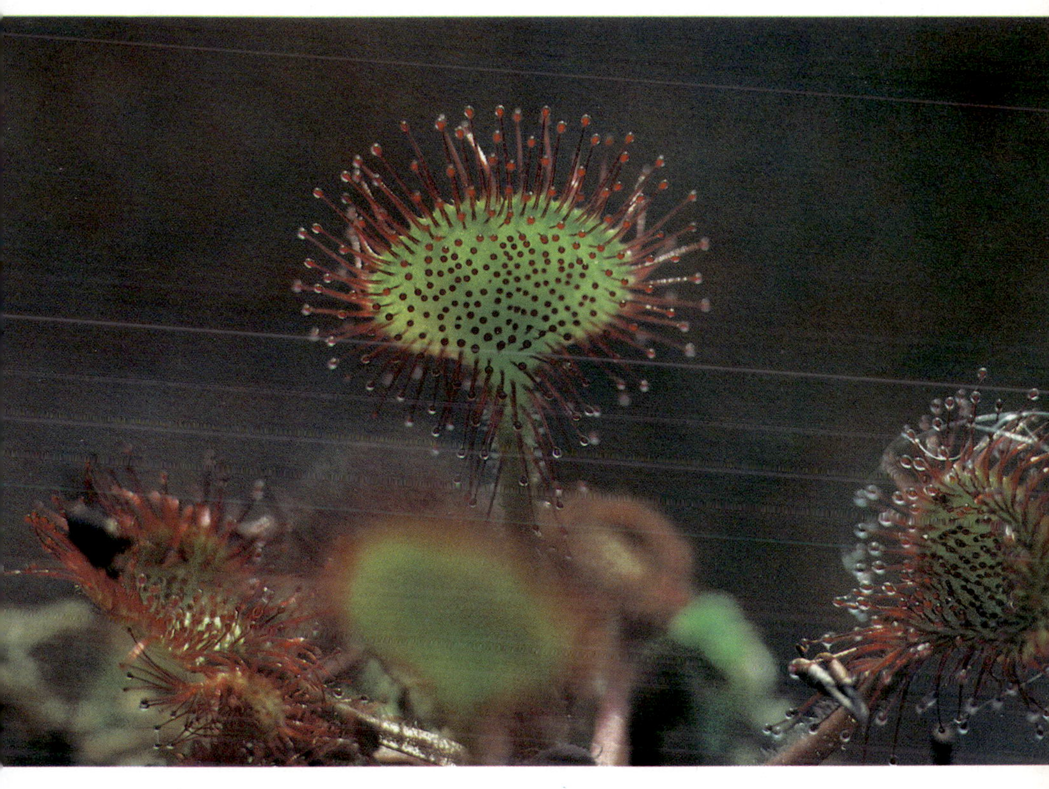

Sun dew. Macro-Elmarit-R 60mm f2.8. Aperture f5.6, 1:1. The relatively large diaphragm was consciously selected in order to draw attention to the sticky hairs on the leaf and to make the background unrecognisable. The plant catches insects on its sticky hairs and then draws them down to absorb their bodies. Photograph: Julius Behnke.

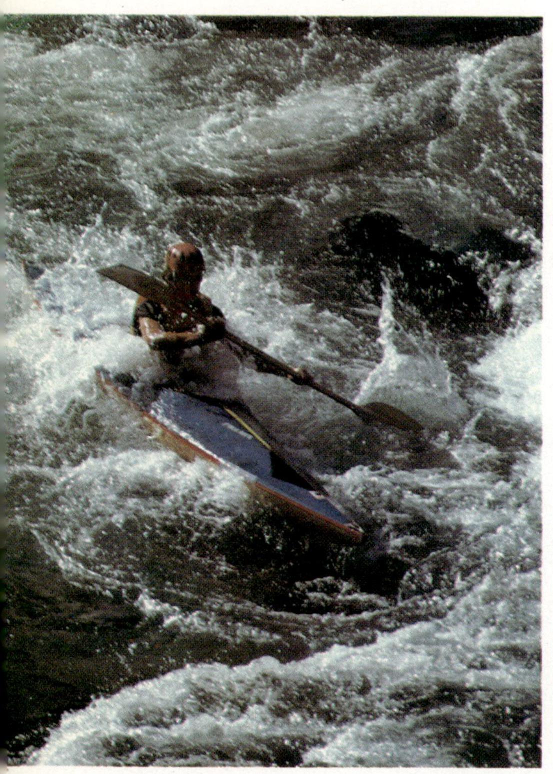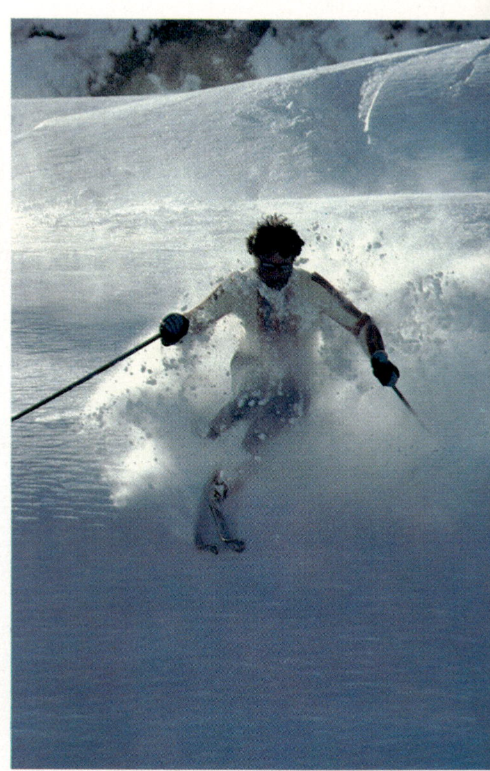

Sports photographs demand a fast shutter speed and fast reactions from the photographer. If you are not familiar with the sport, take an expert with you who can draw your attention to the most important areas. Good sport photographs are rare, even experts are not always successful. One should not be thrifty with film.
Photographs: Theo Kisselbach and Professor F. Hoppichler.

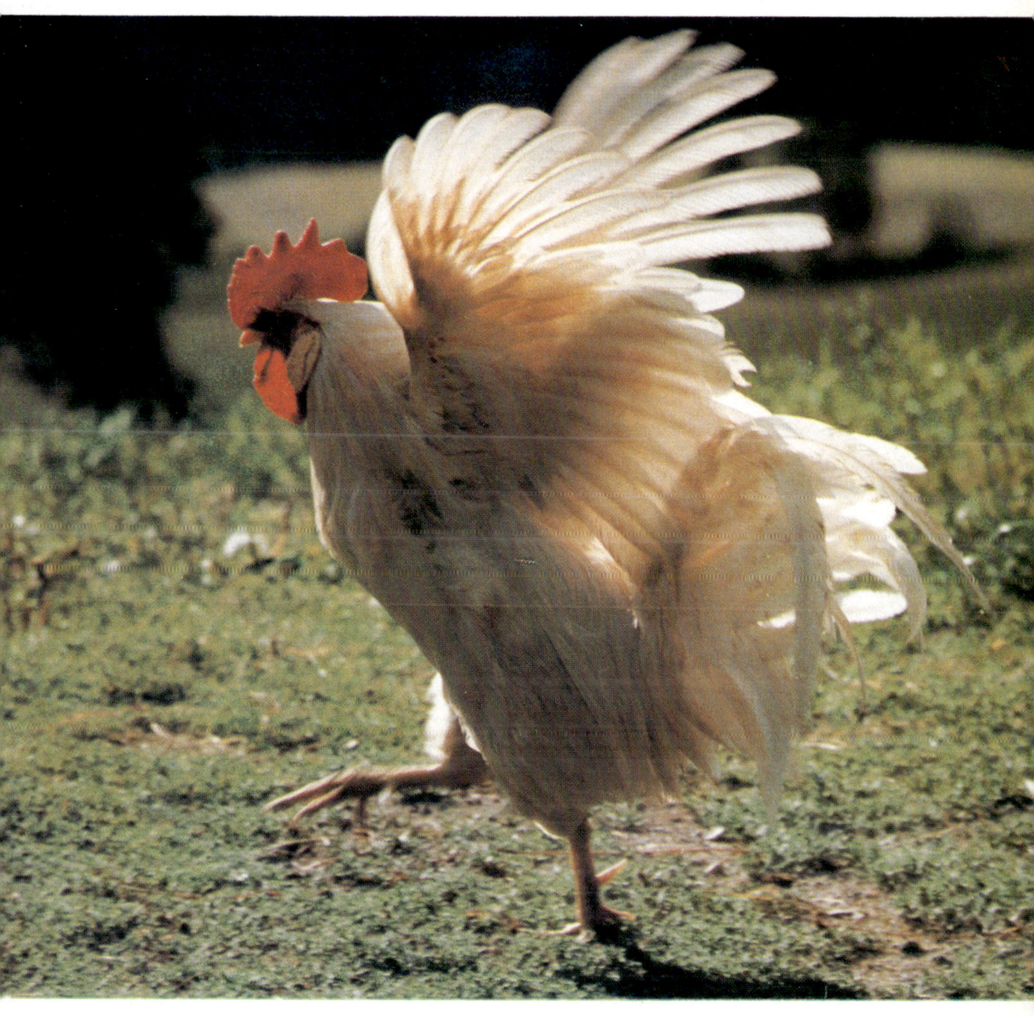

This proud cockerel was photographed with the Apo-Telyt-R 180mm f/3.4 in reflected light. Automatic exposure is a great advantage for snap shots as one can concentrate on focusing. The sideways movement of the bird was useful as it does not alter the range of about 4m. The camera was panned slightly rendering the ground slightly unsharp although the subject did not suffer.

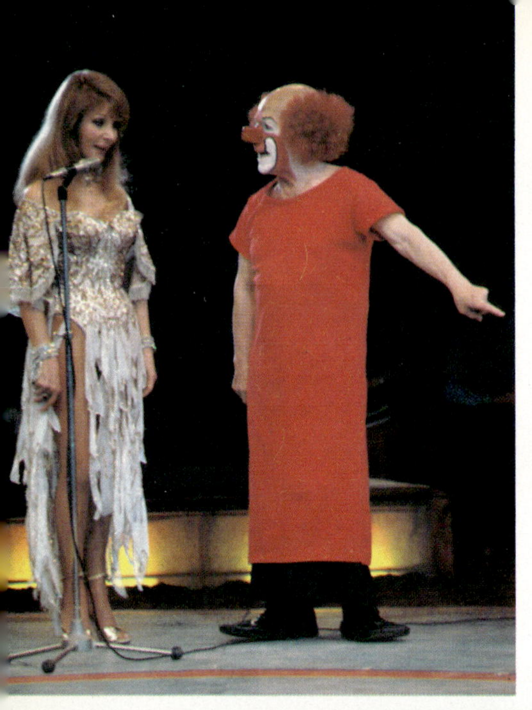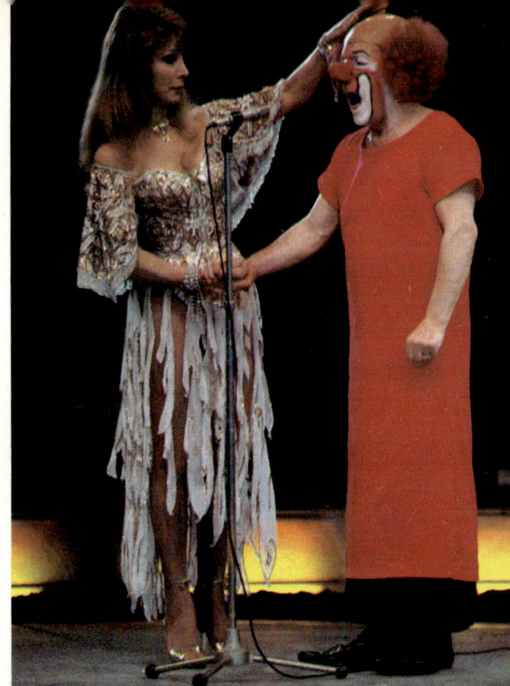

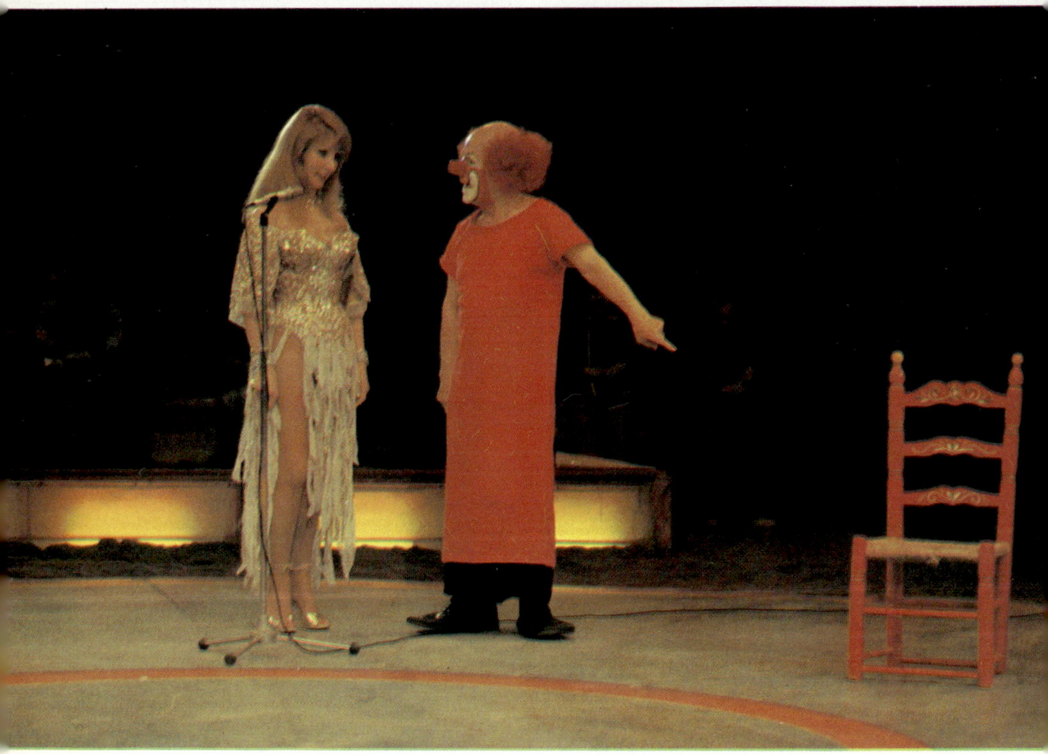

Photographs on (top) artificial light film and (bottom) daylight film. Charlie Rivels in one of his last appearances with the Krone Circus in Munich. Photographs: Theo Kisslebach (top), Inge Springmann (bottom).

THE LENSES

HOW IS A PHOTOGRAPH PRODUCED

The technical side of photography relies on light, the camera and the film. The most important part of the camera is the lens which forms a picture on the light sensitive emulsion. Every lens is in principle exactly the same as a simple convergent lens which gathers together all the rays of light and focuses them to a common point. The distance from the rear nodal point of the lens to the point of focus represents the focal length of a particular lens. Optical lenses have several inherent defects: spherical aberration, chromatic aberration and astigmatism. However these defects can be largely overcome by the use of various optical glasses and configurations of lenses. Slight residual aberrations can be used for artistic results. Stopping down a lens will minimise optical flaws.

FOCAL LENGTH

The focal length of the lens determines the size of the image. A longer focal length produces a larger image while a wide angle lens will produce a reduced image size. The focal length is engraved on the front rim of Leica lenses and on the R4 lenses it is also engraved on the lens barrel for rapid identification.

APERTURES

The f/ number engraved on the aperture scale is a numerical expression of the relative aperture of the lens at its different settings. The aperture number is equal to the focal length divided by the effective diameter of the lens.

FOCUSING

The camera lens produces an image on the light sensitive emulsion, but in order to render the subject sharp the distance between the lens and film is adjusted. Subjects lying closer or further away will be rendered with varying degrees of clarity depending upon the focal length of the lens and the distance of the subject focused on. Depth of field can be controlled to some degree by stopping down the lens. It is essential that the photographer has a firm grasp of the principle involved and learns by experimentation how to control this feature. Near to the aperture ring on R4 lenses there is a depth of field scale which shows the depth of field extending between the two distances engraved between the two aperture scales. In order to make this rather abstract concept of depth of field clearer there are illustrations on the following pages showing the effect of changing the lens aperture and subject distance.

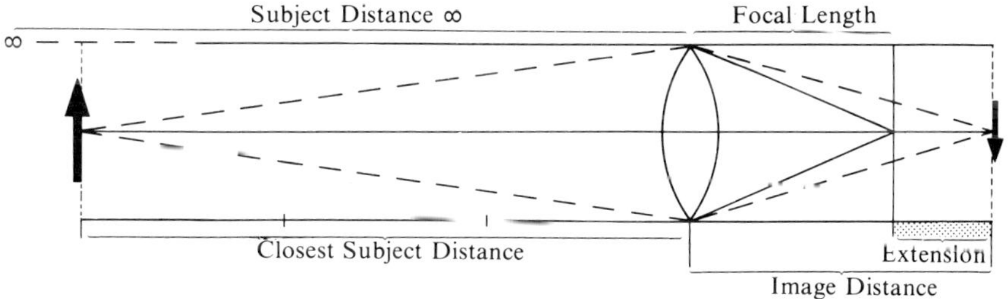

DEPTH OF FIELD

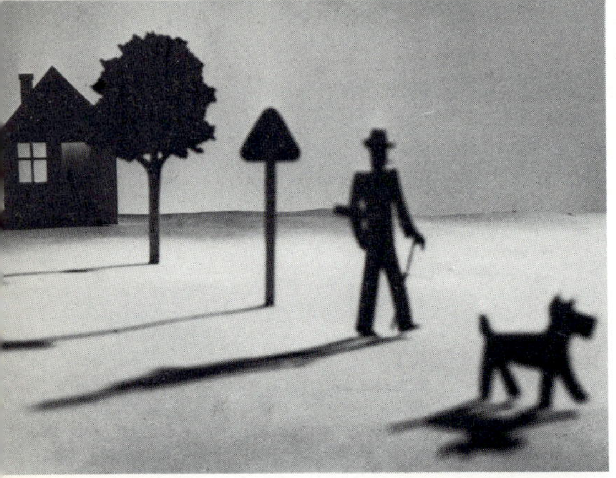

RIGHT
The depth of field changes as the lens is stopped down. In this model the effect is clearly demonstrated. In this first picture taken at f4 the depth of field extends from 4 to 7 metres.

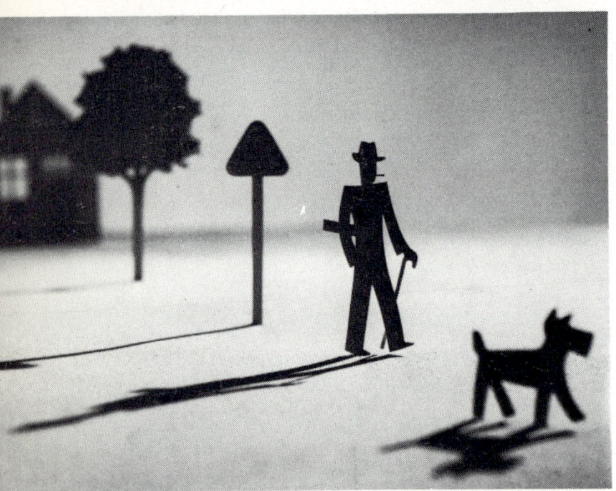

This picture was taken with the lens set at an aperture of f8 the depth of field now is extended so that all aspects between 3.5 to 10 metres are sharp.

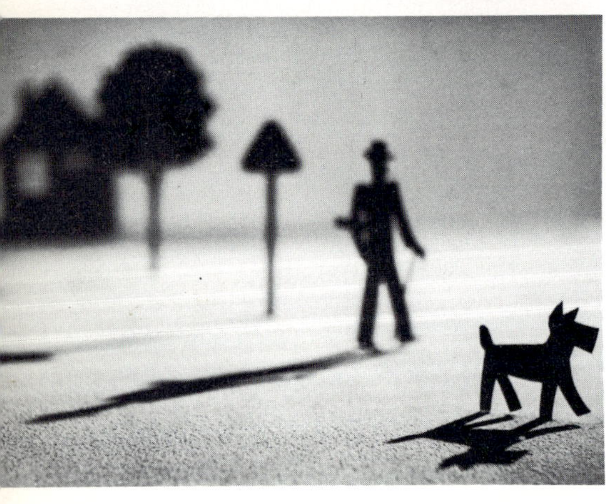

For this illustration the lens was set at its minimum aperture of f16 extending the depth of field from 2.4 metres to infinity.

LEFT
These illustrations show how selective focusing can be used.

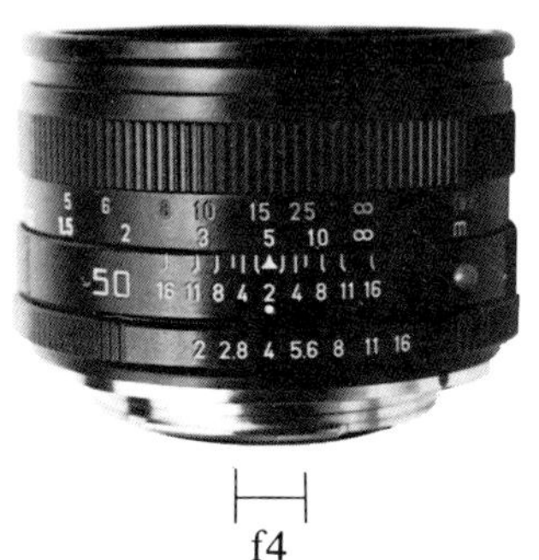
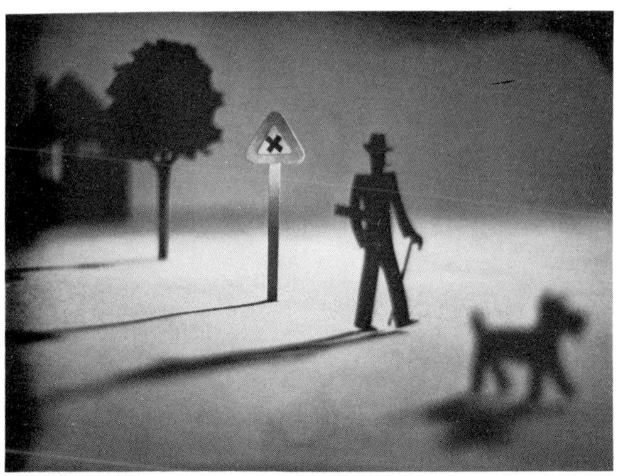

f4

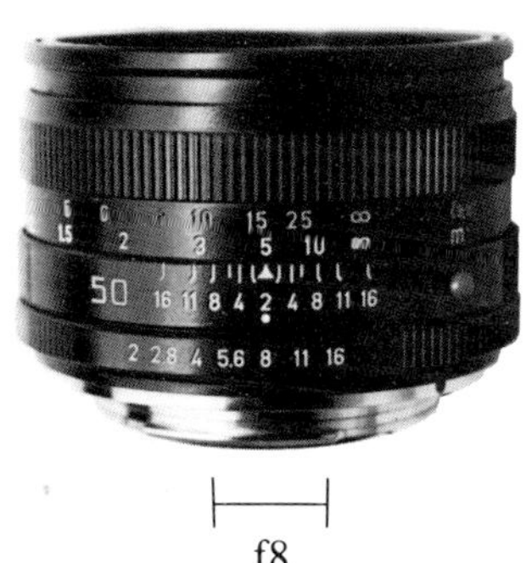
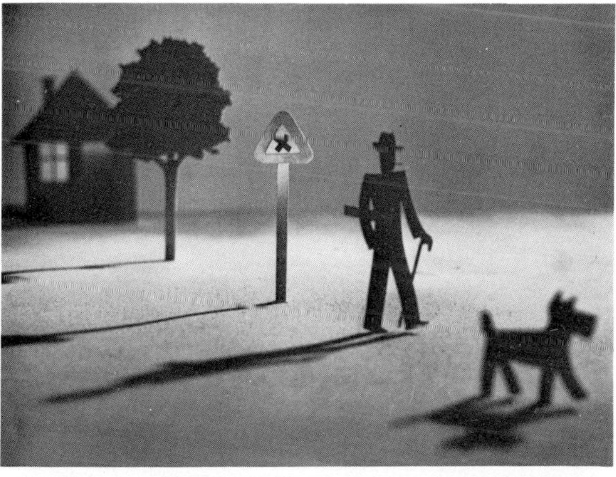

f8

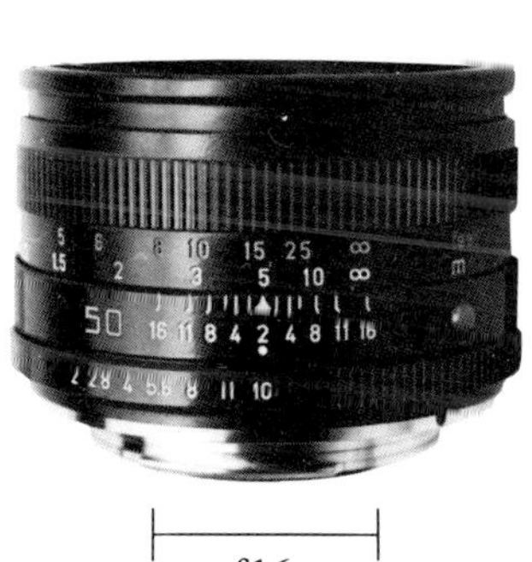
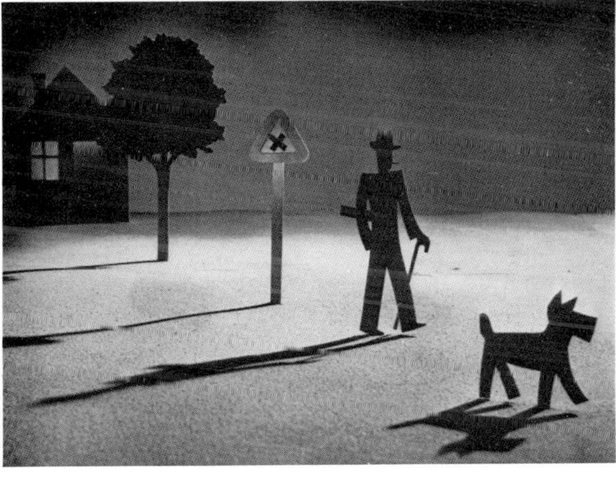

f16

ADJUSTING THE DIAPHRAGM

An adjustable diaphragm is built into the lens which enables the amount of light passing through the lens to be controlled. The diaphragm of the lens works in a similar manner to the iris of the eye. The aperture or diaphragm numbers are engraved on the barrel of the lens, however to simplify the number of individual figures provided only the denominator of the fraction is shown, e.g. 4 = 1:4. The numbers progress in a numerical sequence, hence the next stop down will permit only half the amount of light to be transmitted, one stop up will double the amount of light. The accepted calibration is f/2, 2.8, 5.6, 11, 22. Since relative values are involved the larger the aperture number the smaller will be the diaphragm opening. Leica R4 lenses have click stops at full and half value aperture settings.

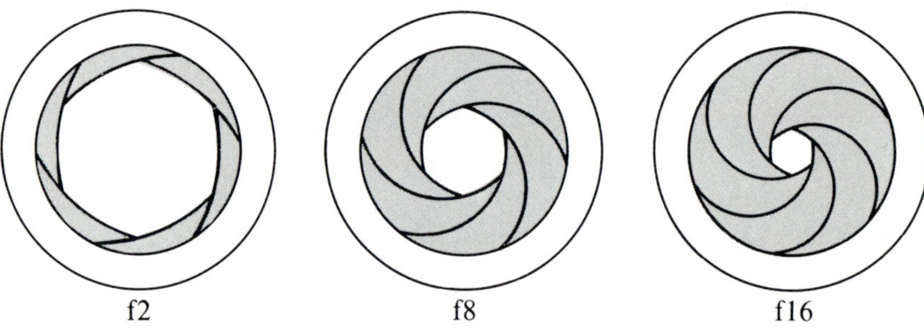

LIGHT LOSSES

The theoretical value of the light intensity is slightly reduced by absorption and internal reflections. Since the advent of lens coating procedures and other technical advances in the production of optical glasses faults have been reduced to an absolute minimum. The Leica R4 aperture scales do take any light loss into account thus giving the photographer the confidence that a marked aperture value is the same as the effective value.

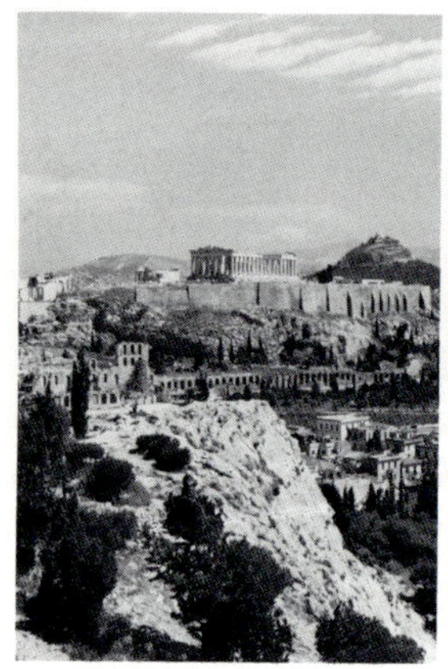
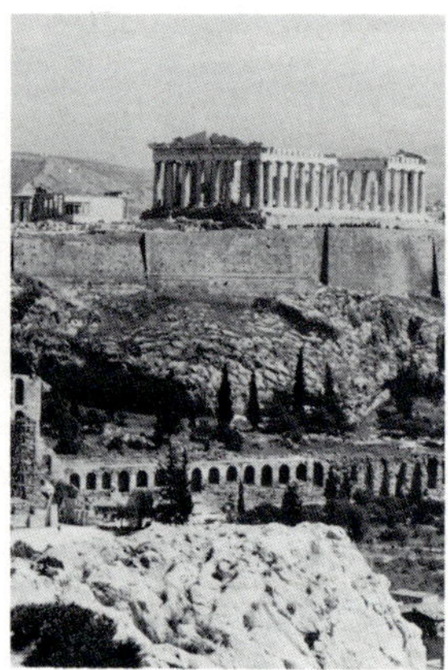
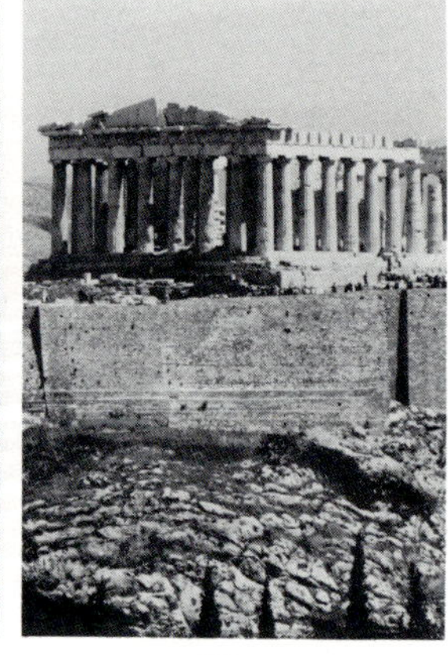

35mm *90mm* *180mm*

These photographs were taken from the same viewpoint with the lenses as indicated.

ANGLE OF VIEW
The angle of view of a lens is related to the acceptance angle measured across the diagonal of the format. Wide angle lenses have a large angle of acceptance and encompass more of the subject than a standard lens, with longer focal lengths the angle of view is proportionally smaller. In practise this is more easily observed through the viewfinder than trying to relate to quoted angles of degrees.

FOCUSING
When a lens is set to infinity (8) the lens to film distance is exactly equal to the focal length. Infinity is usually regarded as being 1,000 times the focal length of the lens. For closer subjects the lens to film distance must be increased proportionally. Leica R4 lenses are provided with a focusing scale which indicates the distance of the object from the film plane. The relationship of the image or the proportion of the image is of interest to those concerned with close up photography, it refers to the relationship in size between the subject and the image. With Leica R4 lenses the metering system is particularly useful in the close up range for as the lens to film plane distance is increased the correct exposure is also lengthened accordingly. Undertaking close-up photography for copy work which involves accurate scaling it is often useful to replace the subject with a piece of 1mm square graph paper which can be related to the 7mm circle of the selective metering system. By counting the number of squares encompassed by the circle it will be possible to work out the exact scale.

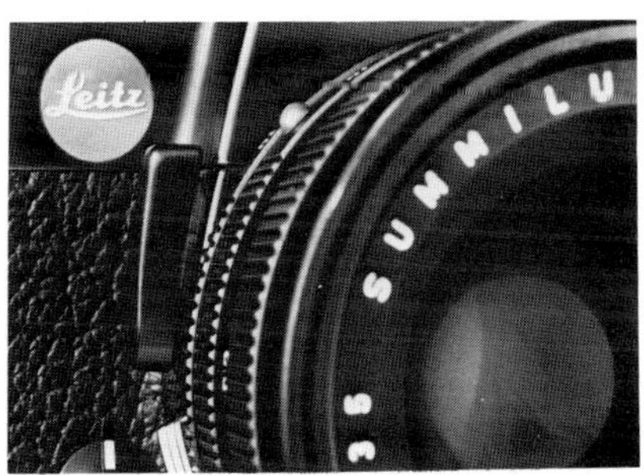

If the preselector lever is operated the lens will close down to the working aperture thus allowing the photographer to see the depth of field. At small apertures the screen becomes very dark. The lever should not be pressed during exposures.

LENSES FOR THE LEICA R4
On the following pages all the Leica R4 lenses from the super wide 15mm to the 800mm telephoto are described. For clarity they have been split into groups according to focal length. Similar lenses with similar characteristics are often found within a group, but by direct comparison it can be decided which lens is more suitable for an individual. Nature photographers will often find lenses of long focal length necessary. However he will often find that extreme close-ups are needed, in this same group he will find lenses perfectly matched to his field of photography. Ultra high speed lenses coupled with fast film will enable the available light photographer to extend the range of working.

THE CONSTRUCTION OF LEICA R4 LENSES

The external construction of all Leica R4 lenses is very similar. The focusing ring rotates in the same direction (23) aperture (21) and depth of field (22) scales are similar. All lenses feature the same robust quick change mount. The red dot ensures that a lens can be located even in the dark. With the exception of the P.C. Curtagon-R and lenses of 400mm and above focal lengths, all lenses have automatic diaphragms, enabling the photographer to focus at maximum aperture and also ensuring that the viewfinder image both before and after exposure can be seen with maximum clarity. However the subject can be viewed to determine depth of field, by pressing the pre-selector button, thus stopping down the lens manually. Release of the preview lever will return the lens to its full aperture. Releasing the shutter ensures that the automatic diaphragm is stopped down to the taking aperture fractions of a second before the actual exposure. Operating efficiency with long life is ensured by the use of ball bearings in the construction, friction is also reduced to a minimum. All lenses previously supplied for the Leica R3 Electro and the R3 MOT are completely compatible with the Leica R4. Lenses and accessories from earlier Leicaflex cameras (without triple cams) can be adapted by the manufacturer. These modifications do not preclude the adapted items being used with the earlier cameras.

THE EXTREME WIDE ANGLE RANGE

This range includes lenses from 15mm to 24mm, the more extreme the angle of view the more dramatic is the reproduction obtained. Lenses of very short focal length can be used for technical and architectural subjects. However great attention and careful use is required. It is essential that the camera is held square to the subject if converging verticals are to be avoided. With very

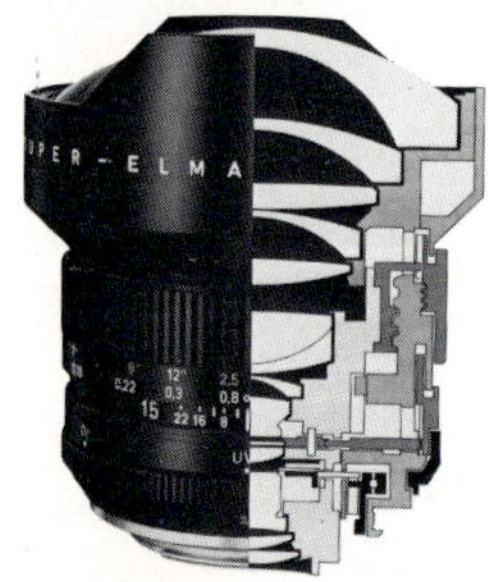

Super-Elmar-R
1:3,5/15mm

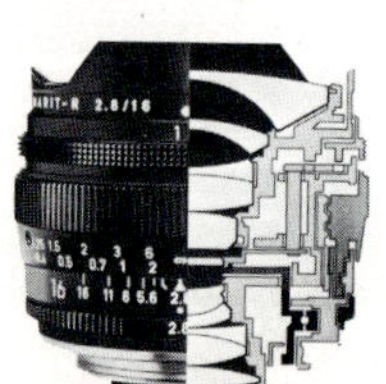

Fisheye-Elmarit-R
1:2,8/16mm

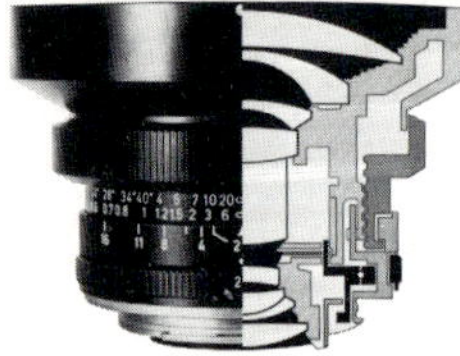

Elmarit-R
1:2,8/19mm

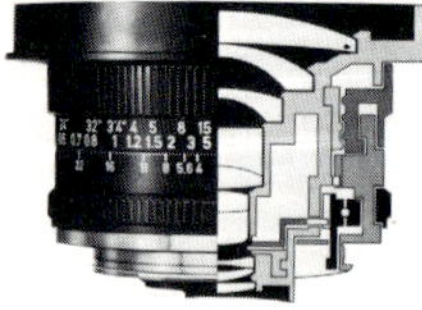

Super-Angulon-R
1:4/21mm

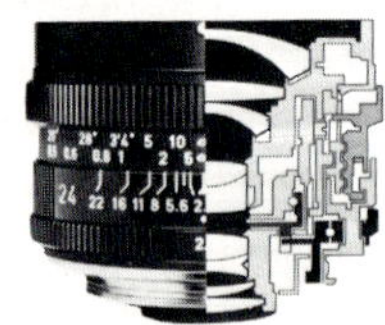

Elmarit-R
1:2,8/24mm

short focal length lenses the depth of field is extreme. However if sharp negatives are required the depth of field scale should be used in the manner previously described.

SUPER ELMAR-R f3.5 15mm

A lens of extreme optical complexity, consisting of 13 elements. It has an angle of acceptance of 110°. Optical quality over the whole focusing range from infinity to 0.6m is achieved by the use of floating elements, as the lens is focused the distance between elements is varied to ensure maximum correction. A built in filter turret houses UVA, yellow, orange and colour correction filters. A filter is always in the light path; for normal photography a UVA is selected. Exposure correction is automatic. A built in lens hood is provided to protect the large front element.

THE FISH-EYE ELMARIT-R f2.8 16mm

A lens of this focal length with the high speed of f2.8 is unusual. The 16mm focal length is only relevant to the centre of the image, becoming shorter towards the edge of the field. Only a section of the circular field is used on the 35mm format. The angle of acceptance is 137° horizontally, 86° vertically, but a true 180° diagonally. The field has a barrel like effect. Straight lines running through the centre of the picture will reproduce as straight, the further away from the centre the more curved they will appear. Circles also become elliptical. At 2m at f2.8 the depth of field extends from 1m to infinity. Four filters are built in, UVA, yellow, orange and blue. This lens is remarkably fast and incorporates a high degree of correction, used properly it is ideal for technical and architectural subjects. At the minimum focusing distance the 96° angle of view covers a field 168 x 702mm. It is also ideal for low light reportage photography. The retrofocus design has nine elements in seven groups.

ELMARIT-R f2.8 19mm

A classical optical design was chosen for this high speed, fully corrected lens. The performance is of the highest quality and is sustained throughout the 12″ to infinity focusing range. The angle of acceptance is 95.7° and at the minimum focusing distance the subject area is 261 x 329mm. The filters M82 x 0.75 are kept in position by the large rectangular lens hood.

SUPER-ANGULON-R f4 21mm

This lens is ideal for those who need a lightweight lens when travelling. It is extremely compact and weighs 150 grams less than the 19mm Elmarit-R and the angle of view is only 4° less. The focusing range is from infinity to 0.2m at which distance the field covered is 148 x 221mm. With lenses of short focal length optical cleanliness is vital, a finger print on the rear element will effect optical performance. Ensure that optics are clean when changing lenses and filters. There are some problems when using polarising filters with short focal length lenses, the light passes through the lens at such extreme angles as to negate the physical properties of the polarising filter to some degree.

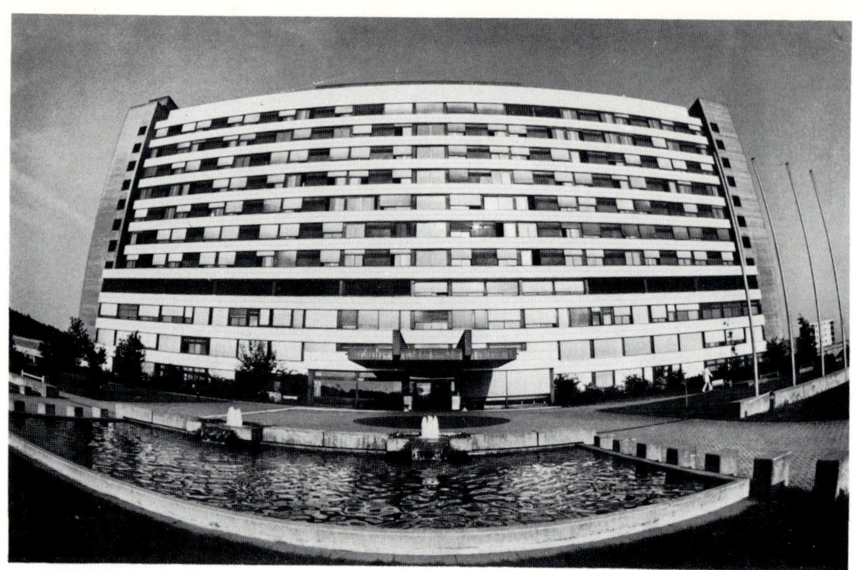

This Architectural photograph taken with the Fisheye Elmarit-R f2.8 16mm is intended as a comparison with the photograph below. Both focal lengths are very similar 16 and 15mm respectfully. The fisheye effect can be seen.

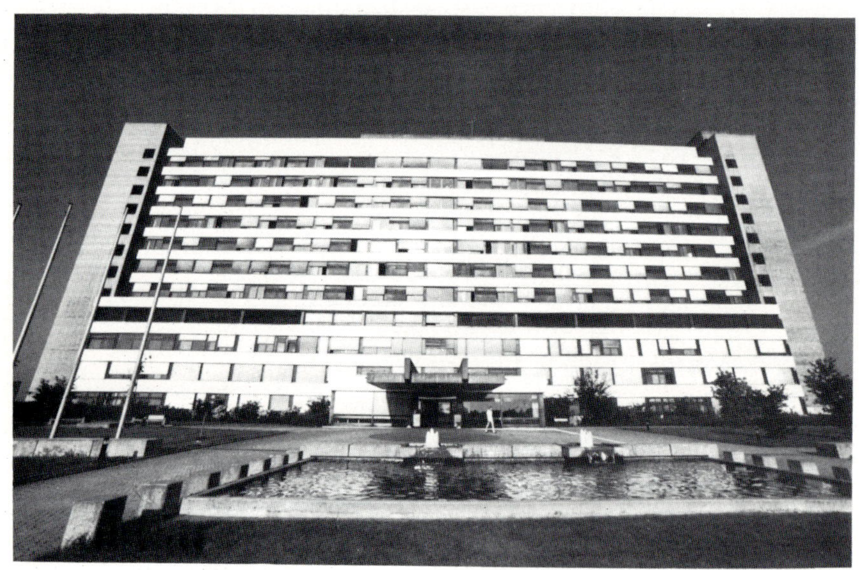

This photograph was taken with the Super Elmar-R f3.5 15mm. Although the verticals are converging due to the camera being tilted it can be clearly seen that straight lines are not distorted and also that the correction is very high.

ELMARIT-R 24mm f2.8

The design of this lens incorporates floating elements which move relative to each other during focusing to achieve maximum correction. The nine elements are arranged in two groups, the front group of three independant floating elements and two cemented, in front of the diaphragm, the rear group has four elements. The focusing range is from infinity to 0.3m at which distance the field of view is 250 x 374mm. The lens is very compact being 46mm long and weighing 420 grams. It is suitable for rapid reportage photography although its high performance also makes it suitable in other fields. This lens cannot be used on the Leicaflex SL or earlier reflex cameras.

WIDE ANGLE LENSES

ELMARIT-R 28mm f2.8

This lens is extremely compact and weighs 275 grams. The 28mm focal length provides an angle of view of 76°, the focusing range is from infinity to 0.3m at which distance the field is 188 x 282mm. An interesting feature of this lens is that the lens hood contains a knob that actuates on the edge of the filter and revolves it, thus one can rotate a polarising filter while observing the effect through the viewfinder. This feature is also incorporated in the 24mm Elmarit-R. The lens design is complex with eight elements in a retrofucus design. This lens with the 50mm and 90mm lenses forms the basis for a very versatile travelling outfit.

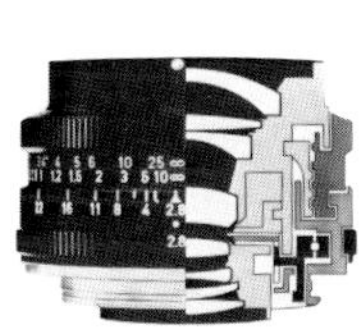

Elmarit-R
1:2,8/28mm

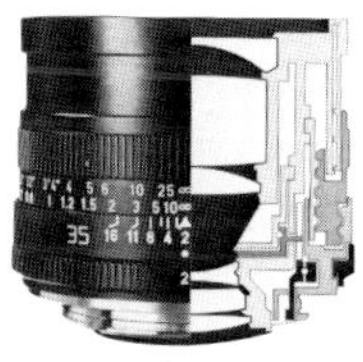

Summicron-R
1:2/35mm

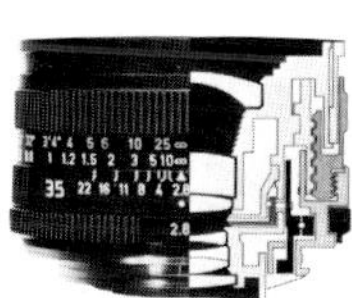

Elmarit-R
1:2,8/35mm

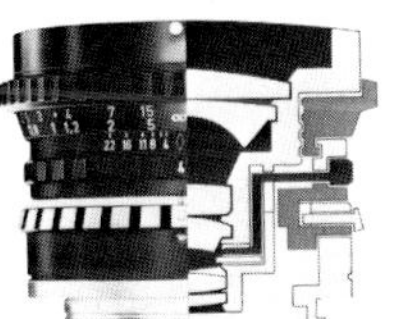

P.A. Curtagon-R
1:4/35mm

ELMARIT-R 35mm f2.8

A 35mm and 90mm lens form a useful basic outfit. If a faster lens is not required the Elmarit-R 2.8 will fulfil the role admirably and is particularly good for travel photography. Candid snap shots can be taken without the subject being aware. Practise by estimating the focal length, set it, point the camera towards the subject from waist level and make the exposure. With experience a high degree of accuracy can be obtained. This method will often enable photographs to be taken that would otherwise be impossible. A useful guide to estimate the limits of the frame is that distance to the subject corresponds approximately to the width of the picture.

SUMMICRON-R 35mm f2

The excellent performance and speed of this lens is a great advantage for photography with colour film or in low light conditions. The new design also shows a considerable weight saving on the previous model. The optical standard is outstandingly good throughout the focusing range from infinity to 0.3m at full aperture. At the minimum focusing distance the field of view is 210 x 140mm. This is the lens that the discerning photographer should chose when the advantages of a wide angle lens coupled with a large maximum aperture are important.

P.C. CURTAGON-R 35mm f4

This is a highly specialised lens that is not made by Leitz but by Schneider. It features a complex system by which the front group of elements can be moved in relation to the rest of the lens up to a maximum of 7mm from its normal position. To achieve this a notched ring engraved with numbers from 0 to 7 is operated, the numbers indicating the amount of displacement. This gives a rising front facility normally only associated with the movements of a technical camera. The facility enables converging lines to be avoided in architectural subjects, thus eliminating the necessity of pointing the camera upwards to include the top of a building which only results in converging verticals. It is advisable to use a tripod when undertaking architectural photography with this lens. Set up the camera ensuring that the back is absolutely vertical in relation to the building. In the event of the angle of acceptance not including the top of the building adjustments to the lens are carried out by viewing the subject and at the same time rotating the operating ring. One can see the angle of acceptance being pushed upwards although the camera is static. It can also be seen that parallel lines remain parallel. The lens can be used to advantage in the horizontal position, for instance when the camera position cannot be altered and some non essential elements are contained within the foreground, lateral displacement can be obtained in the same manner.

The lens is not provided with an automatic diaphragm. After composing and focusing at maximum aperture the lens must be stopped down to its pre-selected stop manually. The focusing range is from infinity to 0.3m at which distance the field of view is 10 x 140mm. The actual lens covers a fully corrected circle of 57mm diameter instead of the normal 43mm that forms the diagonal of the 24 x 36mm frame, thus ensuring that the standard format is covered anywhere within this circle. Note that this lens is no longer manufactured and must be obtained in the secondhand market.

In the event of a larger displacement being necessary it is recommended that apertures of f11 or smaller are used in order to obtain maximum sharpness. To ensure maximum utilisation of this lens the camera should be positioned with precision for which a small spirit level is useful. When attempting this form of photography the standard focusing screen should be replaced. Screen number 4 which incorporates grid lines is perfect for architectural and allied subjects.

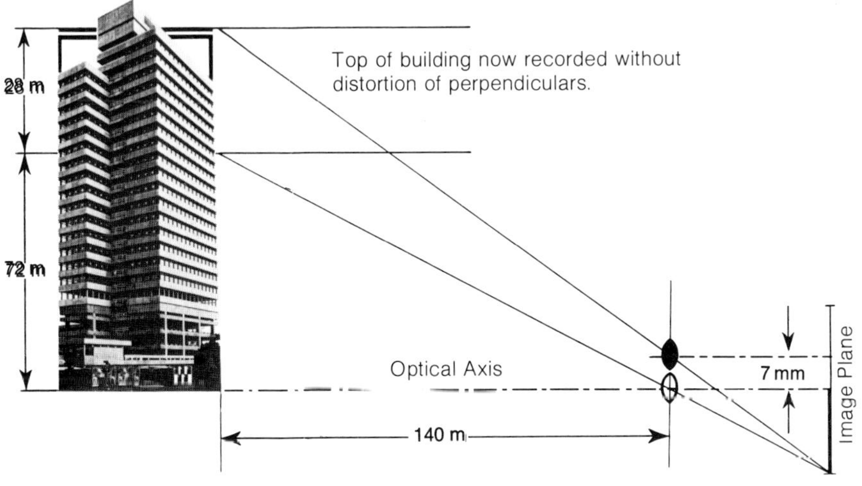

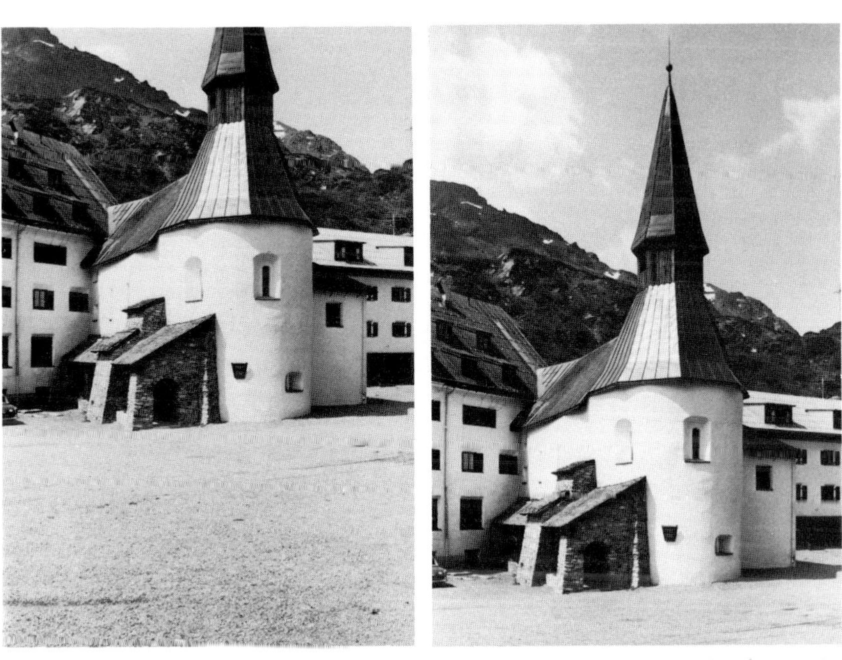

*If converging vertical lines are to be avoided then the camera should not be tilted and it must be
positioned squarely to the subject. With the P.C. Curtagon it is possible to include the top of
buildings without tilting the camera. This is achieved by the ability of the lens to be used with a
controlled degree of optical displacement of the front group of components in relation to the rear.*

67

STANDARD FOCAL LENGTHS

SUMMICRON-R 50mm f2

To most photographers this is the standard lens of the Leica R4 system and provides optical performance by which other lenses are judged. Even at maximum aperture the definition and optical correction is outstandingly good. The design is a Gauss variant of six elements four cemented in pairs to give an almost symmetrical design. The focusing range is from infinity to 0.5m at which distance the field of view is 180 x 270mm. With Elpro 1 and 2 lenses the subject field can be reduced to 62 x 93mm with the Elpro 2. (See page 00 for further information). The lens is supplied with a 3 cam construction and can be used on all reflex cameras. There is a less expensive variant which is only suitable for use with the R3 and R4 and is engraved as such on the barrel.

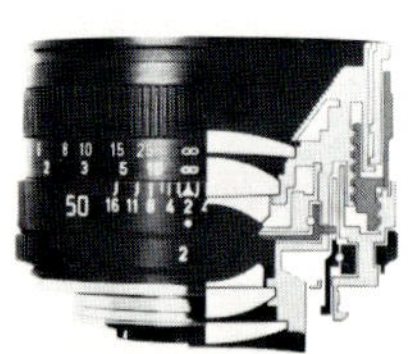

Summicron-R
1:2/50mm

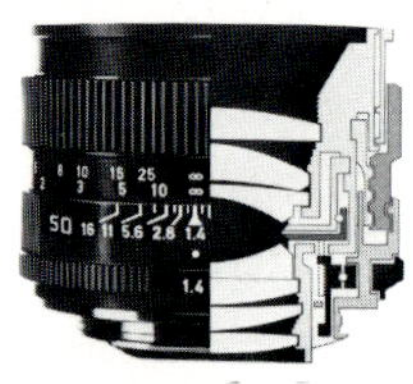

Summilux-R
1:1,4/35mm

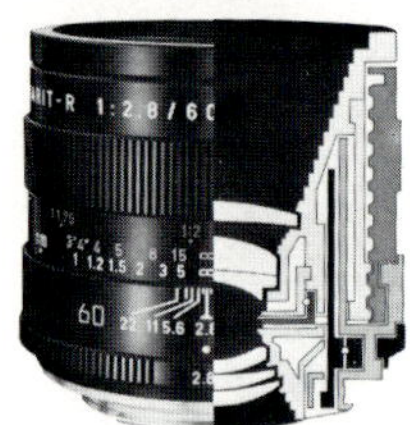

Macro-Elmarit-R
1:2,8/60mm

SUMMILUX-R 50mm f1.4

This is the fastest standard lens being effectively twice as fast as the Summicron f/2. The lens provides an extremely high correction, comma and flare being virtually eliminated. It is ideal for reportage photography in low light conditions or when slow colour films have to be used. The focusing range extends from infinity to 0.5m and performance is equal throughout the range. At maximum aperture the depth of field is very restricted compared to the normal 50mm lens.

MACRO-ELMARIT-R 60mm f2.8

This is a Gaussian lens design comprising six elements, two of which are cemented. It is provided with a deeply recessed front element and has the ability to focus from infinity to 0.27m. With the adapter ring the reproduction ratio can be reduced to 1:1. As implied by the prefix 'Macro' this lens is primarily designed for close-up work and particular attention has been paid to high image quality, however it is also a most useful standard lens. It should be noted that the lens and adapter have an interlock system to ensure that they are coupled in the correct manner so that the automatic diaphragm will read correctly. When fitting the lens and adapter ensure that both are set to their minimum aperture of f22. The lens alone provides a maximum reproduction ratio of 1:2, i.e. half life size, by means of the adapter (order number 14256) the close-up range is increased to 1:1 and the automatic metering system is still fully operational. When using this lens for close-up photography try presetting the appropriate scale or the required film to object distance on the focusing ring and varying the distance from the object by moving backwards and forwards. The subject can be quickly and accurately focused. This method has the advantage that small subject movements can be quickly compensated for.

For accurate scaling when undertaking technical, scientific or record photography the subject can be laid on a sheet of 1mm graph paper. Areas of view at set ratios can be read from the table on the next page, depth of field will of course decrease as the subject to film distance is shortened.

Because of its special optical construction the Macro-Elmarit-R 60mm f/2.8 does not lose performance in the extreme close-up field. For line reproductions an aperture of f/8 is recommended for a scale between 1:3 and 1:2, from 1:2 to 1:1 the lens should be stopped down to f/11, although for some subjects this lens is highly usable stopped down to f/16 or f/22 when maximum depth of field is required. The Macro-Elmarit-R can also be used with extension rings or the bellows unit.

MEDIUM TELEPHOTO LENSES

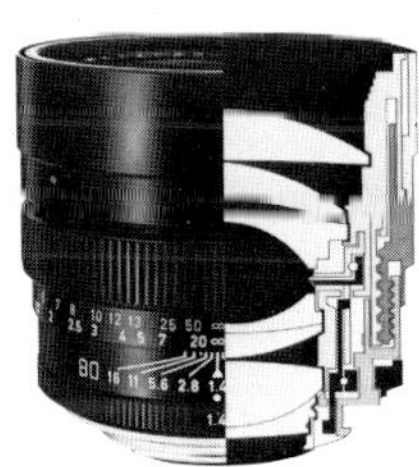

Summulux-R
1:1,4/80mm

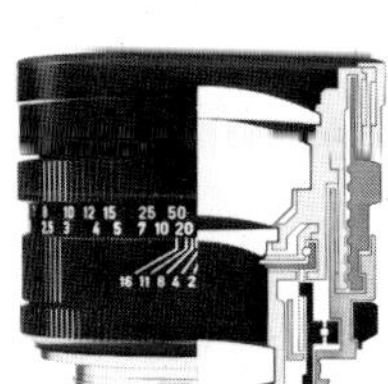

Summicron-R
1:2/90mm

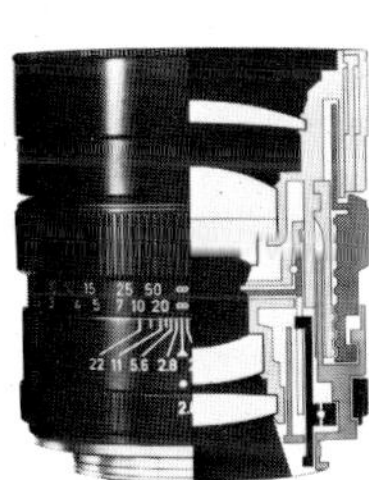

Elmarit-R
1:2,8/90mm

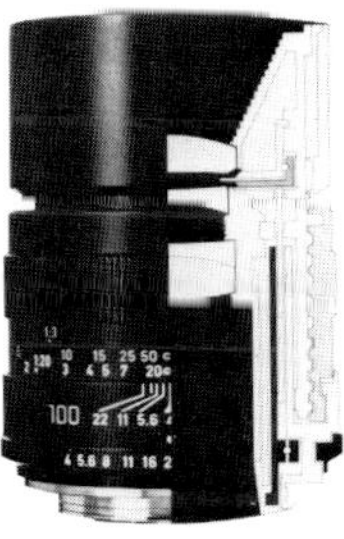

Macro-Elmar-R
1:4/100mm

This group contains four lightweight short telephoto lenses ranging from a maximum aperture of f/1.4 to f4 and from 80mm to 100mm with acceptance angles between 30° to 35°. Only the individual photographer can chose which lens suits him best. For many years the Elmarit-R 90mm f/2.8 has been my particular favourite. I like the ability of this focal length to achieve tight, frame filling composition and the relatively small depth of field coupled with the focusing range from infinity to 0.7m makes it particularly suitable for my style of photography. Close-up photographers will prefer the Macro-Elmar-R f4.

SUMMILUX 80mm f1.4

This lens is particularly useful for low light reportage photography. With this lens Leitz have achieved an extremely large maximum aperture without the normal inherent loss of quality. This has been made possible by the use of new optical glass techniques. It is an extremely light and compact lens and stopping down only marginally increases its performance, although in the close up field stopping down is recommended for maximum performance.

ELPRO CLOSE-UP ATTACHMENTS

Unlike usual supplementary lenses these do not affect the reproduction quality of the lens with which they are used. The exposure time is not increased and there is no interference with the functioning of the light measurement systems at full aperture or with the fully automatic pre-set diaphragm. Like filters, the Elpro components are quickly and easily attached to the front of the lens.

PERFORMANCE WITH THE ELPRO AND COMBINATION RINGS

Three part combination ring Order number 14159 for use with lens	Elpro	Range from	Ratio of Reproduction	Size of object field in cm
50mm Summicron-R f2	1/VIa		1.1:1	22x32
	1/VIa	0.5	1.2:1	20x30
	1/VIb		1.2:1	20x30
	1/VIb	0.5	1.4:1	17x25
90mm Elmarit-R f2.8	3/VIIa		1:1.4	33x50
90mm Summicron-R f2	3/VIIa	0.7	1:1.1	26x39
135mm Elmarit-R f2.8	4/VIIb		1:2	48x72
	4/VIIb	1.5	1:1.6	38x56
	3/VIIa		1:1.4	33x50
	3/Viia	1.5	1:1.2	28x42

The use of Vario Elmars with Elpro's and rings is not recommended.

Note all figures are rounded off.

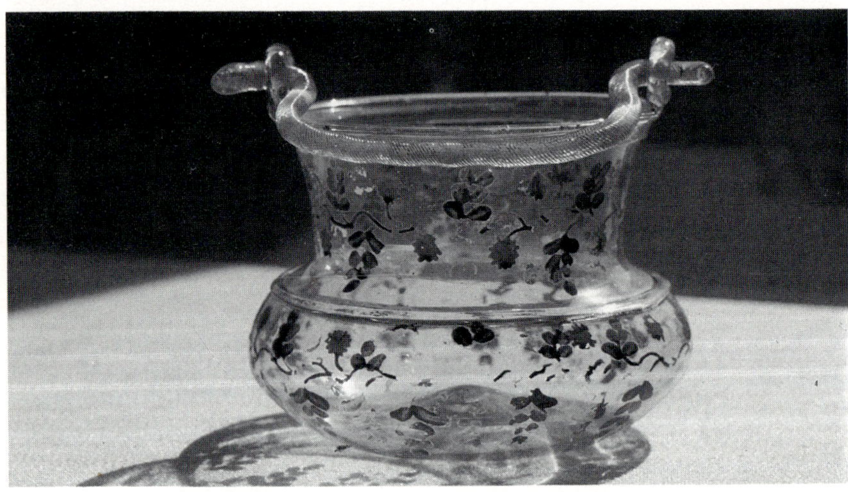

Murano near Venice has been a centre of the glass industry since the middle ages. This vase was photographed with the Macro Elmarit-R f2.8 60mm whilst in its showcase against the light.

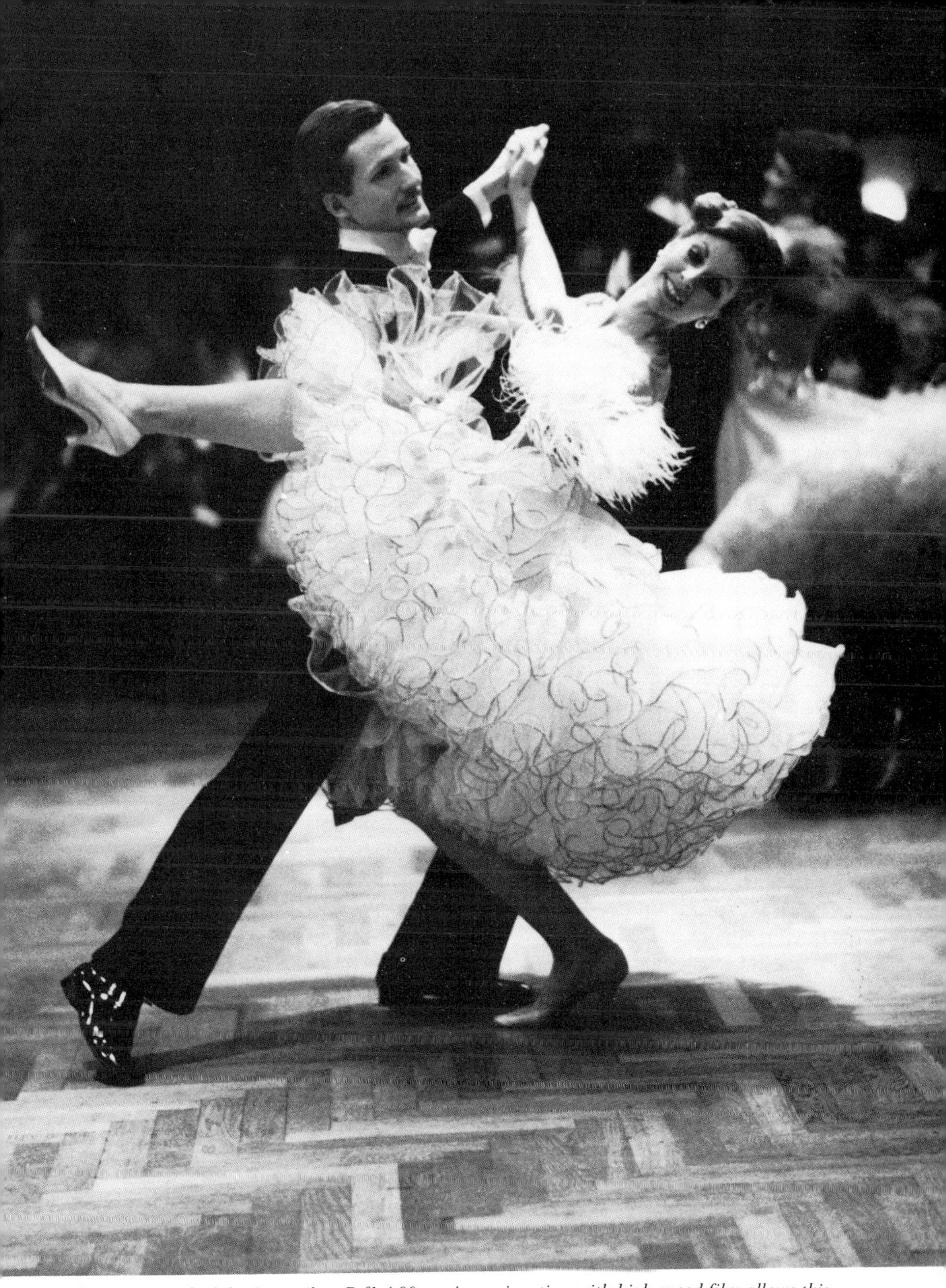

The great speed of the Summilux-R f1.4 80mm in conjunction with high speed film allows this type of snapshot to be taken using the existing light. (Photo: Rudolph Seck)

SUMMICRON 90mm f2

The extremely compact construction of this lens has been achieved by using a sophisticated telephoto construction which has kept the lens to only 62mm. Although slower than the Summilux 80mm the aperture of f/2 enables the photographer to work in adverse lighting conditions. The portrait photographer will find that this is a most useful lens. The focusing range from infinity to 0.7m can be further extended by using the Elpro attachments or other close-up accessories. Lenses of these focal lengths are useful for colour slides. Tight composition is necessary to achieve impact. The landscape photographer will find this focal length suitable, the slight compression of distance provides a more balanced composition. Photographers undertaking photographs of children, travel and close-up work will also find this kind of lens extremely valuable. The portrait photographer will find this lens approximately 1.5m from the subject will provide a full frame image. This distance is not close enough to make the subject nervous. The large apertures of the Summicron and Summilux lenses enable candid portraiture even in low light conditions without necessitating supplementary lights. Also the limited depth of field renders backgrounds unobtrusive.

ELMARIT-R 90mm f2.8

This is a light, handy, medium length telephoto lens which gives a completely corrected image throughout the focusing range from infinity to 0.7m even at maximum aperture. This lens is suitable for use with all the available close-up accessories of the Leica R4 system. Used in conjunction with the Elpro 3 the subject field can be decreased to 72x108mm. These accessories do not interfere with the automatic functions of the camera. This is an ideal lens for candid portraiture.

MACRO-ELMAR-R 100mm f4

Due to the extraordinary 32mm length of the helical focusing thread this lens is capable of focusing down to a scale of 1:3 providing a subject field of 72x108mm. When used in conjunction with the Macro-Adapter-R (order number 14256) the close-up field is extended and a field of 38x57mm is covered. The range of applications of this lens is similar to that of the Macro-Elmarit-R 60mm although with this lens the extra focal length enables greater subject to camera distances. The Macro-Elmar-R 100mm f/4 is also ideal for general purpose photography, in particular portraiture, as with its extended focusing range everything from a full length figure shot to a frame filling close-up of a person's eye can be achieved. With the Elpro 2 a ratio of 1:2 is attained. The lens was first introduced in a simple short mount and required the bellows for focusing from infinity to 1:1. It had a non automatic diaphragm. The new version introduced in 1978 has a focusing mount similar to that of the Macro-Elmarit-R 60mm. It focuses to 0.6m and retains full automatic operations.

MACRO-ELMAR-R 1:4/100mm:

100mm MACRO-ELMAR-R f/4	ELPRO	Distance scale at	Distance in cm		Object field size in mm	Repro-duction scale
			object to film plane	object to front lens		
	4	∞	150.5	136	323 x 484	1:13
		0.6	48.6	31	61 x 92	1:2.5
With close-up focusing ring 14262	4	∞	48.5	31	63 x 94	1:2.6
		0.6	40.6	20	34 x 51	1:1.4
	3	∞	75.5	61	145 x 218	1:6
		0.6	41.6	24	48 x 72	1:2

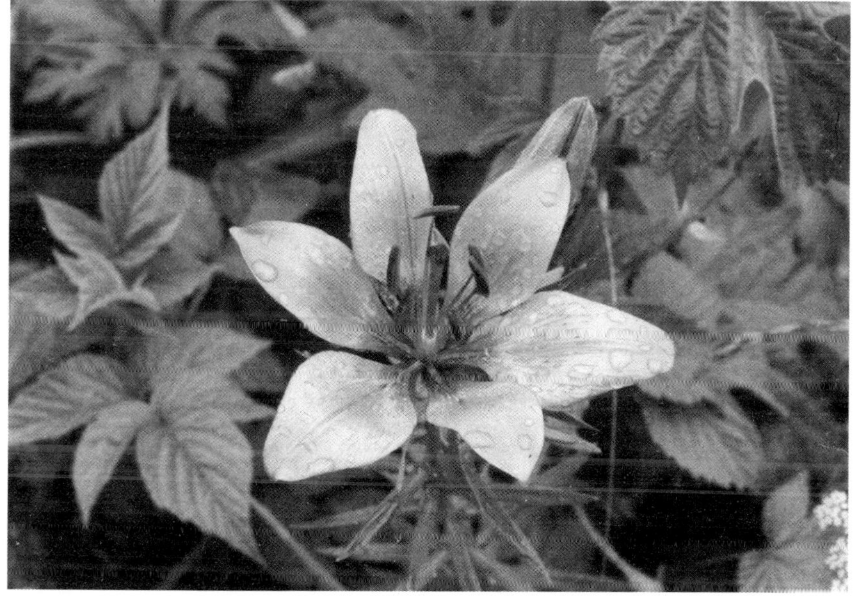

A protected species photographed in the Alps. Photographed with the 100mm Macro-Elmar-R f4. Using the macro lens has enabled the photographer to preserve this 'Firelily'.

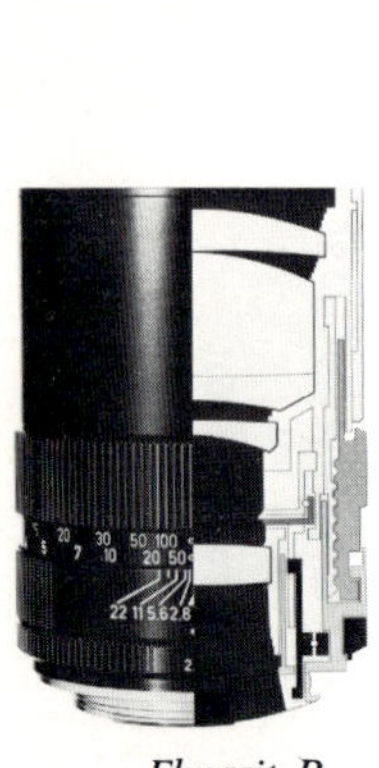
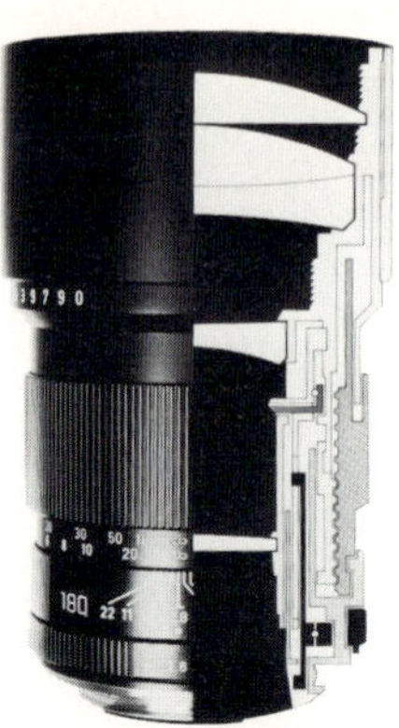
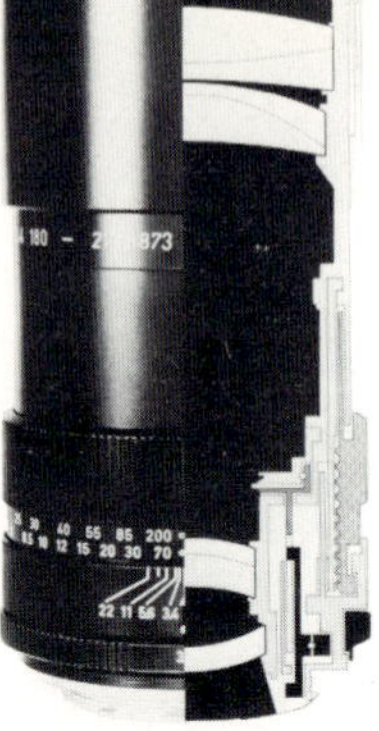
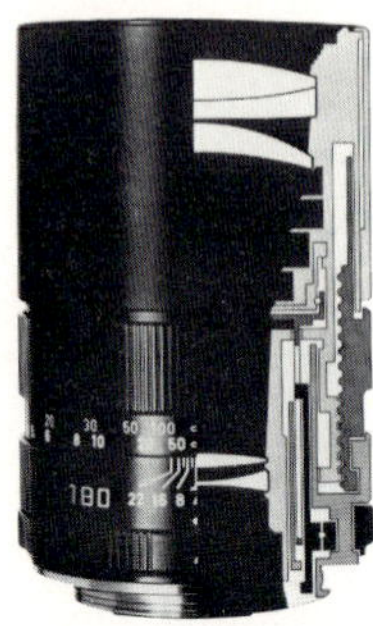

| *Elmarit-R* | *Elmarit-R* | *Apo-Telyt-R* | *Elmar-R* |
| *1:2,8/135mm* | *1:2,8/180mm* | *1:3,4/180mm* | *1:4/180mm* |

LONG FOCAL LENGTHS

Standard focal length lenses have an angle of acceptance of between 40° and 60°. Lenses with angles of view of less than this are regarded as being of long focal length. The term telephoto refers to a lens which has an optical construction comprising of two groups of lenses. The front group acts as a converging lens whilst the rear group which is often separated by an appreciable distance from the front group, acts as a diverging lens. Each group within itself may be quite complex and consist of up to three elements and sometimes more. The back focus (i.e. the distance from the rear element of the lens to the film,) is shorter than the focal length of the lens when focused at infinity. Improved techniques in optical glass and computerised lens design have enabled telephoto lenses to be designed which are very compact.

ELMARIT-R f2.8 135mm

This telephoto lens consists of five elements arranged in two groups. Advances in optical glass manufacture have enabled a high degree of optical performance to be achieved, resolution, even at full aperture is remarkable. Stopping down will increase the depth of field but not the performance. To retain compactness the focusing range is restricted to from infinity to 1.5m, or closer when used with the close-up attachments. The R4 viewfinder enables quick and accurate focusing. The focal length of the lens combined with its relatively large maximum aperture produce a fairly heavy lens although its compact construction ensures that the lens balances and handles correctly. When fitted to the camera the weight makes it steadier to hold. The filter size is E55 and the lens is supplied with a collapsible lens hood. The 135mm focal length provides the photographer with the ability to get in close to a subject while remaining relatively far away. This is useful for photographing sport or at official functions when access to the subject is restricted. This focal length is admirably suited to portraiture especially when frame filling character studies are required. Many of the comments related to the 90mm lenses are relevant, although of course the 135mm lens is somewhat larger and heavier. The

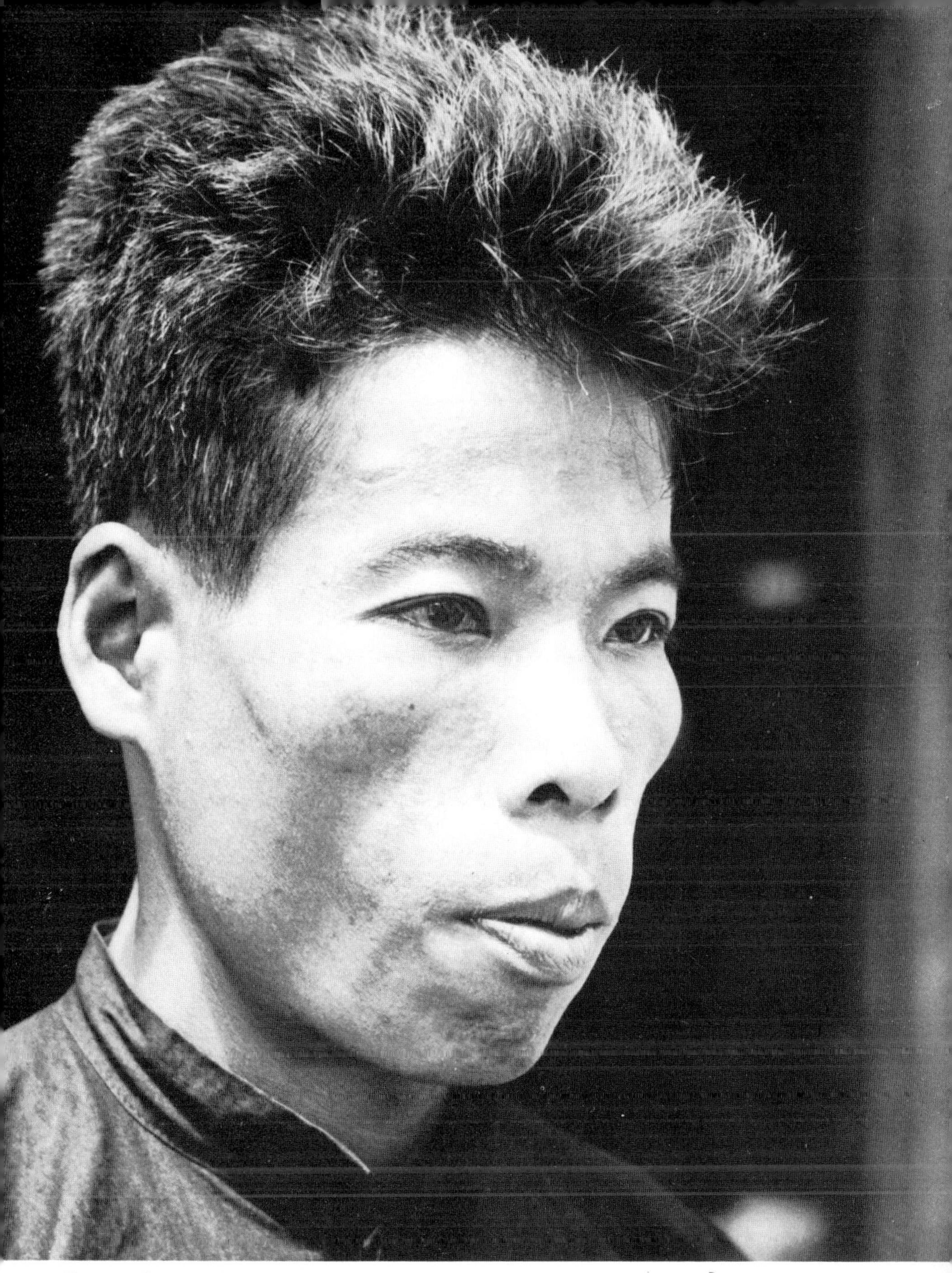

Portrait showing the modelling effect of soft sunlight, which enhances plasticity. The black
background is thrown out of focus by the 90mm Elmarit-R f/2.8 which is a great advantage in
portraiture. (Photograph: Rudolf Schauß).

landscape photographer will find the 135mm lens is extremely useful in that it compresses the subject and reduces apparent distance.

180mm LENSES
The focal length of 180mm is represented in the Leica R4 system by three lenses, which differ in their maximum aperture, weight and of course cost. Many photographers find this focal length most useful and it is for this reason that Leitz produce three lenses in this group. It is the photographer's responsibility to chose which of the lenses is best suited to his purpose.

ELMARIT-R 180mm f2.8
This lens, with a relatively large aperture of f/2.8, opens up the scope of photography to both the amateur and the professional user. The combination of large aperture and fast film ensures that photography can be achieved even in the worst lighting conditions. Even in low light the viewfinder image is extremely bright and therefore focusing can easily be achieved. With practice the lens can be used for hand held photography even at relatively long exposure times. The focusing range is from infinity to 1.8m at which distance the subject field is 200 x 300mm. The aperture settings are provided with click stops at full and half values and the lens stops down to f/22. The lens is provided with an extendable lens hood.

APO-TELYT-R 180mm f3.4
The prefix Apo- indicates that this lens is fully apochromatically corrected. The extremely high degree of correction of residual abberations has been made possible by the development of new optical glass. This allows an unsurpassed degree of colour rendition and the ability to resolve the finest detail. Another advantage of apochromatic correction is that it brings all the colours of the spectrum both visible and invisible to a common point of focus. In infra-red photography no focus shift is experienced. The resolving power of this lens can only be exploited when used in conjunction with the finest available film, which enables the photographer to achieve standards of technical perfection hitherto unobtainable with small format photography. The focusing range of this lens extends from infinity to 2.5m enabling a subject field of 276 x 414mm to be covered at the closest focusing distance.

ELMAR-R 180mm f4
This is the choice for photographers who cannot justify the high cost of the Apo-Telyt and who do not require the maximum aperture of the Elmarit-R 180mm f/2.8. This lens is extremely compact and weighs a mere 525 grams. It is 21mm shorter than the Elmarit-R 180mm and 215 grams lighter. The photographer who requires high technical performance combined with light-weight will value this lens highly. The focusing range extends from infinity to 1.8m at which distance the field covered is 175 x 262mm. Filter size E55.

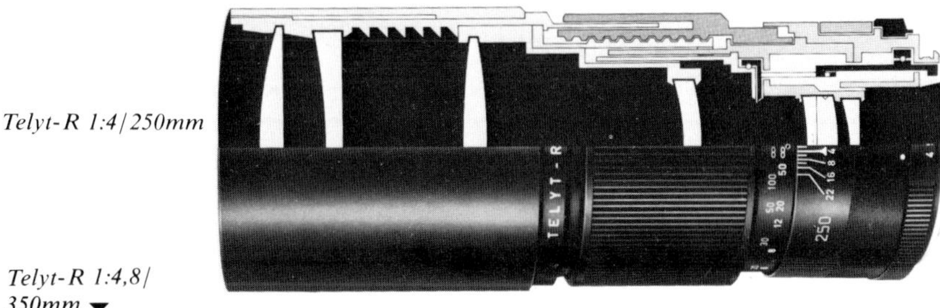

Telyt-R 1:4/250mm

*Telyt-R 1:4,8/
350mm* ▼

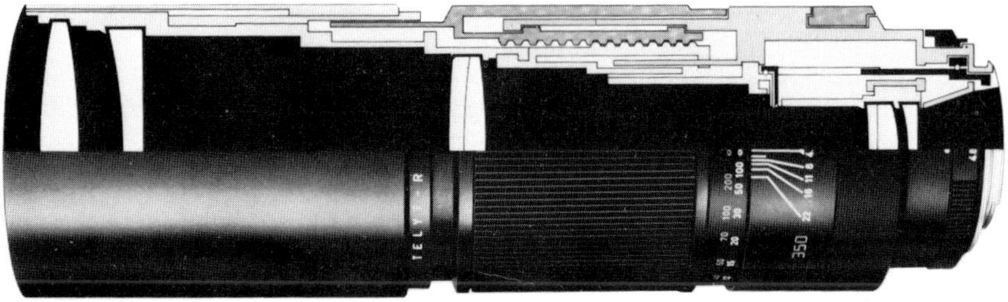

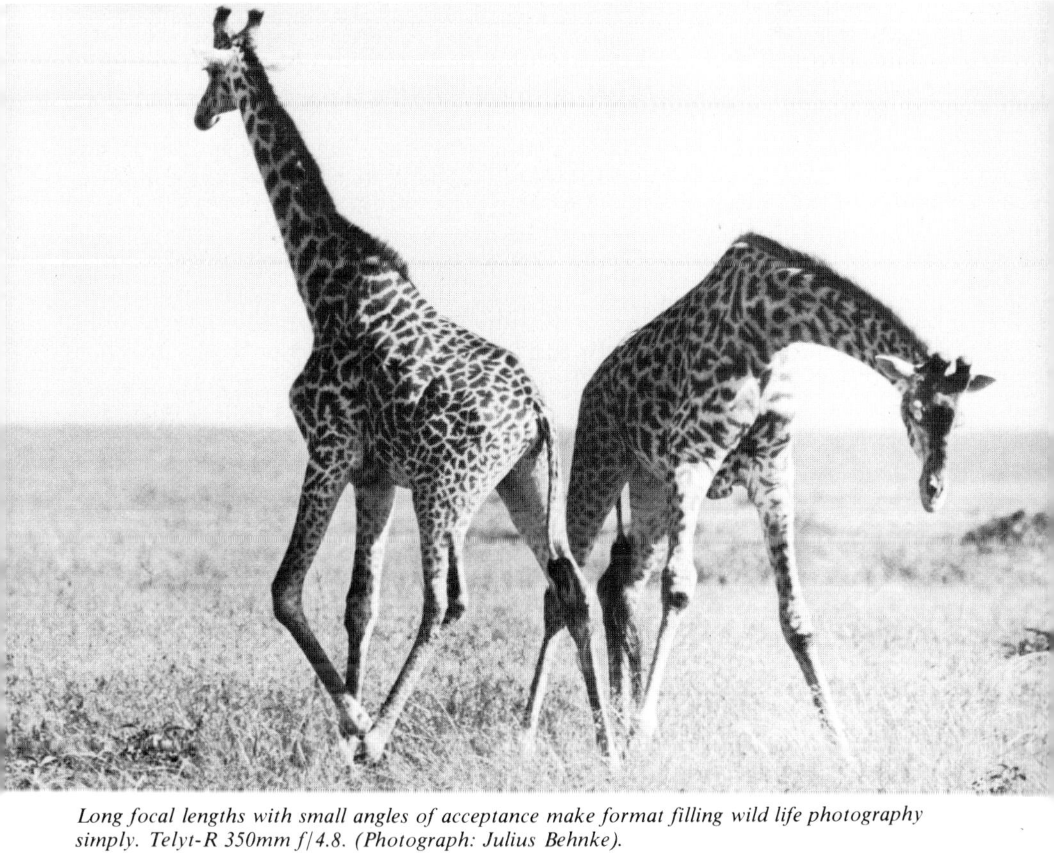

*Long focal lengths with small angles of acceptance make format filling wild life photography
simply. Telyt-R 350mm f/4.8. (Photograph: Julius Behnke).*

CLASSICAL TELEPHOTO LENSES

For many sports photographers and for reportage work telephoto lenses are the only ones capable of solving physical restrictions of subject to camera distance. Optical quality must be first class as often the resulting negatives will be subjected to extensive enlargement. Wildlife photography also comes under this heading. The layman photographer often compares telephoto lenses to binoculars or telescopes and does not realise that different parameters are used. If I use a telephoto lens with a focal length of 400mm then from a distance of 40m (100') an area 2.4 x 3.6m is covered. If a subject is for example a stag at a distance of 50 to 60m then by our calculations using a lens of 180mm according to the following formula:-

$$\frac{\text{focal length}}{\text{distance}} = \text{scale of the image} = \frac{180\text{mm}}{54000\text{mm}} = \frac{1}{300}$$

then the subject will appear on the negative approximately $\frac{1}{300}$th of its actual size, i.e. 2-3mm high.

TELYT-R 250mm f4 and TELYT-R 350mm f4.8

These two telephoto lenses are grouped together since they are both in the same category. The front group of four lenses are moved internally in relation to the rear group. This focusing design (internal focusing) requires only a small change in the relative distances to achieve focusing over the complete scale, thus focusing is very rapid. With the Telyt-R 250mm f/4 the focusing range is from infinity to 1.7m at which distance the field is 120 x 186mm. The 350mm lens focuses from infinity to 3m and the smallest subject field is 171 x 257mm. Both lenses are equipped with built in tripod sockets which are suitable for both vertical and horizontal photography as they rotate through 360°. The universal hand grip with the shoulder support (Order number 14188) can be attached to both lenses. The use of the shoulder support enables the lens to be used with a high degree of success when hand held for relatively long exposure times.

THE SNAP SHOT TELEPHOTO LENSES,
TELYT-R f6.8 400mm and 560mm

These lenses can be used with the simplicity of operation normally associated with shorter focal lengths because the focusing mechanism is constructed in a different way. It is unlocked by means of a button and then the front of the lens barrel can be moved backwards and forwards precisely but with great ease. The viewfinder image snaps in and out of focus very quickly because of the long focal length and focusing should be carried out using the outer area of the standard screen. The lenses are outstandingly corrected and the lens coating helps to produce an image of extremely high contrast. The lenses consist of two elements which are cemented together. With only two air to glass surfaces there is minimal light loss within the lens and the exposure time is marginally shorter than with lenses of complex design. With photographs taken over long distances contrast plays an important role because light loses through haze and atmosphere will reduce the contrast of the subject. The high brillance of the viewfinder image of the Leica R4 ensures that the subject is viewed with greater clarity thus facilitating composition and focusing. There telephoto lenses are not provided with focusing scales, a printed scale is issued with the instructions and can be fixed onto the lens barrel with sellotape. A real advantage with this type of focusing is the large range that is possible. With a movement of 60mm the 400mm combination provides a range of focusing from infinity to 3.6m and in combination with the 560mm optical head from infinity to 6.4m. For transportation the lens heads with the focusing tubes and mounts can be separated. For close-up work an intermediary ring (Order number 14182) can be attached. The 400mm lens can be used to a close focusing distance of 2.8m covering a field of 80 x 120mm. When used in conjunction with the 560mm lens head close focus is decreased to 4m giving a subject area of 120 x 180mm. A slot is provided in the lens tube into which a series 7 filter can be fitted. The filter slot is provided with a cover, to expose the slot this is pushed back towards the camera. For ease this cover is spring loaded. Focusing must be carried out with the filter in position as the filter is within the optical path of the lens. The only filters suitable are those which are optically flawless. The aperture scale is provided with click stops at full and half values and are not automatic in operation. According to the light conditions it is possible to focus even when f/8 is selected. Fully automatic metering facilities can be used with the lens set at its working aperture. Lenses of these focal lenghts should be used on a tripod or with the shoulder support. The total weight with the 400mm lens is 1,800 grams and with the 560mm 2,300 grams.

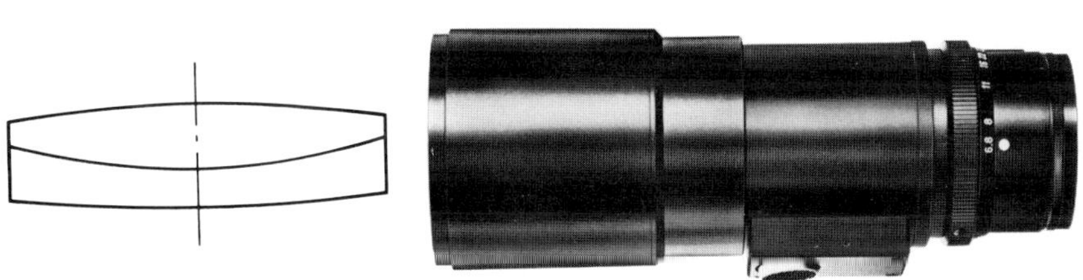

Telyt-R f6.8/400mm.

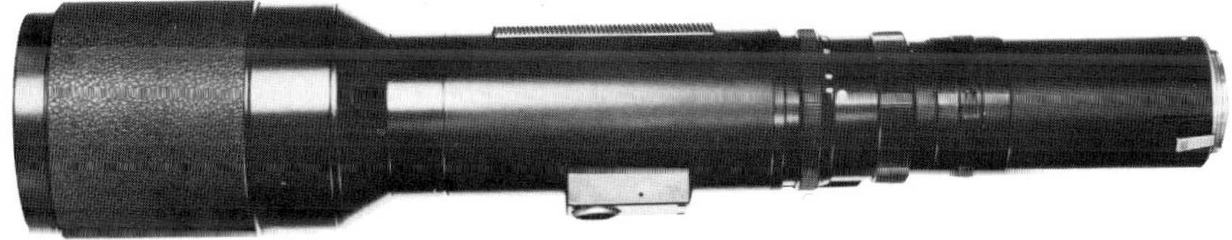

Telyt-R f6.8/560mm.

MIRROR LENSES

Mirror lenses have been used in astronomy for many years and have recently become popular for some photographic uses. Although they have some drawbacks they also have many advantages, such as light weight, compactness and handling. With this method of construction it is possible to produce long focal length lenses with a high degree of correction that are extremely small in size. The construction of a catadioptric (mirror) lens is that the light rays are reflected by a large mirror within the light path. This reflection is then reflected onto another mirror located coaxially, back onto the photographic emulsion. Lenses located behind and in front of the mirrors correct the image. Mirror lenses because of their construction do not have a variable diaphragm. However to cut down light intensity it is possible to use filters that are inserted in the light path.

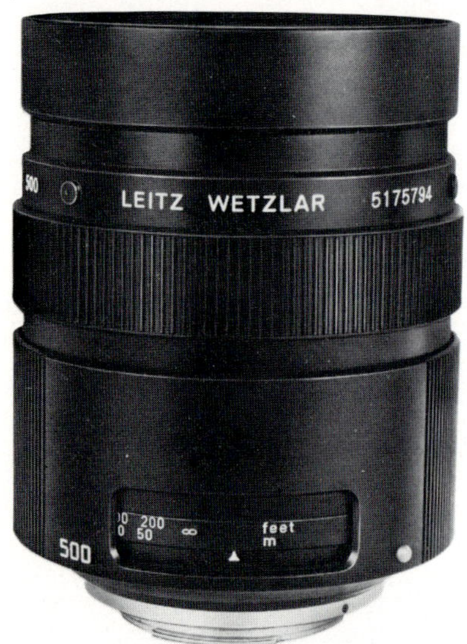

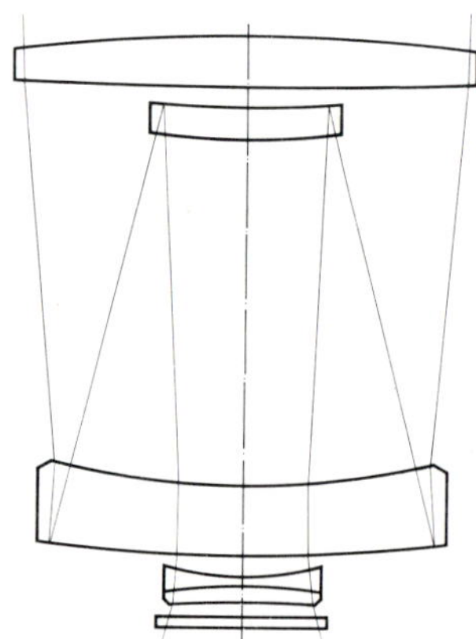

MR TELYT 500mm f8

Mirror lenses of this aperture are small and easily handlable. The standard screen of the Leica R4 produces a somewhat dim image but the full matt number 2 screen can be used to advantage. Since it is not possible to stop this lens down from f8 the transition from sharp to unsharp is very marked. The focusing range for this lens is form infinity to 2.4m. Because of the long focal length and the relatively small aperture it is advisable that films of high sensitivity are used in order to utilise short exposure times.

SUPER TELEPHOTO LENSES
THE TELYT-S 800mm F6.8

Telephoto lenses of extremely long focal length provide difficult problems for optical designers. The chromatic flaws become more and more apparent as the focal length increases. Today many designers incorporate the use of Calcium Fluorite crystals in order to obviate this difficulty. However glass

manufactured in this way is not stable, it is affected by changes in temperature
and humidity and is physically very delicate. Leitz have succeeded in
producing new glasses which approach the performance of Calcium Fluorite
but without having the disadvantages. This newly developed glass enables an
'achromat' lens to be produced containing three elements surpassing the
performance of all earlier lenses and almost equalling that of an
apochromatic lens. High performance in the field of colour photography has
been achieved. The optical design of this lens involves three elements
cemented in one group providing only two air to glass surfaces thus enabling
light transmission loss to be minimised. The lens has a diaphragm with click
stops down to f/32. A filter slot is incorporated within the focusing tube
taking series 7 filters. The weight is 6,800 grams and the lens must be used
mounted on a tripod. The lens barrel is provided with two tripod sockets, one
located at the point of balance, the other at the front for extra stability. An
interesting feature of this lens is that because of its extremely small angle of
view a sighting device faciltating subject location is provided in the form of a
gun sight attached in the form of a carrying handle. The focusing range
extends from infinity to 12.5m, at this distance the field of view is
approximately 300 x 450mm. For transportation the lens is dismantled into
five major components and is carried in a specially designed aluminium
transport case. Since modern films have improved so much it is advantageous
to use faster films, the faster exposure times will help to overcome the
problem of camera shake.

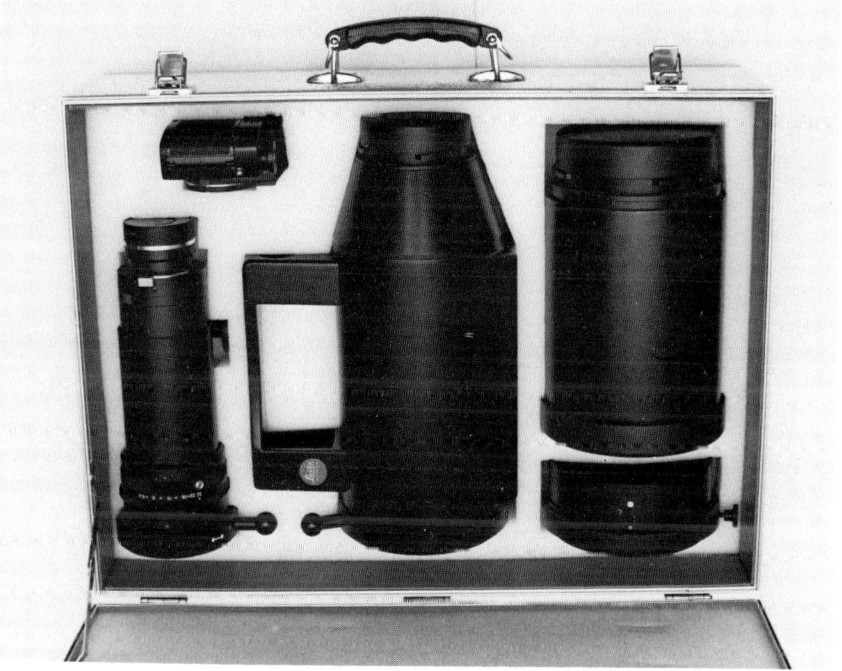

Telyt-S f6.8/800mm dismantled in aluminium travelling case.

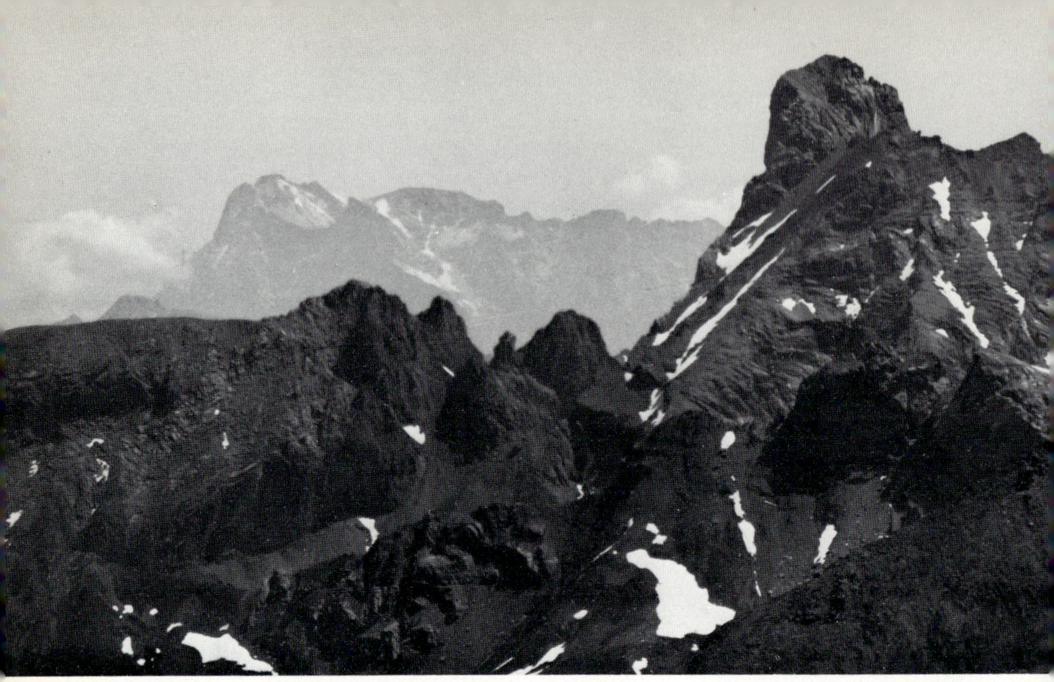

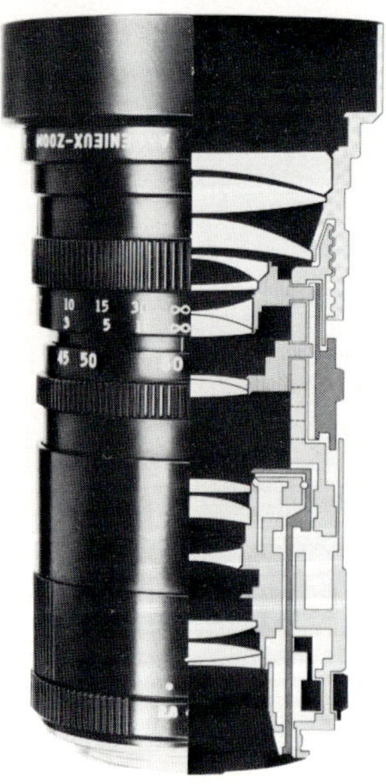

The Zugspitz-Massive taken from the Valuga summit (Arlberg) a distance of 64 kilometers, taken on the Telyt-R 560mm. The problem in this type of photography lies not in the lenses but in the weather conditions, such as air turbulence.

VARIABLE FOCAL LENGTH LENSES

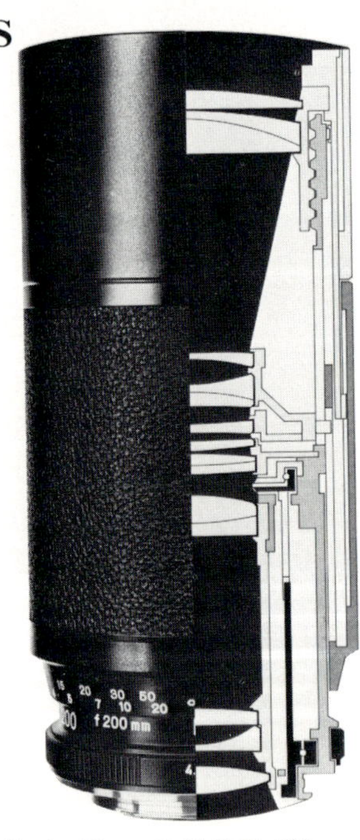

Angenieux-Zoom f2.8/45–90mm

Vario-Elmar-R f4.5/75–200mm

ANGENIEUX ZOOM 45-90mm f2.8

This zoom lens is manufactured by Angenieux. It has an automatic diaphragm with a minimum aperture of f22. Zooming is possible between 45-90mm, focusing remains constant. The optical construction is complex, incorporating fifteen elements in the twelve groups. Light transmission losses are high but compensated for by the automatic metering facility. The zoom lens enables the photographer to frame the subject precisely. Colour reproduction is slightly warmer than a typical Leitz optic.

VARIO-ELMAR-R 75-200mm f4.5

This is a very useful lens whose 2.5:1 zooming range covers the focal lengths of five prime lenses. Focusing and zoom control is operated by a single large sleeve that rotates for focusing and slides back and forth for zooming. The complex lens design contains 15 elements in 11 groups. The focusing range extends from infinity to 1.2m at which distance the field is 160 x 107mm. The maximum aperture of f4.5 allows a compact design and a light weight of 725 grams. Elpro attachments can be used to increase the focusing range. Under extreme conditions 'Vario' lenses will not perform as well as prime lenses, but the difference is minimal, and under normal conditions may be outweighed by their convenience. Light transmission losses are high but compensated for by the automatic metering. Contrast also suffers, with so many optical surfaces the danger of flare is increased. However the lens offers the unique possibility of zooming during exposure to give unusual effects. To practise mount the camera on a tripod and stop down to minimum aperture to increase exposure time. During exposure zoom in or out, the subject will appear to explode and produce an interesting print. This can be effective on the right subject but should not be used too frequently.

VARIO-ELMAR-R 75-200mm f/4.5	ELPRO	Distance scale at	Distance in cm		Object field size in mm	Reproduction scale
			object to film plane	object to front lens		
	4	75 mm/	156	135	414 x 621	1:17,3
		200 mm/1.2	80	58	62 x 93	1:2.6
	3	75mm/	82	61	187 x 281	1:7.8
		200mm/1.2	61	38	41 x 62	1:1.7

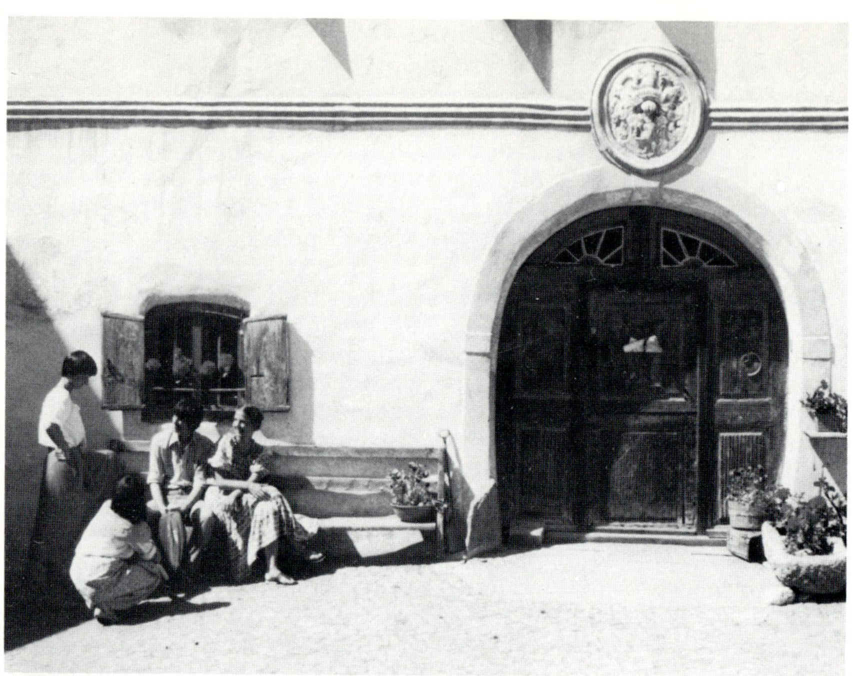

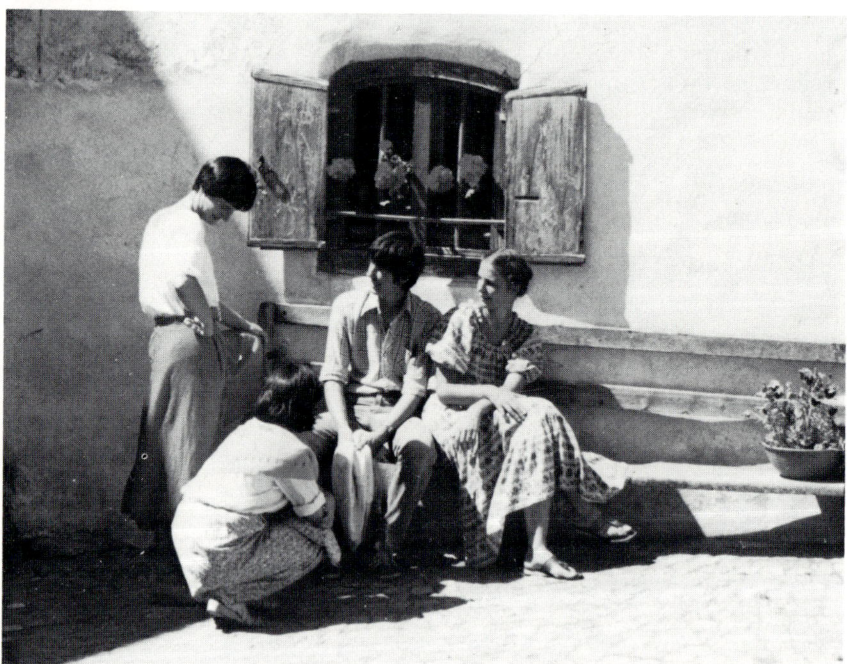

The advantage of the Vario lenses is that it is possible to alter the picture area very quickly without changing the lens.

MACRO ELMAR-R 100mm f4

This is a special model to use in conjunction with the Leica R4 bellows unit. The main difference from the Macro-Elmar-R previously described is that it has no means of focusing and therefore can only be used on the bellows unit. This combination allows for focusing from infinity to a scale of 1:1 at which point it covers a field 24 x 36mm. The lens apertures are provided with click stops at full and half values and the minimum aperture is f/22. The diaphragm is non automatic and therefore metering is carried out at the working aperture. Apertures can be preselected and focusing is carried out at full aperture, by means of a double cable release the lens can be stopped down to the preselected value. This lens is extremely well corrected for the close-up range, although performance is outstanding throughout. The filter size is E55, adapter 14225 allows series 7 filters to be used. The internal thread 0.75 x M55 enables the Elpro lenses to be used. As the exposure time is measured at the working aperture the bellows extension is automatically taken into account and the exposure compensated for accordingly.

THE BELLOWS UNIT

The new Leica R4 Bellows unit is a precision made piece of equipment enabling the scientific and technical photographer a large degree of control over the close focusing range. It provides controlled extension up to a maximum of 100mm, the intermediary ring no. 168863 can be used with the bellows unit thus allowing the following 'M' series lenses to be used: Elmar 65mm f3.5, the lens head Elmarit 90mm f2.8 and the lens head Tele-Elmar 135mm f4. The lenses can be adjusted from infinity up to the following close-up ranges 65mm 1.5:1, 90mm 1.1:1 and 135mm 1:1.3 with all these lenses the apertures must be selected manually. Other Leica lenses can be used in limited photographic areas via means of the ring 14167. The Leitz Photar lenses which are specifically corrected for extreme scales of reproduction can be attached by means of the Photar adapter order number 14259.

Focusing the bellows is achieved by rotating the large knob on the left hand side. In order to open the diaphragm press inwards on the circular plate that is located conveniently around the focusing knob. When this button is released the diaphragm automatically closes down to the preselected aperture. If the automatic diaphragm is to be used on the Leica R4 lenses then hold the diaphragm open by means of the small lock, then using the double cable release the lens will automatically close down to the taking aperture. When using this ensure that the adjustment of the cable release is correct so that the sequence of: first operation, close down aperture, second operation, release shutter, is maintained. A measuring scale is engraved on a rod which can be rotated to provide scales for various lenses. The fourth side of this square section rod indicates the amount of extension being used. If the photographer wishes to duplicate a photograph at a later date the reading should be noted. The same shot can then be repeated by setting the bellows extension at that distance, then focusing is achieved by moving the whole bellows unit in relation to the subject by means of the secondary focusing knob which is secured by means of a winged screw.

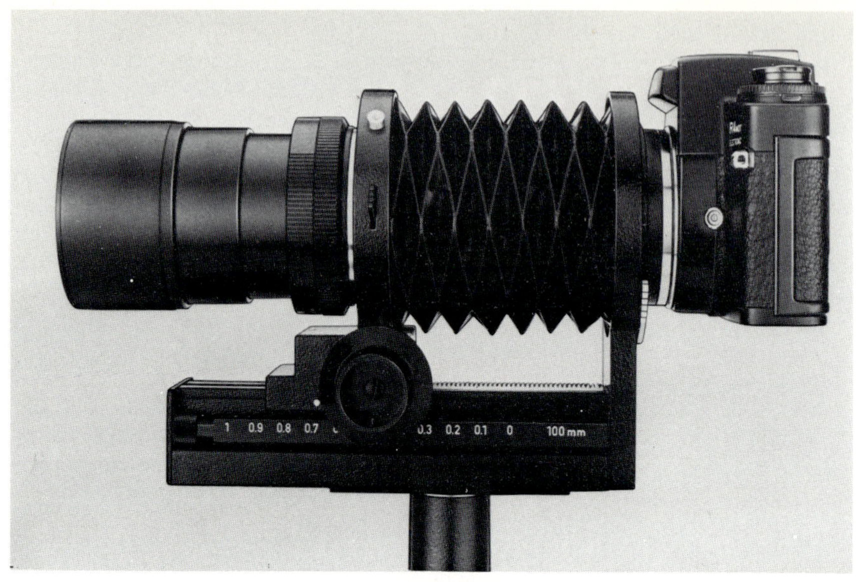

The Bellows Leica R4 Unit

THE EXTENDER-R X2

This is a highly corrected optical system consisting of five elements, it doubles the focal length of Leica R4 lenses. Lenses from 50mm to 80mm can be used and fully automatic diaphragm functions are retained. Exposure programmes (m), (A), [A], can be used. Doubling the focal length of the lens is a useful facility in certain circumstances and the use of the tele-extender X2 enables this to be accomplished easily. With early tele-extenders the results were most disappointing. However the advent of modern optical glass manufacture and technology has overcome these difficulties.

With colour reversal film it is extremely desirable to take photographs in which the subject fills the frame and the tele-extender makes this possible. The lens aperture value is halved which necessitates the exposure factor being increased by approximately x4. In practice this factor is often increased by amounts up to x5 because the five elements of the tele-extender absorb light. This also reduces the brightness of the image in the viewfinder although this makes little difference if apertures of f/5.6 or larger are used. The excellent characteristics of modern colour emulsions can compensate for the light loss. For example on a journey to Greece, because of weight limitations I selected the following lenses a 28mm, a 50mm and a 135mm and the Extender-R X2. By utilising the tele-extender I effectively had lenses of 28mm, 50mm, 100mm, 135mm and 270mm. I used a film of 200 A.S.A. In full daylight I could achieve exposure times of $^1/_{500}$th of a second using the tele-extender and a medium diaphragm setting. Of course with a longer focal length the danger of camera shake increases, therefore a focal length of 270mm requires extreme care.

86·

I do not have any problems with the exposure times when using the extender because of the automatic metering. When my Summicron-R is set to f/5.6 with the extender, an aperture of f/11 is indicated. Only when taking flash photographs does one have to take account of light loss. When using the Summilux f1.4 50mm or 80mm a correction setting of +1 should be used. With the two Macro lenses the use of the extender provides another useful feature. Not only the focal length but also the scale of the image is doubled, it is possible to achieve 1:1 ratios without using the Macro adapter. Results are particularly good when using the extender with the Macro-Elmar-R 100mm f/4 if the lens is stopped down to a small aperture and a tripod used.

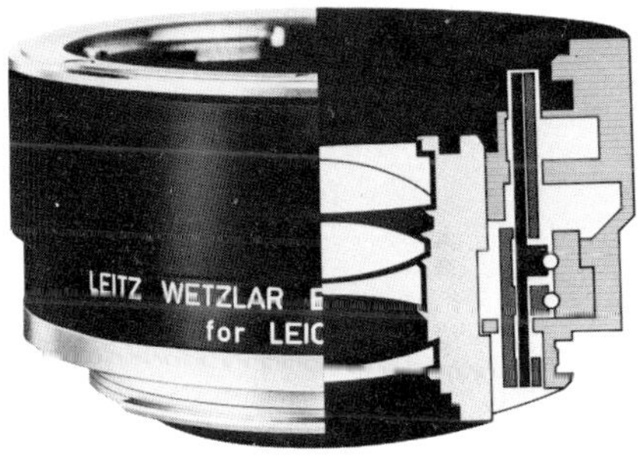

The Extender-R X2 doubles the focal length of the lens. To determine the exposure both the time and manual programmes can be used. The spring diaphragm on the R4 lenses is also incorporated into the extender.

Photographs with the Elmarit-R 90mm f2.8 alone (right) and with the Extender-R (below).

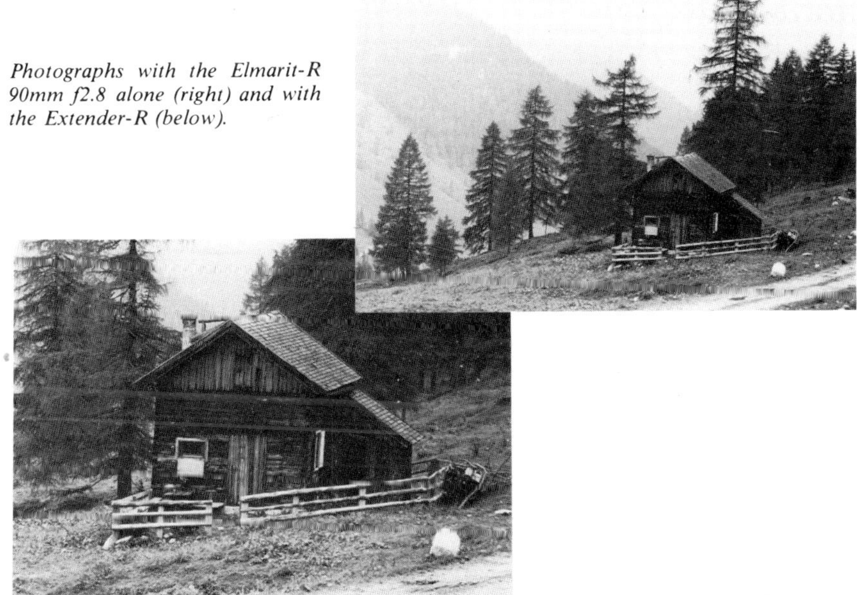

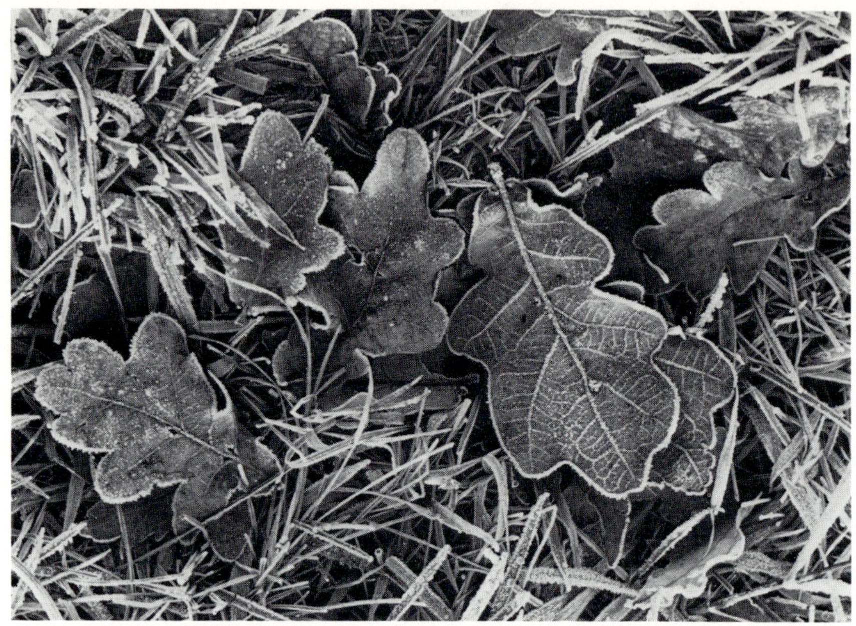

Hoar frost gives grasses and leaves a fine outline. With the Elpro 3 close-up attachment the focusing area of the Elmarit-R 90mm f/2.8 is increased up to a scale of 1:3.

ELPRO CLOSE-UP ATTACHMENTS

These should not be confused with simple close up lenses, they are superbly designed achromat lenses in their own right. Each Elpro consists of two elements cemented to form one group which are specifically calculated to provide the maximum performance in the close-up field. They extend the close-up range and improve the performance of lenses not intended for close-up work. The automatic diaphragm remains fully operational, no correction of the automatic metering is needed. If extension tubes or Macro adapters are used in conjunction with the Elpros the increase of exposure is taken into account by the metering system. The thread size is the standard E55 similar to many of the Leica R lenses. The latest models are marked 1, 2, 3 and 4. Earlier models are marked 6a, 6b, 7a, 7b. The table shows the lenses, the size of the image and the object field. The Elpro number 1 and 2 are intended for use with the Summicron-R f/2 50mm however they can be used on earlier Summicron lenses with the appropriate adapter. The Elpro number 3 is the most versatile, the Elmarit-R 90mm, the Summicron-R 90mm, the Macro-Elmar-R 100mm, the Elmarit-R 135mm and the Vario-Elmar-R 75-200mm can be used with it.

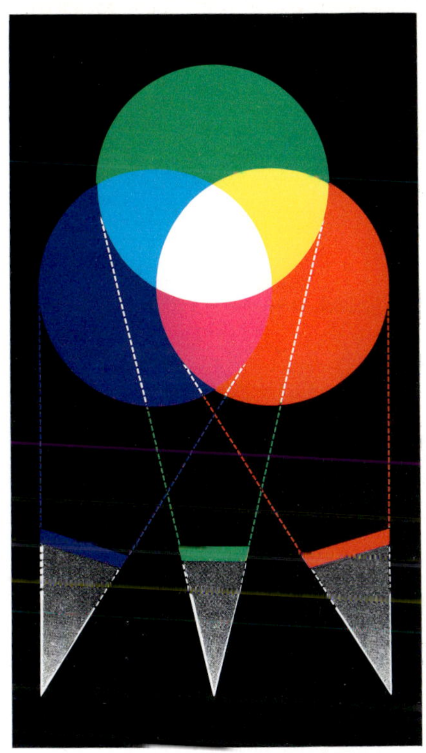
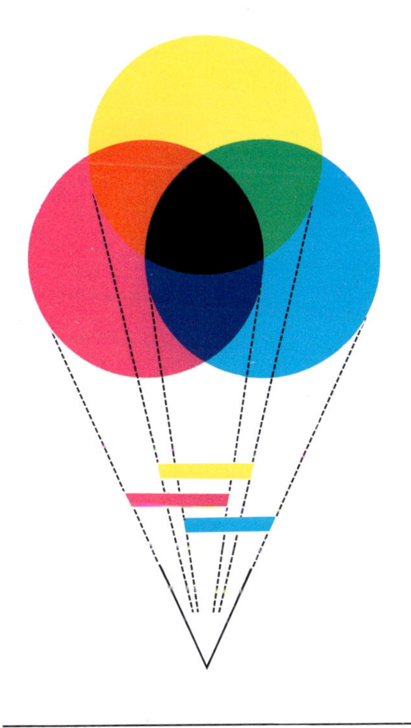
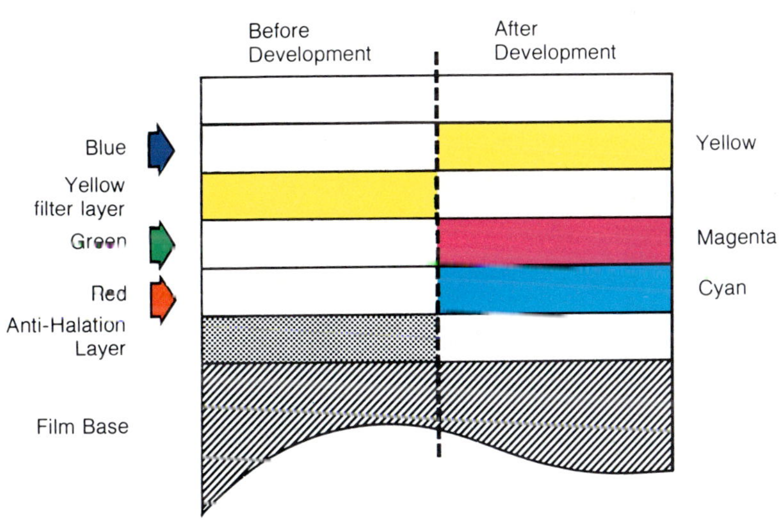

Layer construction of colour material.

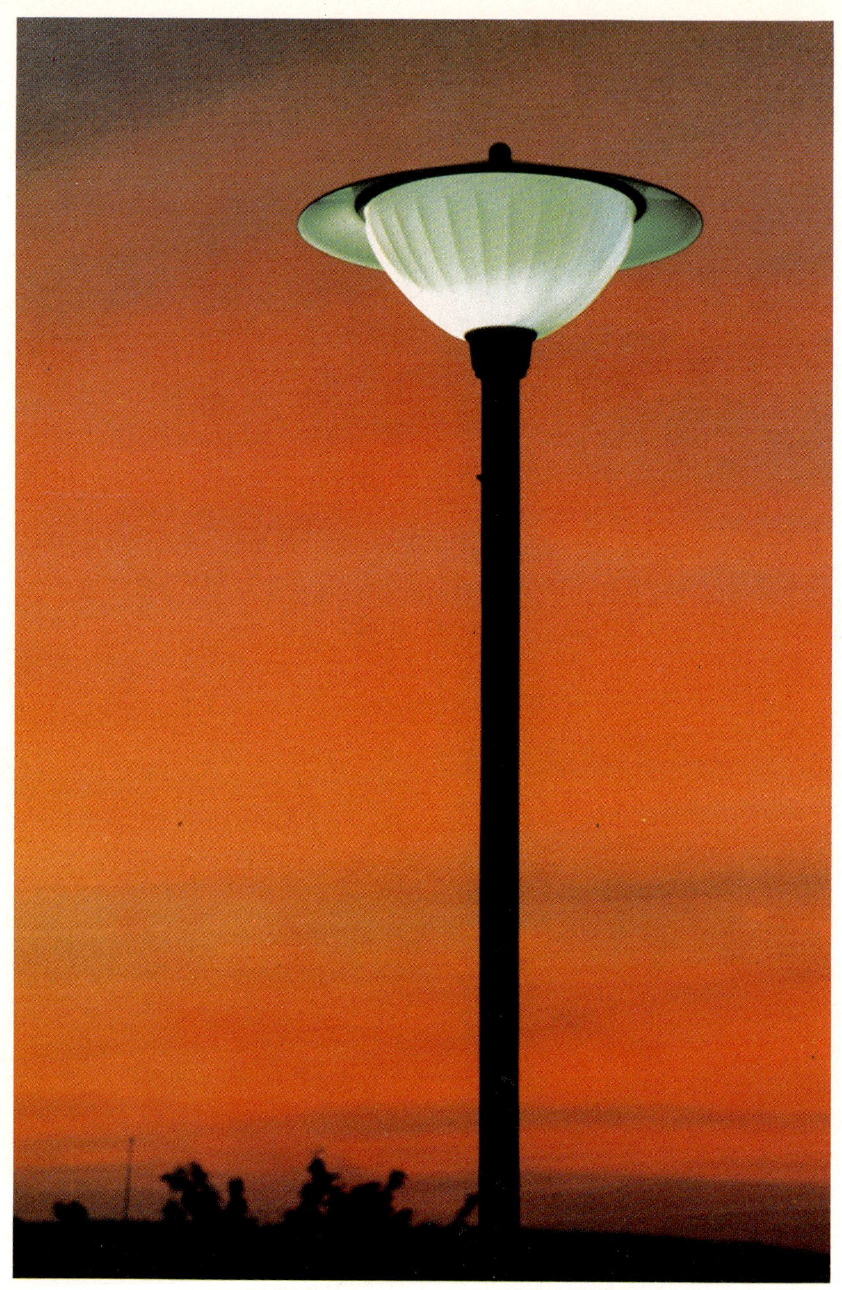

The attraction of this photograph lies in the contrasting illumination between the warm tones of the evening sky and the cold colours of the modern street lamp.

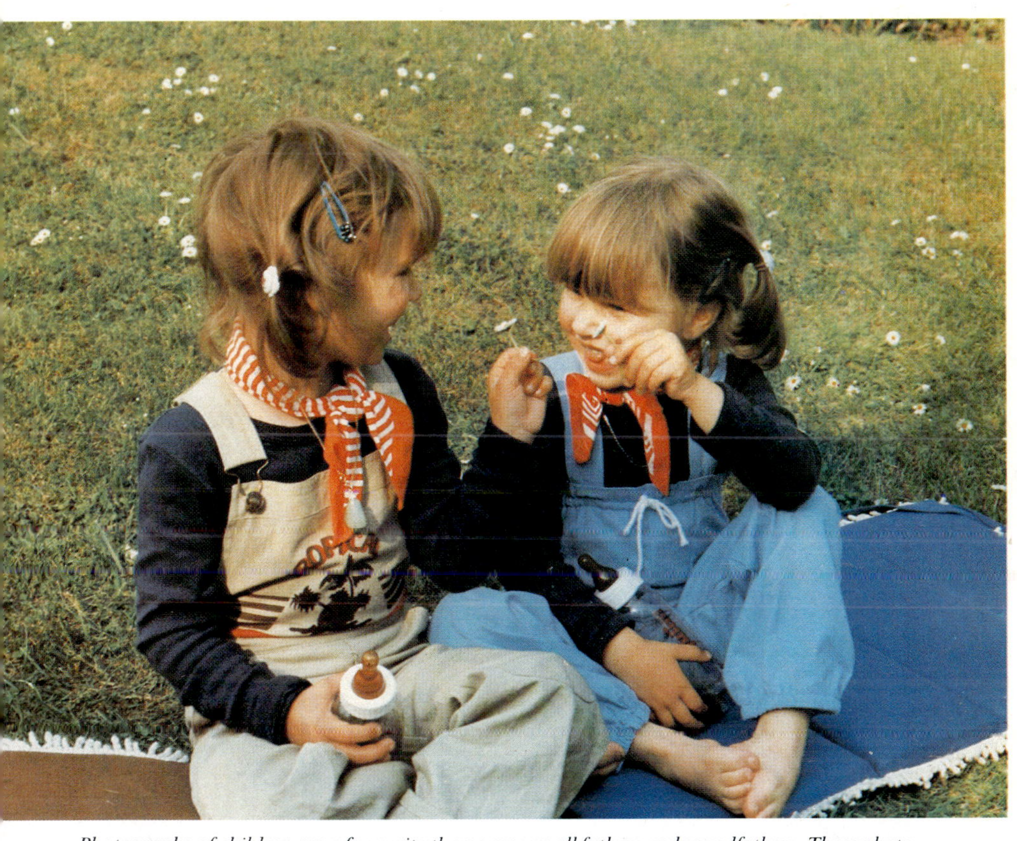

Photographs of children are a favourite theme among all fathers and grandfathers. These photographs show how important the different expressions of the eye can be, and how this is effected by indoor and outdoor lighting. Bright sunlight leads to squinting which is not obstrusive in pictures of children playing but would be inappropriate for a character study. Beautiful photographs of children can be taken indoors by the light from windows or skylights. When using colour film it may be necessary to brighten the shadows if illumination is uneven. This can be done by placing a projection screen or a white table cloth on the opposite side to the window. In most cases the selective metering of the face and hair is appropriate (if this is not light blonde). The camera should not be above the child's nose height. The picture above shows the effects of bright sunlight and wrong camera position. See next page also.

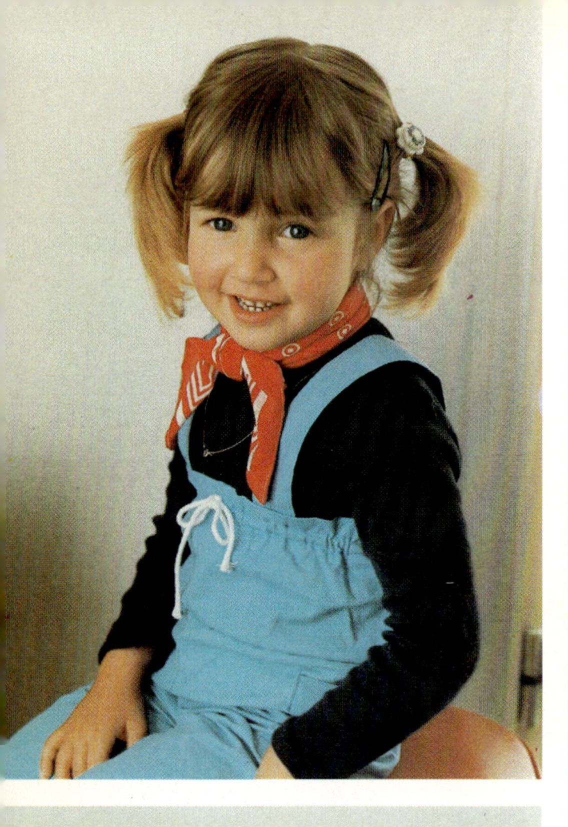
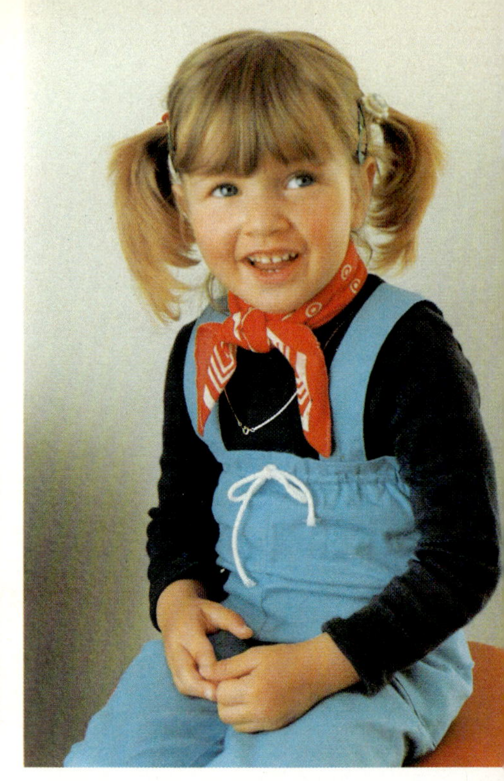
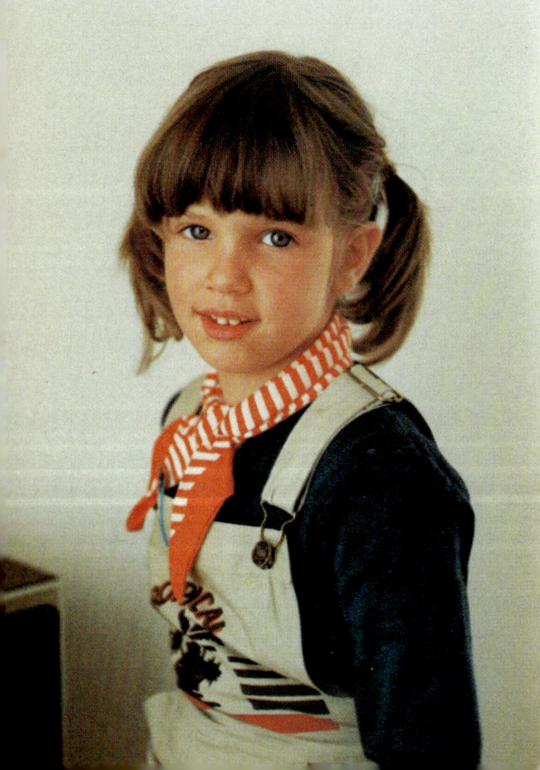
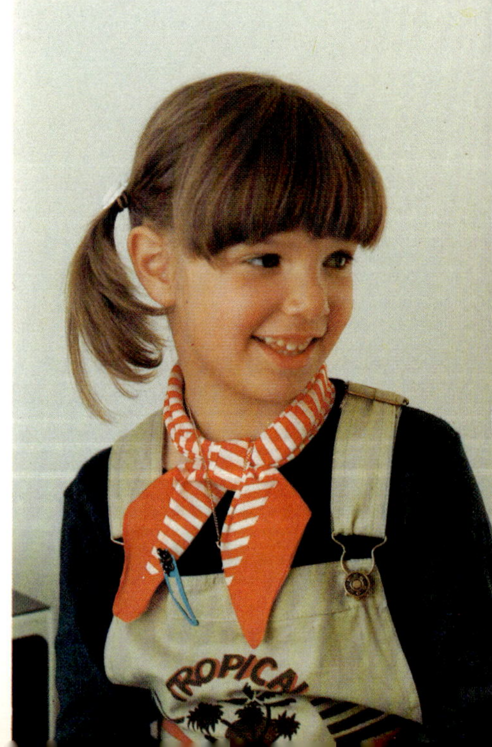

The Elpro number 4 is mainly used on the Elmarit-R 135mm. This close-up attachment produces an improvement in optical quality even when used in combination with other lenses, however it offers no increase in the focusing range when compared with the Elpro no.3. The use of two Elpro close-up attachments in conjunction with each other is possible, because the front ring of the Elpro accepts an E55 filter. However this is not to be recommended as there will be no improvement in optical performance. If using two Elpros an aperture of at least f/11 will be needed to obtain maximum sharpness.

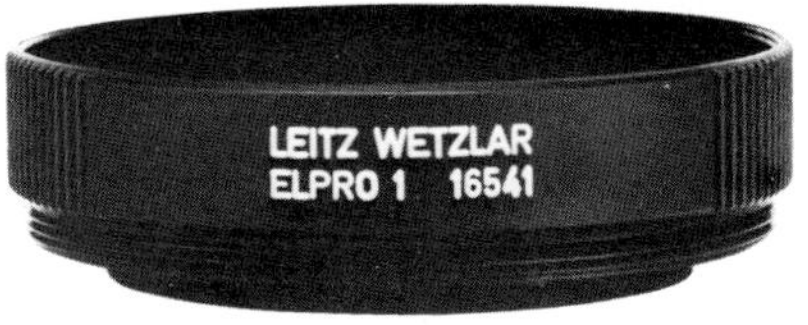

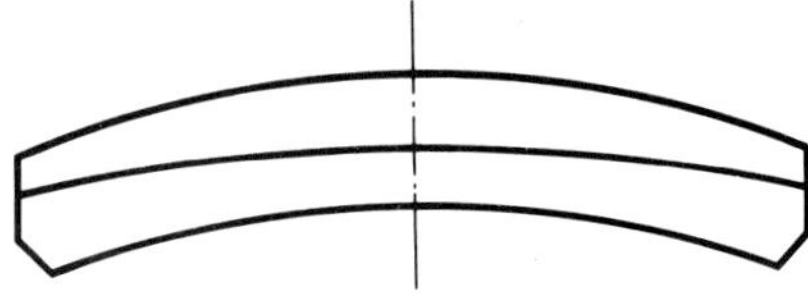

ELPRO near-focusing attachments for LEICA-R lenses

Lens	ELPRO Code No.	Focusing scale at	Distance in cm object to film	object to front lens	Object field size in mm	Reproduction scale
50mm SUMMICRON-R f/2 (E55)	1 16541	∞ 0.5	50 31	41 21	184 x 276 91 x 137	1:7.7 1:3.8
from No. 2777651 11215/11216	2 16542	∞ 0.5	30 24	21 14	94 x 141 62 x 93	1:3.9 1:2.6
90mm ELMARIT-R f/2.8 from No. 2809001 (E55) 11239	3 165543	∞ 0.7	74 44	61 30	161 x 241 72 x 108	1:6.7 1:3.0
90mm SUMMICRON-R f/2 from No. 2770951 (E55) 11219	3 16543	∞ 0.7	74 44	61 30	161 x 241 72 x 108	1:6.7 1:3.0
100mm MACRO-ELMAR-R f/4 (E55) 11232	3 16543	∞ 0.6	75.5 41.6	61 24	145 x 218 48 x 72	1:6 1:2
	+ MACRO-ADAP.-R 14256	∞ 0.6	42 37.4	24 17	49 x 73 29 x 44	1:2 1:1.2
	4 16544	∞ 0.6	150.5 48.6	136 31	323 x 484 61 x 92	1:13 1:2.5
	+ MACRO-ADAP.-R 14256	∞ 0.6	48.8 40.4	31 20	63 x 94 34 x 51	1:2.9 1:1.4
135mm ELMARIT-R f/2.8 from No. 2772619 (E55) 11211	3 16543	∞ 1.5	76 58	61 42	107 x 160 66 x 99	1:4.5 1:2.8
	4 16544	∞ 1.5	150 84	135 68	237 x 355 106 x 159	1:9.9 1:4.4
180mm ELMAR-R f/4 (E55) 11922	3 16543	∞ 1.8	77 63	61 45	80 x 120 48 x 72	1:3.3 1:2
	4 16544	∞ 1.8	151 93	135 75	176 x 267 80 x 120	1:7.4 1:3.3
75-200mm VARIO-ELMAR-R f/4.5 (E55) 11226	3 16543	75mm/∞ 200mm/1.2	82 60	61 38	187 x 281 41 x 62	1:7.8 1:1.7
	4 16544	75mm/∞ 200mm/1.2	156 80	135 58	414 x 621 62 x 93	1:17.3 1:2.6

all values round

THREE PART RING COMBINATION

This combination consists of three different rings or tubes which are fitted together in accordance with the illustration below. The middle ring is 25mm long and combinations of two and three rings can be used together. The ring with the lens bayonet is equipped with a semi-automatic diaphragm control. For focusing the lens diaphragm can be locked at its maximum setting by pressing down on the button. Using the double cable release the diaphragm will close semi automatically to the working aperture. The Summicron-R f/2 50mm in conjunction with three extension rings achieves a scale of 1.09 :1 at its closest focusing setting. The table on the following pages shows the subject fields which are produced for the 25 and 50mm rings on lenses with focal lengths between 50mm and 350mm focal lengths. With the Leica R4 the exposure must be carried out at the working aperture. It is possible to meter at an open diaphragm and to adjust the exposure required for the working diaphragm manually. At very small apertures the centre of the screen will darken, then the use of the no. 2 screen will be found ideal, or one can focus using the matt area of the standard screen.

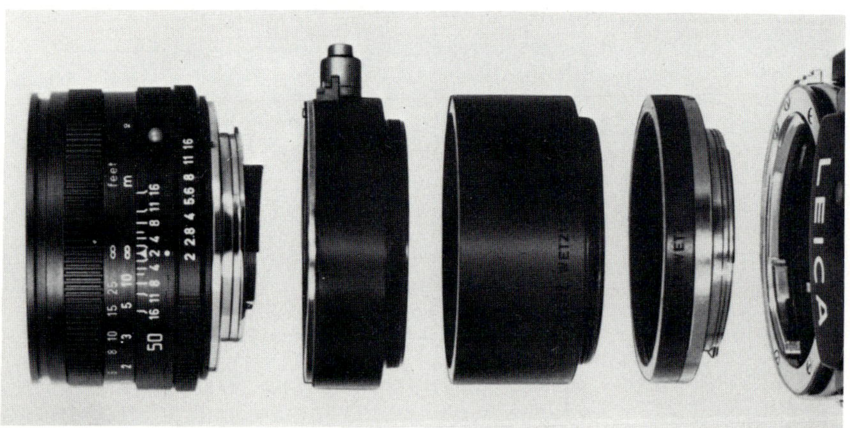

Three Ring Combination.

Lens	Distance scale at	Ring combination					
		2-part (length 25mm) 14158			3-part (length 50mm) 14159		
		Distance in cm object - front lens	Reproduction scale	Object field size in mm	Distance in cm object - front lens	Reproduction scale	Object field size in mm
50mm SUMMICRON-R f/2	∞	13.5	1:2.1	50 x 75	8.1	1:1.04	25 x 37
	0.5	11.2	1:1.6	38 x 58	7.5	1.09:1	22 x 33
90mm ELMARIT-R f/2.8	∞	37.6	1:3.6	86 x 130	21.4	1:1.8	43 x 65
90mm SUMMICRON-R f/2	0.7	25.2	1:2.2	53 x 79	17.6	1:1.4	34 x 50
135mm ELMARIT-R f/2.8	∞	87.2	1:5.4	130 x 195	50.7	1:2.7	65 x 97
	1.5	59.7	1:3.4	81 x 121	42.3	1:2.1	50 x 75
180mm ELMARIT-R f/4	∞	161	1:7.2	172 x 258	96.6	1:3.6	86 x 129
	1.8	97.2	1:3.6	87 x 130	75.4	1:2.4	58 x 87
180mm APO-TELYT-R f/3.4	∞	154	1:7.2	172 x 258	89.4	1:3.6	86 x 129
	2.5	104	1:4.4	106 x 159	74.0	1.2.7	66 x 99
180mm ELMARIT-R f/2.8	∞	146	1:7.2	172 x 258	81.2	1:3.6	86 x 129
	1.8	84.9	1:3.8	91 x 137	61.3	1:2.5	60 x 90
250mm TELYT-R f/4	∞	299	1:10.1	242 x 363	172	1:5.0	121 x 181
	1.7	104	1:3.2	76 x 114	85.8	1:2.3	55 x 82
350mm TELYT-R f/4.8	∞	558	1:13.9	334 x 501	316	1:7.0	167 x 250
	3.0	187	1:4.4	105 x 157	153	1:3.2	76 x 114

all values round

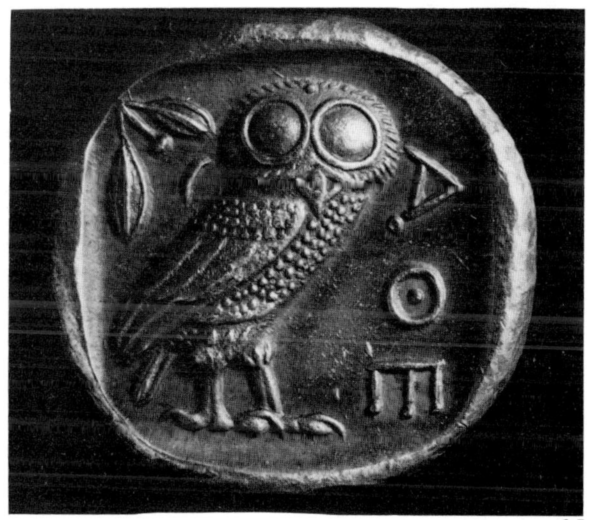

Ancient Greek coin. Photograph taken with the 50mm Summicron-R f/2 without the middle ring but with the focusing adjusted to 50cm.

MACRO ADAPTER-R

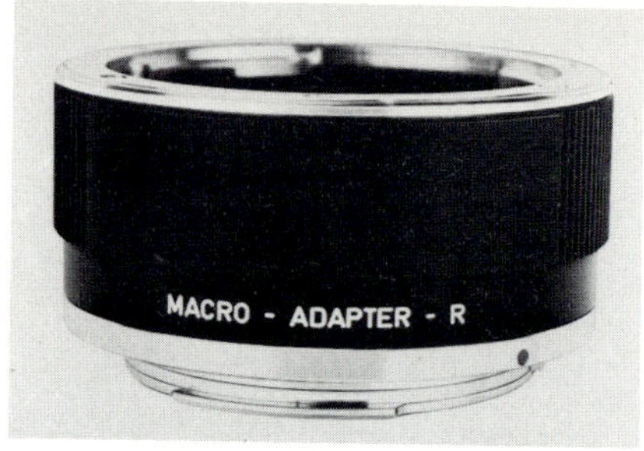

For the R4 system there is the new Macro adapter-R which serves as an inter-mediate ring retaining the full automatic diaphragm operation (order no. 14256). This adapter fits 11 Leica lenses. It is 30mm long and is particularly useful in the close-up area. The following table shows which lenses are suitable and focusing and image scales. This new Macro Adapter-R does not fit the earlier Leicaflex models. With the Leica R4 all metering modes remain operational.

Macro-Adapter-R for LEICA-R lenses

Lens	Distance scale at	Distance in cm object - front lens	Repro-duction scale	Object field size in mm
50mm SUMMICRON-R f/2	∞ 0.5	11.6 9.9	1:1.75 1:1.42	42 x 63 34 x 51
60mm MACRO-ELMARIT-R f/2.8	∞ 1.2	16 9.7	1:2 1:1	48 x 72 24 x 36
90mm ELMARIT-R f/2.8 90mm SUMMICRON-R f/2	∞ 0.7	32 23	1:3 1:2	72 x 108 90 x 72
100mm MACRO-ELMAR-R f/4	∞ 0.6	42 25	1:3.3 1:1.6	80 x 120 39 x 59
135mm ELMARIT-R f/2.8	∞ 1.5	75 55	1:4.5 1:3	108 x 162 72 x 108
180mm ELMAR-R f/4	∞ 1.8	140 91	1:6 1:3.3	144 x 216 79 x 118
180mm APO-TELYT-R f/3.4	∞ 2.5	133 95.6	1:6 1:3.9	144 x 216 95 x 142
180mm ELMARIT-R f/2.8	∞ 1.8	124 78.4	1:6 1:3.4	144 x 216 82 x 123
250mm TELYT-R f/4	∞ 1.7	256 99.1	1:8.4 1:2.9	202 x 303 70 x 105
350mm TELYT-R f/4.8	∞ 3.0	477 178	1:11.6 1:4.1	278 x 417 97 x 146

all values round

THE RIGHT ANGLE VIEWFINDER

The standard viewfinder of the Leica R4 has many advantages but in certain fields of photography it will be found to be slightly inconvenient. This is very apparent when carrying out tasks such as copying, with the camera mounted in a vertical position. It then becomes physically very diffciult to look through the viewfinder, this is also true when taking photographs from low levels near to the ground. For such applications it will be found that the right angle view finder provides the perfect answer. It is located by pushing the attachment prongs into the accessory shoe and provides the facility for viewing at an angle of 90°. The viewfinder can be rotated through 360°. It is also provided with an ocular correction allowing for eyesight corrections between –5 to +3 diopters. The easiest way to adjust the correction lens is to set it to –5 and slowly rotate it until the engraved lines in the viewfinder appear at their sharpest. Once this setting has been obtained it can be marked with a strip of sellotape.

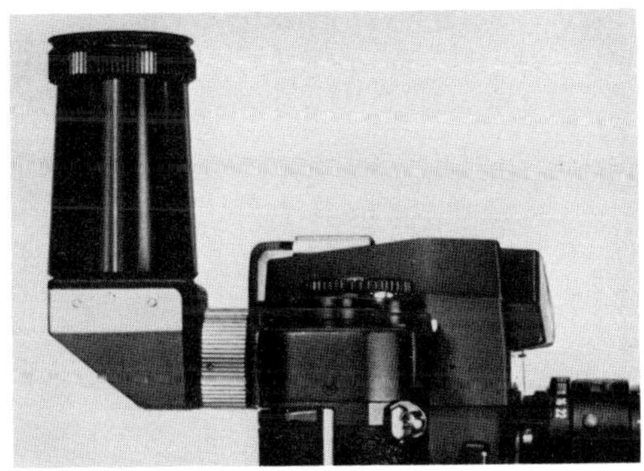

THE BRIDGE TO THE LEICA M SYSTEM

The ability to use M Leica lenses on the R camera can only be accommodated to a limited extent as the lens mounting systems are completely different. The lens throat size of the R4 camera is 47mm and on M models 27.8mm. In addition to this the bayonet mount of the R4 is considerably deeper. Therefore Leica M lenses cannot be used directly on the R4 camera. However since some of the M lenses are intended for use with the Visoflex reflex viewing system these can be used on the R4 via an adapter (order number 14167). This adapter has the R4 bayonet on the camera side and the M bayonet on the lens side. The Leica M series lenses are not provided with an automatic diaphragm so this operation is carried out manually. In order that the exposure meter operates at the working diaphragm the adapter must be provided with the appropriate camming, earlier models did not have this facility. Only the programmes ⓜ, Ⓐ, Ａ, are suitable for controlling exposure. All in all the use of Leica M lenses on the R4 camera is only a makeshift device.

Accessories for LEICA-R lenses

LEICA-R lens:	Code No.	Lens hood	Lens cap	Rear cover	Filters or screw thread	Series	Adapter for Series filters	A Ø in mm
15mm f/3.5	11213	built-in	14294	14162	built-in		–	83.5
16mm f/2.8	11222	built-in	14089	14162	built-in		–	65
19mm f/2.8	11225	12529	14221	14162	M 82 x 0.75		–	88
21mm f/4	11813	12506	14145	14162	–	8.5	lens hood	75
24mm f/2.8	11221	12523	14184	14162	–	8	lens hood	63.7
28mm f/2.8	11204	12509	14172	14162	–	7	lens hood	51
35mm f/4	11202	12514	14184	14162	–	8	lens hood	63.7
35mm f/2.8 from No. 2928901	11231	built-in	14133	14162	E 55 or 7		14225	63
35mm f/2 from No. 2791417	11115	built-in	14133	14162	E 55 or 7		14225	63
50mm f/2 from No. 2777651	11215 11216	built-in	14133	14162	E 55 or 7		14225	63
50mm f/1.4 from No. 2806501	11776	built-in	14133	14162	E 55 or 7		14225	63
60mm f/2.8 from No. 3013651	11212	built-in	14133	14162	E 55 or 7		14225	63
80mm f/1.4	11880	built-in	14265	14162	E 67 or 8		14264	75
90mm f/2.8 from No. 2809001	11239	built-in	14089	14162	E 55 or 7		14225	65
90mm f/2 from No. 2770951	11219	built-in	14144	14162	E 55 or 7		14225	70
100mm f/4	11232	built-in	14133	14162	E 55 or 7		14225	63
100mm f/4 for Bellows R from No. 2933351	11230	built-in	14089	14162	E 55 or 7		14225	65
135mm f/2.8 from No. 2772619	11211	built-in	14089	14162	E 55 or 7		14225	65
180mm f/4	11922	built-in	14089	14162	E 55 or 7		14225	65
180mm f/3.4 from No. 2947024	11242	built-in	14281	14162	E 60 or 7.5		14263	66
180mm f/2.8 from No. 2939701	11923	built-in	14265	14162	E 67 or 8		14264	75
75-200mm f/4.5	11226	built-in	14144	14162	E 55 or 7		14225	70
250mm f/4 from No. 3050601	11925	built-in	14265	14162	E 67 or 8		14264	75
350mm f/4.8	11915	built-in	14294	14162	E 77		–	83.5
400mm f/6.8	11960	built-in	14152	14162	–	7	filter slot	78
500mm f/8	11243	built-in	14294	14162	E 77	–	–	83.5
560mm f/6.8	11865	built-in	14295	14162	–	7	filter slot	98
800mm f/6.3	11921	built-in	on request	14162	–	7	filter slot	152

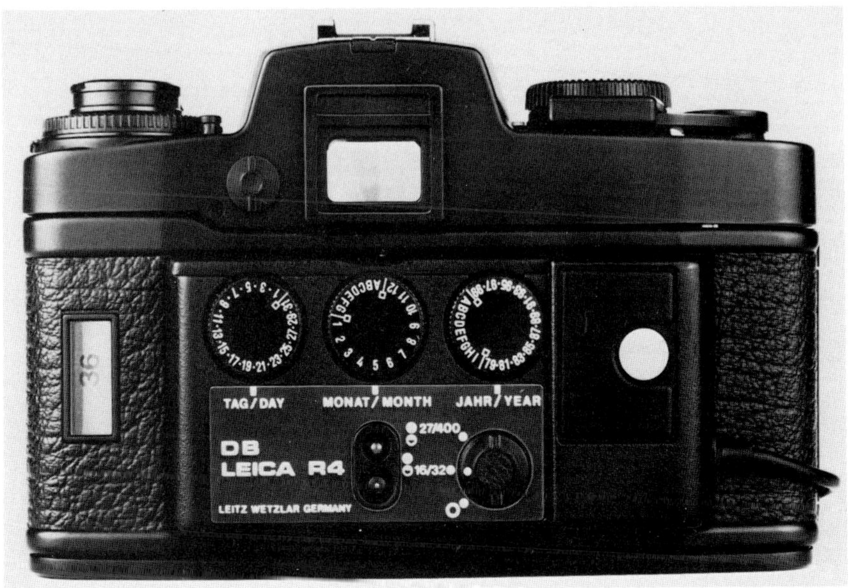

Data-Back DB Leica R4

DATABACK DB LEICA R4

The standard camera back of the Leica R4 can be removed after opening, the hinge is on a spring which can be depressed to release the back from its fixing location point. If a data back is attached it is possible to take an exposure and record details such as dates etc. directly onto the film in the bottom right hand corner at the time the exposure is made. For scientific and technical applications it is particularly useful, enabling easy identification of subjects. The data is exposed from the back of the film by means of a small flash diode and the connection is made by means of a short flash cable which is attached to the camera's flash contact. An on/off switch is provided and a control which is set in accordance with the film's sensitivity. There is a choice of three screens showing the day month and year, two of the screens also have letters. The size of the exposed area on the film is approximately 0.7mm x 4.5mm. The flash diode needs two silver oxide batteries of 1.5 volts each (standard camera batteries). The unit can be used in conjunction with the motor winder and motor drive. The weight of the data back is approximately 50 grams more than the standard back.

250 EXPOSURE BACK

The 250 exposure back can be fitted in place of the standard one. It incorporates giant size cassettes allowing 250 exposures to be made on a film 11 metres long. The film counter is incorporated within the unit.

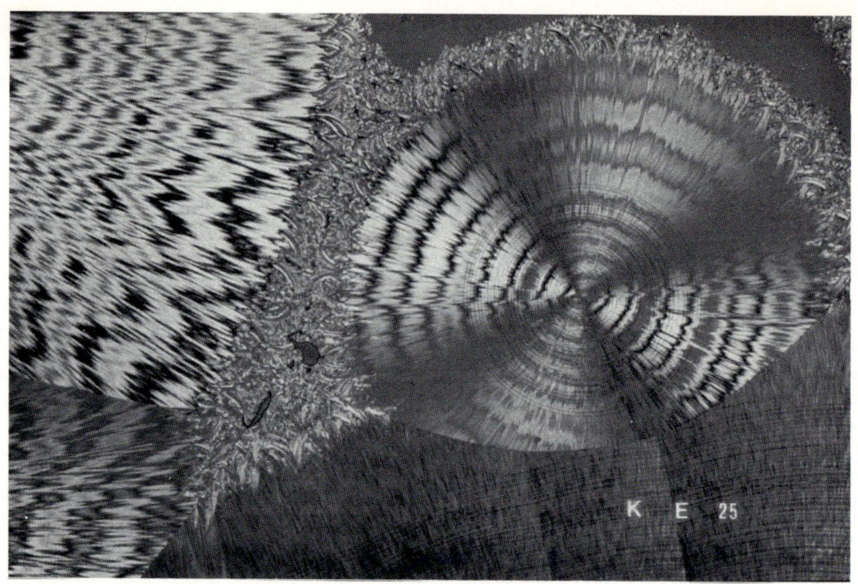

Close-up photograph showing data recording. If the date is to be recorded take care that this is done in reverse in accordance with the new International Ruling. First the year number, then the month number, then at the end, the day.

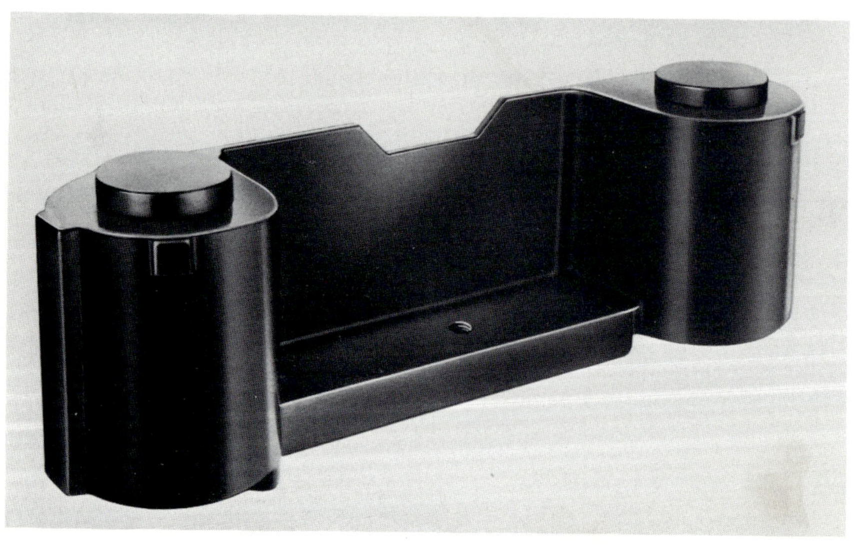

250 Exposure Back Leica R4

CASES

The owner of a valuable Leica R4 system would like to be able to transport everything about safely and easily with everything necessary to hand. However the system of lenses has now grown to a considerable number and there are so many combinations that it would be easy to fill pages on the subect of cases. The individual must choose which case best meets his needs. A factor which is often forgotten is the maximum weight with which the photographer wishes to be encumbered. With increasing age one becomes more and more aware of the weight problem therefore only the basic cases are described below.

EVEREADY CASES

The standard camera case made out of leather was altered in such a way that the broad camera strap does not need to be taken off the camera but is retained as the camera strap for the eveready case. There are two types of case which differ from each other in that one is supplied with the front cover of sufficient depth to contain the camera complete with a lens of standard focal length, and the large nosed model which will contain lenses from 16mm to 90mm.

COMBINATION CASES

These combination cases which are made of soft leather come in two models, one is designed for the use of the camera complete with motor winder or motor drive attached and the other, slightly smaller case, for the camera alone. With both cases up to four lenses according to size can be accommodated in addition to the standard lens. Both models are also supplied in khaki sail cloth and are known as the 'Safari cases'.

THE UNIVERSAL or REPORTER CASE

This large leather case will accommodate two Leica R4 bodies with or without motor winder or motor drive attachments and up to six lenses according to focal length. Its external dimensions are 360 x 210 x 240mm (length x breadth x depth). The bag is unlined.

Note: All above 'soft' cases have a hard protective insert to protect cameras and lenses.

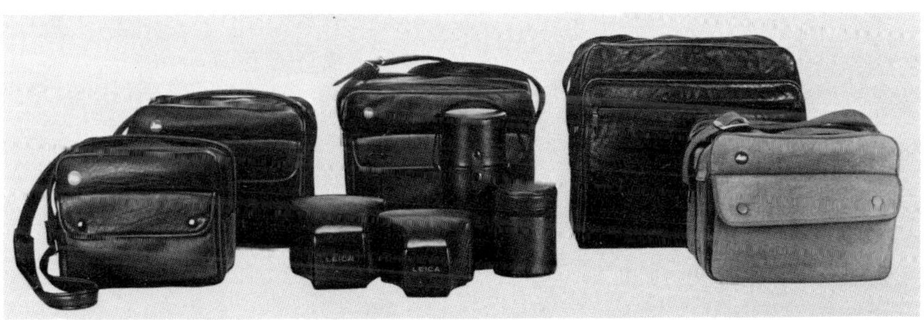

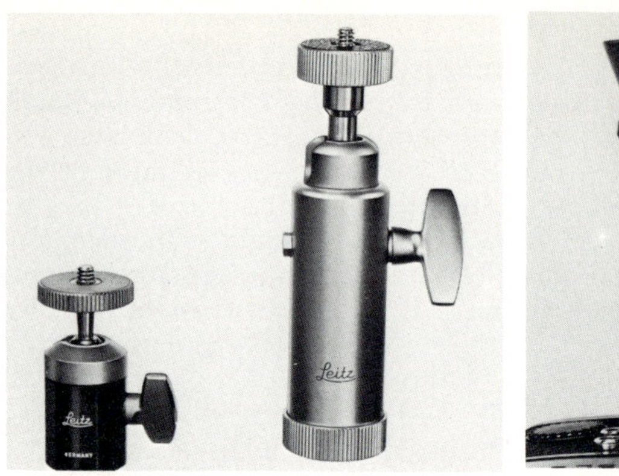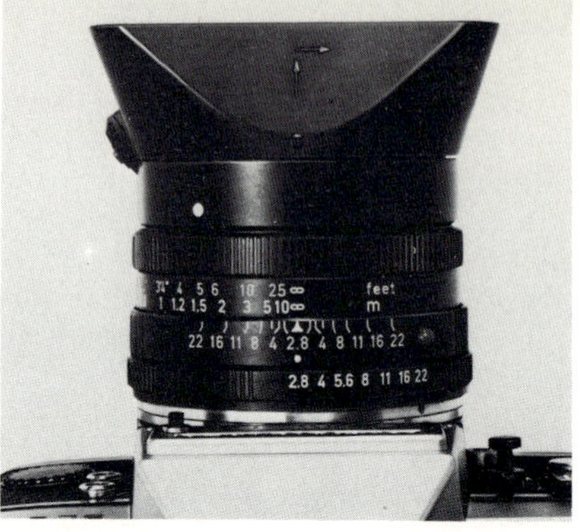

Left: Small and large ball and socket heads. Right: Lens hood with filter rotating control.

LENS HOODS

Lens hoods are basic and play a vital role in the production of flare free photographs. They ensure that stray light sources are kept away from the front surface of the lens, they also protect the lens from rain and accidental damage. They help to prevent finger marks appearing on the lens as well. There are several types of hoods. Most R lenses are provided with built-in collapsible hoods which are extended for use. A few focal lengths have a separate hood and these hoods also provide an adapter for the use of series filters. To remove them from the lens, pull the lenshood slightly forwards and turn it in an anti-clockwise direction. To attach these lens hoods the white dot is lined up with the bayonet pin and turned in a clockwise direction until it is felt to lock in position.

FITTING THE CAMERA ONTO OPTICAL EQUIPMENT

For fitting scientific equipment to the Leica R4 the rear part of the ring combination (order no. 14158 is suitable for use as a connecting piece and can be ordered from the Technical Service Department of Ernst Leitz. This ring also provides full metering facilities to be retained. The length of the adapter is 9.5mm and the front is provided with a thread M51.5 x 0.75.

FILTERS AND THEIR APPLICATIONS

Colour sensitivity is also applicable to black and white photography even though it is not the colours themselves but the tonal range which is altered. Brilliant differences in colour such as that between green and red, yellow and blue under certain circumstances will produce an almost identical shade of grey. By using a suitable filter a better tonal contrast can be achieved. In order to select the most appropriate filter its effect on the sensitive emulsion, and not the visual effect on the eye must be taken into account. In colour photography ultra violet and polarising filters are most commonly used and for black and white films yellow and orange are the most usual. The properties of filters are that they allow light of their own colour to pass freely through and lighten its reproduction whilst light of the complementary colour is weakened and thus appears darker on the final print.

FILTERS FOR BLACK AND WHITE FILMS

YELLOW
This filter is indispensable for winter sports, otherwise the shadow of the snow would have too little contrast despite illumination of the sun. In the summer it is particularly useful in landscape photography, however a delicate blue sky with white clouds will not be sufficiently effected by this filter. The exposure factor is X2.

YELLOW GREEN
This filter is similar in characteristics to the yellow filter, it lightens green shades in landscape photography, enhancing grass and foliage. Another advantage is that sun tanned skin is reproduced somewhat darker than with the yellow filter. The exposure factor is X3.

ORANGE
The orange filter produces a considerable contrast effect with cloud or snow scenes. It is effective in reducing haze thus enabling long distance shots to be taken with enhanced clarity. Care should be taken when photographing people with this filter as skin tones are considerably lightened. The exposure factor is X3.

FILTERS FOR BLACK AND WHITE AND COLOUR FILMS

ULTRA VIOLET FILTERS
UVA filters are capable of absorbing ultra violet light. The new Leica R4 lenses are specially coated so that ultra violet light is automatically compensated. However under extremely bright lighting conditions the UVA filter will have an effect. It also serves as a very useful protection for the delicate front element of the lens. This filter can normally be left permanently on the lens and its effect is not detrimental to performance. The following exception should be noted, night shots when very strong sources of light are included within the area of the subject can cause internal reflections, similarly flare can also appear if the sun is included in the photograph. The increase in the exposure with the UVA filter is so minimal that it can be ignored.

CIRCULAR POLARISATION FILTER

Ernst Leitz have been producing these filters for a considerable time. Circular polarising filters enable the automatic metering system of the Leica R4 to give the correct reading. This filter can be used in many circumstances and is particularly useful in colour photography. It is worth testing the effect by

Screw-thread Filters

	Screw-thread				
	E 32*	E 55	E 60	E 67	
UV	13400	13373	13381	13386	
Yellow	13403	13236	–	–	
Yellow-green	–	13391	13392	13393	
Orange	13402	13312	13383	13388	
Red	13401	–	–	–	
Neutral density 4x	13405	–	–	–	
Circular polarising	–	13357	13376	13377	
Polarising	–	13374	–	–	

Series Filters

	Series filters				
	6	7	7.5	8	8.5
UV	13012	13009	–	13018	13024
Yellow	13013	13006	–	13019	–
Yellow-green	13014	13007	–	13021	–
Orange	13011	13008	–	13017	13023
Circular polarising	–	13370	–	13372	–
Filter adapter	14160 (E 44)	14161 (E 54) 14225 (E 55)	14222 (E 59) 14263 (E 60)	14165 (E 72) 14264 (E 67)	

viewing the subject through the viewfinder and slowly rotating the filter through 180°. Under many lighting conditions the effect is that the colour is enhanced. The normal use of this filter is to cut out spectral reflection when photographing glass or liquid. The filter holder has a yellow dot on one side, when it is inserted into the lenshood care should be taken that this dot is on the top. Technically the elimination of reflections is caused by the fact that polarised light only has one direction of vibration, whilst normal light vibrates in all directions. If normal light falls on a reflecting non-metallic surface then a large percentage is reflected as polarised light. Since a pol filter only allows light to be transmitted in one direction of vibration the reflected light can be reduced by using a polarising filter. The filter is used at an angle to the direction of vibration of the reflection, the degree of polarisation depends on the angle of reflection and therefore complete elimination is not achieved. When using wide angle lenses the avoidance of all reflections does not always give the best effect. Take care when changing from vertical to horizontal format since the effect of the filter will be strongly influenced by the 90° turn of the camera and must be corrected accordingly.

USING FILTERS ON THE LEICA R4

Automatic metering does not always make full adjustment for filters because the silicon diodes of the metering system remain constant in their sensitivity to the spectrum. However different films vary in their light sensitivity and the manner in which they respond to different areas of the spectrum. An exposure correction of +1 should be used with yellow, yellow green and orange filters. With red filters it is impossible to give an overall factor as films vary enormously in their sensitivity to red.

USING THE CAMERA

COLOUR PHOTOGRAPHY

In many instances colour photography is easier than black and white. However a few points should be observed regarding the correct lighting and exposure. The exposure metering which is suitable to the contrast of the subject no longer provides any difficulty with the Leica R4. The production of colour film is quite a technical achievement. Small variations in the colour balance are unavoidable since the way that the film is kept with regard to age and temperature will effect the film, therefore it is important that it is used as fresh as possible. Any reserve of film should be kept in a cool place such as the vegetable compartment of the refrigerator. It is important that colour film is not left for months loaded in the camera. Once the film is exposed it should be processed as soon as possible. It is not important that the photographer should be fully acquainted with all the technical and physical complexities of film production in order that good photographs can be taken. It is of greater importance that the photographer is aware of balances and blends of colour. White light is composed of all the colours of the spectrum combined. Modern colour film is made up of at least three different layers of emulsion in a sandwich, which together are capable of resolving all visible colours. Each layer is sensitive to either blue, green, or red, the three primary colours.

COLOUR REVERSAL FILM

With reversal film the colour film is turned directly into a colour transparency by a complex process. A projected picture can be viewed. For colour rendition and subtlety of colour balance the colour transparency is unsurpassed. Additionally it is also possible to produce colour prints from them. For the best results the original slide should not contain a very large contrast range.

Reversal films are normally processed pre-paid, the price of the film also contains the price of the processing. The glassless type of mounting has become more popular since it is apparent that glassless mounted slides keep better than those mounted between sheets of glass. With colour reversal films the exposure is governed above all by the highlights of the picture. The slide becomes too dense when the film is under-exposed or too bright when over-exposed. The accurate metering of the Leica R4, particularly in the selective mode, is invaluable. For subjects containing a bright contrast range it is necessary to view the most important subjects very carefully and expose accordingly. If lighter slides are required for projection then the film sensitivity should be set to a speed of 1/2 DIN lower than the actual rating of the film.

DAYLIGHT AND ARTIFICIAL LIGHT COLOUR FILMS

There are two groups of reversal emulsions. Daylight film which is set to a colour temperature of 5,600° K and artificial light film which is set to 3,200° K. Different films are necessary because the colour reproduction of daylight film if used with tungsten lighting differs so much in its colour balance that an artificial colour rendition is reproduced. Tungsten lighting contains a much smaller range of blue than daylight. However daylight film can be used in artificial light if the colour balance is adapted by means of a salmon coloured filter. The loss of transmitted light when you are using this filter is equivalent to a decrease of film speed of 2/3 DIN. It is not recommended that artificial film is used under daylight conditions as it would be necessary to use a very dark blue filter. The decrease in effective film speed would be 6 DIN.

REVERSAL COLOUR FILM DEVELOPMENT

Reversal colour film development requires very special equipment and great care. The majority of producers carry out this work in their own laboratories and so the processing costs including the postage is already contained in the purchase price, some firms return the slides pre-mounted in cardboard or plastic mounts. It is therefore important when comparing prices that the mounting costs are included for those films which are sold without processing costs involved. The manufacturers provide a complete processing kit and instructions to enable the user to process the films themselves. Home processing is no less costly than commercial processing. The tolerance when processing is extremely small. In order that consistent results are obtained a well equipped laboratory with temperature control and very accurate processing procedures are required. The use of colour equipped darkrooms amongst amateurs is becoming more and more common. For those wishing to embark on this, valuable tips will be found in the book "Home Laboratory Practice in Colour" by Rudolph Sect published by Heering Verlag.

COLOUR NEGATIVE FILM

In the development of colour negative film a negative colour picture is produced in the subtractive basic colours, yellow, purple and blue/green. In order to improve the reproduction of colour there are no ideal colour dyes. The mask is employed to remove faulty absorption by means of correction. Colour negative film is always sold exclusive of processing costs. Negative film is suitable for both daylight and tungsten lighting conditions.

COLOUR TEMPERATURE

Colour temperature is a measure of the spectral mixing of light and is expressed in the term 'KELVIN'. The base of this scale is equal to $-273°$ C. In order to determine the colour temperature of a light source we must know the distribution of its spectrum. The most important source of light is daylight. In normal daylight conditions, with the sun shining and white clouds, the colour temperature is equivalent to $5,000°$ K. Since we take photographs in changing conditions the photographer must be aware of changes. Under a deep blue sky in the high mountains the light will be approximately $20,000°$ K (without direct sunlight.) The higher the blue portion of the sky so the colour temperature increases. When the sun is low the blue parts of the sunlight are less apparent. Because of the greater distance the light is travelling through the earth's atmosphere the more yellow or red it appears. The eye is capable of rapid changes according to colour temperature. A sheet of white paper appears as white to the human eye under lamp light (2,800 K) as under sunlight (5,700 K). Only when we compare the two types of illumination do we notice the difference clearly.

Contrast also plays an important role. Apart from the appropriate colour temperature the illumination contrast also plays a part. Every photographic subject displays differences of brightness, apart from the differences of colour, which can be influenced by means of illumination. Although this effective light and shadow is extremely important with black and white photography it should not exceed a certain limit in colour photography. The colour reproduction will be altered if the contrast in illumination between the lightest and darkest parts of the subject exceeds a ratio of 1:4. This can be controlled if the exposure is taken from a sheet of white paper located at the brightest part of the subject, this is repeated in the darkest area and the difference in the result gives the reference to determined contrast ratio. This contrast ratio has nothing to do with the general brightness of the object being photographed, a brightly illuminated snow scene can have a low illumination contrast. On the other hand it makes a great difference if we are photographing with direct light, side lighting or 'contra jour'. In the last case the illumination contrast increases so much that it is very easy for it to exceed the latitude of the colour emulsion. This does not occur if the shadows are well lit as is the case with snow or beach photography.

TIPS FOR COLOUR PHOTOGRAPHY

All colour materials are demanding in their storage. The colour balance will become distorted if films are stored at too high a temperature. It is therefore recommended by the manufacturers that films should be kept in a cool place (less than 18°C). This is done most conveniently if films are kept in a plastic bag in a domestic refrigerator. Cameras should always be loaded and unloaded in the shade and the film speed indicator checked for the emulsion being used. The leaders of exposed films should always be marked by some standard method and replaced in their original containers. Cartridges are seldom light tight and should not be left lying around. Exposed film should be sent for processing as soon as possible, particularly in hot conditions. If colour films which have not been fully exposed are left for a long time the latent image fades and the colour will become distorted. Exploit the format, go close to the subject, fill the frame and be sure that all superfluous details are omitted. Long focal length lenses are often useful in this respect. If possible brighten up the shadows that are too dark, sunshine with white clouds is more balanced than sunshine with a completely clear blue sky. Frontal lighting produces glowing colour slides, side lighting produces plasticity in the subject. Take care when shooting against the light, the selective metering mode of the R4 is particularly useful for this type of photography. Photographs of distant objects are only successful when the atmosphere is clear, the best effect being produced when the foreground contains strong shapes. Although you are using colour film it is very important that colour is used correctly. It is often true that the colour photograph or slide containing the fewest colours is the most successful. Foggy and rainy conditions produce interesting photographs, particularly in cities and towns. Use a fast lens and a short exposure time. Night photographs are most successful in the last phases of twilight. In towns, shop windows and hoardings often produce delightful subjects. Use the integrated metering to measure the overall light intensity and the main subject will be considerably over exposed, the selective mode is the one to use. The use of filters in night photography is to be avoided as they introduce extra glass to air surfaces increasing the risk of reflection.

The absolutely correct rendition of an original subject with colour film is almost impossible. The photographer can be sure that if an original grey is reproduced accurately then he has achieved the most that can be expected. Subjects that are essentially monochromatic in colour content are often very successful in colour photography. Warm colours (yellows and reds) have a better effect in the foreground, cold colours (blues and greens) are more successful in the background. Although of course it is not always practical, beware of coloured reflections, people beneath trees, umbrellas etc. Select an exposure time that is as short as possible unless a special effect is required. It is better that lenses are used at larger apertures so that shorter shutter speeds

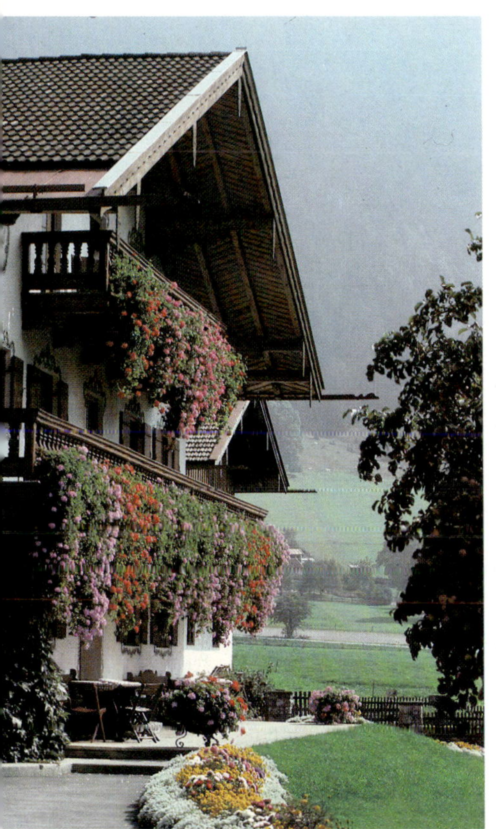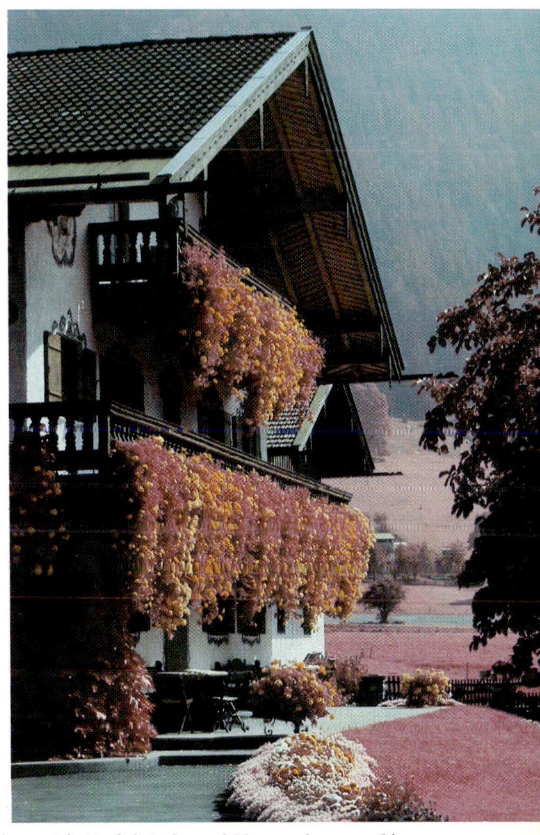

Comparison photographs. Left normal, right taken with Kodak Infra red film, and orange filter. The film has three layers, sensitive to infra red, green and red. An orange filter negates the blue sensitivity of the film. Infra red is strongly reflected from green leaves (chlorophyl) it is therefore easy to recognise plant diseases very early with this film. Photograph Rudolf Seck.

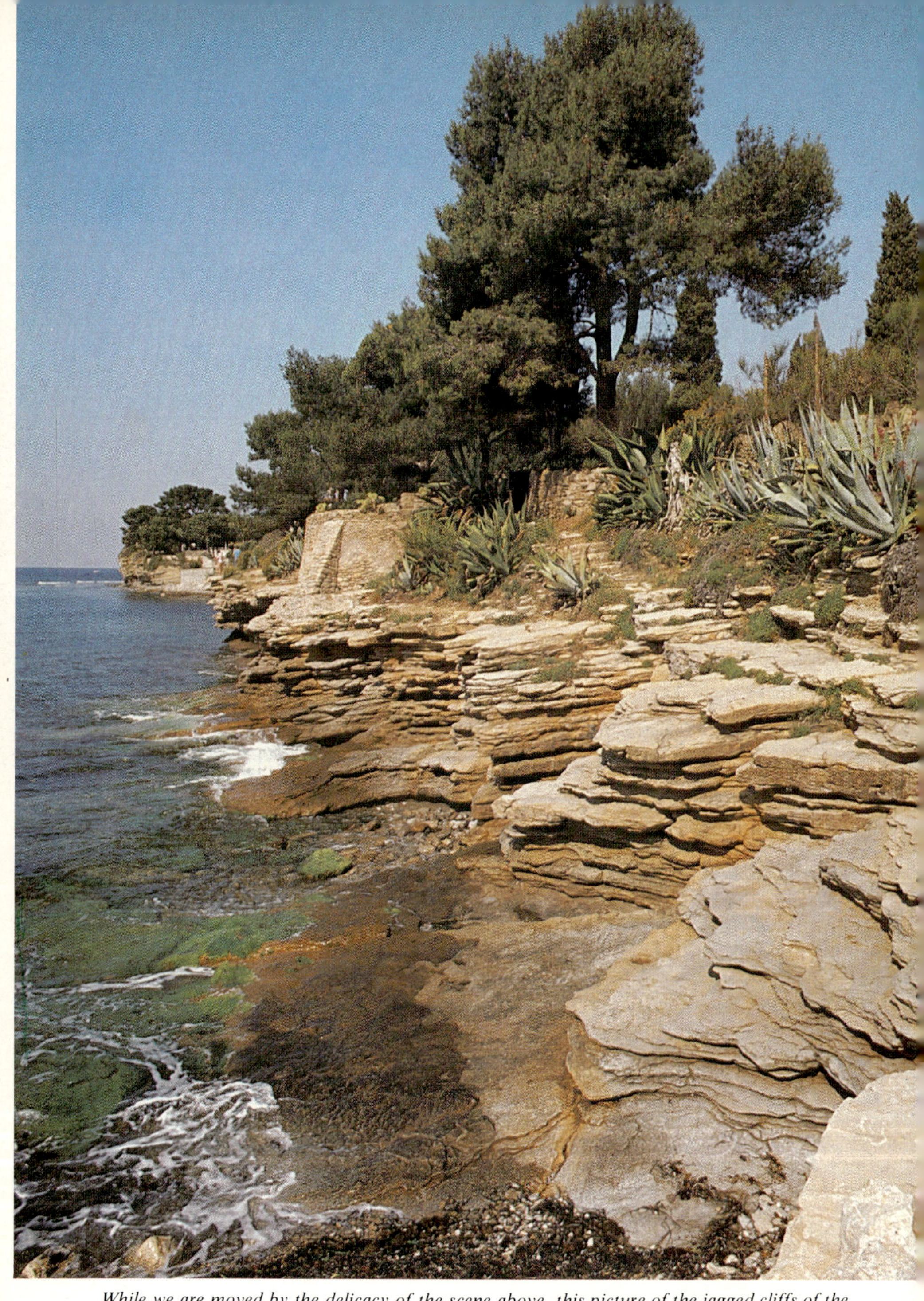

While we are moved by the delicacy of the scene above, this picture of the jagged cliffs of the Mediterranean coast on the Cote D'Azur leaps out at us because of its strong colours. The exposure is no problem and therefore particularly suitable for integral metering. Photograph: Theo Kisselbach, Elmarit-R 28mm f/2.8 $^1/_{250}$th of a second at f/8.

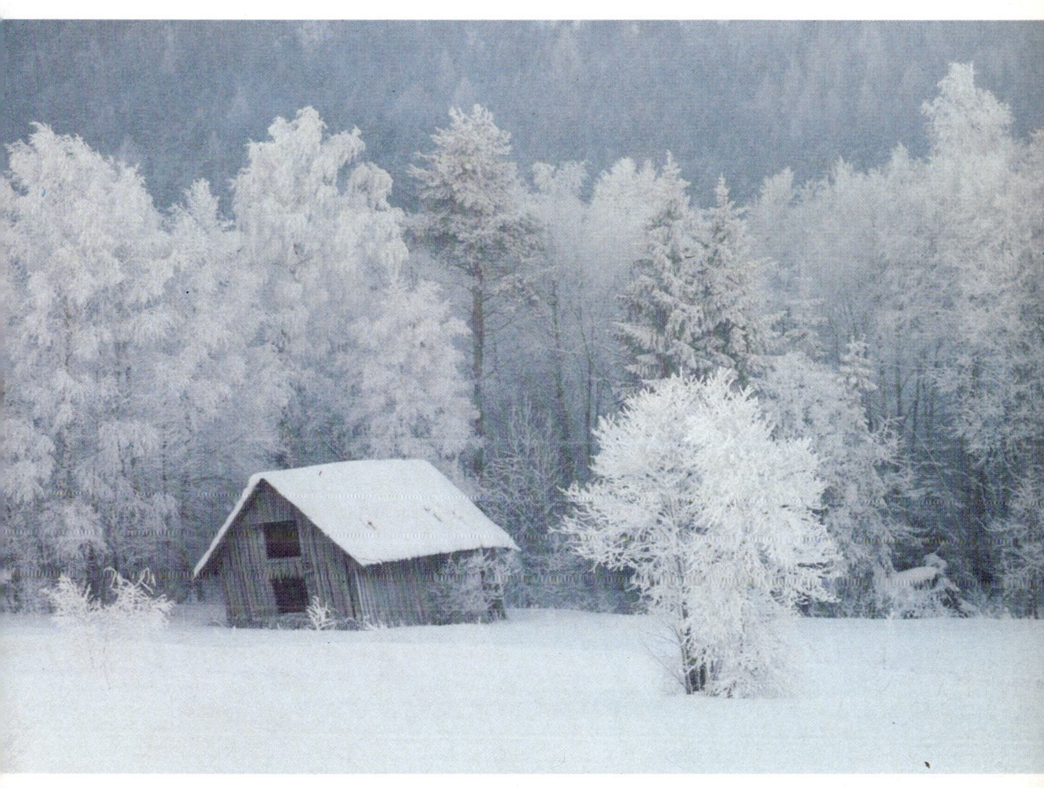

This winter photograph in delicate pastel colours is a good example of the fact that colour photographs without sunshine have their own special charm. The correct exposure is important, since the snow can give a false impression of brightness. Once you are familiar with the R4 metering in snow you will quickly adjust by an exposure over ride factor of up to +2, in this case +1/2 was sufficient. Photograph: Inge Springmann.

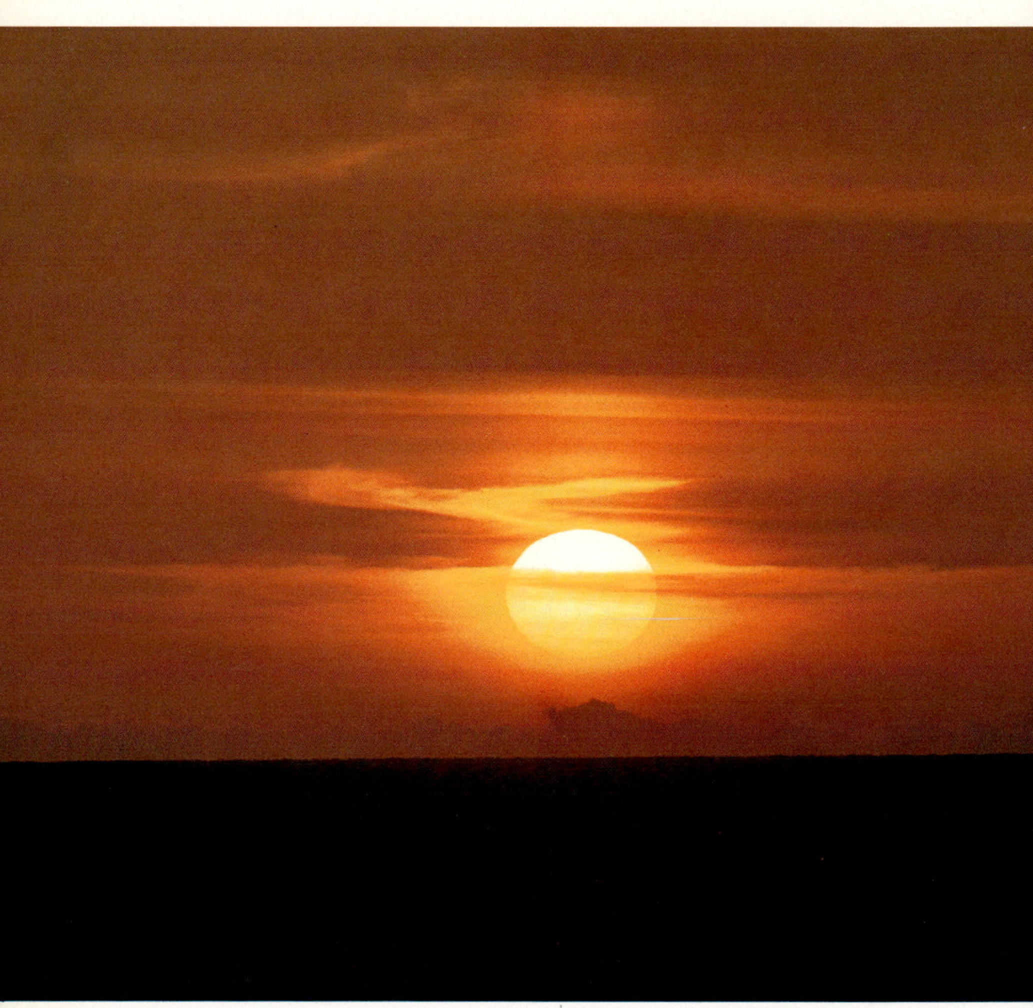

Sunsets are popular subjects but are more difficult than one supposes. On a 50mm lens the sun appears as 0.5mm large on the negative or slide. Therefore it is always advisable to use long focal lengths. For every 10mm of focal length the sun will appear 1mm large. Meter the sky and then divide the time by 2 or 3 for a more accurate exposure time. Beginners can guarantee a satisfactory result by taking a series of bracketed exposures. Examining the results will be helpful in teaching him to gauge exposure values for sunsets.

can be used to obviate camera shake. An exposure time of $1/125$th of a second is the maximum that can be recommended unless particular attention is paid to steadying the camera. High shutter speeds are particularly important when using lenses of longer than standard focal length. For a lot of subjects a large aperture can be used to throw the background completely out of focus. In colour photography this often lends a beautiful plasticity to the subject. When photographing people soft lighting is normally very successful, under harsh lighting most people tend to squint or frown. Indirect flash lighting should be used with care as the material used to reflect the flash light, if it is coloured, will add to the colour of the illumination. Electronic flash units alter their colour balance with age and the sharp fall of their light intensity produces colour deviation. For colour photography lighting should be soft and well balanced. For sunsets the colour temperature is reduced to less than $3,000°$ K and with an artificial light emulsion the redness of the sun is increased rendering a more natural appearance. Sunsets can only be reproduced to an acceptable scale when lenses of longer focal length are used. For every 100mm of focal length the scale of the sun is increased by 1mm. Adapting daylight film by means of the blue conversion filter KB9 or KB12. When using this filter the light transmission loss is in the order of 4 to 6 DIN. For sunsets normal metering does not provide acceptable results therefore it is best if the exposure meter reading is bracketed.

These rules are intended to give the novice some points of reference and to help him avoid disappointment. The advanced photographer knows that in some areas hard and fast rules do not apply and it is often the breaking of a rule that enables a beautiful photograph to be taken. Colour prints have become more and more popular over the last few years. Modern printing and enlarging machines are capable of turning out colour prints at very economic prices. The standard size of enlargement is now 9 x 13cm but it is not so commonly known that reasonably priced machine copies can also be produced in larger formats, prints of 13 x 18cm and 25 x 20cm can make admirable presents.

FAULTS WITH COLOUR REVERSAL FILMS

Light stripes running across the film at right angles to the perforations on one or more frames at the beginning of the film is caused by light entering through the mouth of the film cartridge. This can normally be avoided if the film is loaded and unloaded in the shade. A much more common cause is that the exposed film was left lying about and not replaced in the original container. If the pictures are too light overall and the colours are very pale this is caused by over-exposure. If the picture is too dark the cause is under-exposure, for very low lighting conditions an exposure must be given in excess of that indicated this is caused by reciprocity. If the whole film is too dark there can be several reasons. The film sensitivity was set too high or a previously selected exposure override factor was left uncorrected. If the entire film is dark with no trace of an image the film was not exposed. It is essential that after the film is loaded the correct procedures (as previously described) are followed. If there is a slight blue cast, particularly in the shadow areas, the colour temperature was too high. If there is a strong blue cast, artificial light film was used in daylight without the appropriate correction filter. If there is a yellow or yellowish brown cast the photograph was taken either very early or very late in the day or a daylight film was used without the correct filtration. If black and white and colour film is being used at the same time then mark the camera loaded with colour film with a piece of tape. Disturbing colour reflections appear when the light is reflected onto the subject from a large coloured surface, particularly sensitive are light neutral colours such as grey and white. For example a portrait taken with the sitter underneath a coloured sun shade will often result in a disturbing colour cast over the subject.

FILMS AND THEIR CHARACTERISTICS
In spite of the obvious advantages in photographing in colour, black and white prints are often more acceptable. Those who wish to set up their own dark room for black and white photography will find that the cost is less than that of colour as the basic equipment is more simple. Just as in art, graphics and painting have existed alongside each other for centuries, so with colour and black and white photography. Colour photography certainly has its place but black and white photography has some distinct artistic merit. With the advent of modern photographic processes it is possibly more easy for the beginner to produce an acceptable result in colour than in black and white.

GENERAL SENSITIVITY
The exposure time is governed by the sensitivity of the emulsion so this value must be known. In Germany it is normal practice to rate film speed in DIN values. The film is rated in such a way that an increase in number of 3 DIN is equivalent to a doubling of the emulsion speed and vice versa, 3 DIN lower will signify a film half as sensitive. Film manufacturers are allowed a tolerance of +/- 1 DIN. Average values are used for the gradation and outline of the subject. A usable sensitivity of a black and white emulsion can be increased by lengthening the development process. This will result in contrast becoming higher or in other words the negative will contain more contrast. Under normal photographic circumstances this method of increasing the sensitivity of the film is not recommended, it should be reserved for taking photographs which are not possible in any other way. The American term for speed rating is ASA and it is internationally accepted. This method of rating is extremely simple. A film rated at 100 ASA will be exactly twice as fast as one rated at 50 ASA. Conversely a film rated 200 ASA will be twice as fast as one rated 100 ASA. With the Leica R4 the film sensitivity setting can be used for both DIN and ASA ratings.

It is important to note that some commercial developers will affect the film speed rating and it is advised that the photographer carefully reads the instructions enclosed with the developer. If an important photographic assignment is to be undertaken with colour reversal films it is essential that the exact film speed for that batch of film is known. In order to achieve this it is advised that a film is tested. The test film should incorporate as many different subjects and lighting conditions as possible in order to give an overall picture. Each subject should be photographed with small exposure corrections. The easiest way to achieve this is with the camera in the manual mode and adjusting the lens diaphragm by means of the click stops which give half values. The exposure meter of the R4 with for example a film speed setting of 19 DIN may read f/11 ^{1}/125th of a second. The first exposure is made at f/16 then f/11 then through the half values. When the film is returned from the processor we will receive 5 slides of varying densities. These five slides will enable the photographer to decide exactly where the film speed rating should be set. When making this judgement it is important to consider whether slides are required for home projection or for use in public halls where a long projector to screen distance is envisaged. If we wish to carry out the test when using a different metering mode, for instance (A) or [A] the alteration must be carried out by means of the film sensitivity setting ring.

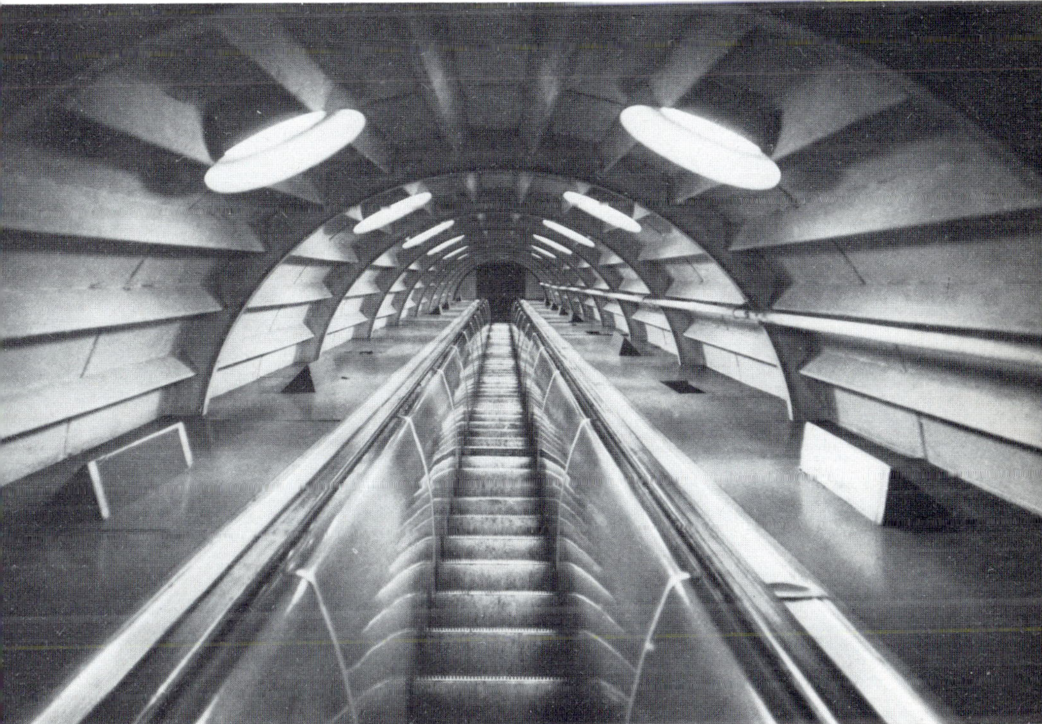

Available light, hand-held shot of the escalator at the Brussels Atomium taken with the Elmarit-R 1:2,8/35mm.

COLOUR SENSITIVITY OF BLACK AND WHITE EMULSIONS

Paradoxically we only speak of colour sensitivity related to black and white emulsions. Standard photographic emulsion is only sensitive to the blue end of the spectrum. With the addition of certain dyes during manufacture the emulsion can be made to respond to other areas of the spectrum. Orthochromatic films are sensitive to green and yellow. Panchromatic films are sensitive to the whole range of the visible spectrum. Infra red films are sensitive to the red end of the spectrum and are capable of resolving light invisible to the naked eye. The beginner often finds difficulty in realising that under certain conditions such widely different colours as green and red will be rendered as the same shade of grey. Often the tones in the final print do not correspond exactly with the tonal value of the subject, because in daylight, films tend to be more sensitive to the blue end of the spectrum. For example if we take a photograph of a blue sky with white clouds the picture will often be disappointing unless the colour sensitivity is changed by means of a yellow or orange filter. The way in which colours can be altered by filters can be found in an earlier section of this book in the chapter on filters. In black and white photographs it is therefore recommended that the photographer takes more notice of the actual contrast of the subject, that is the balance between the light and shade, than the actual colour content.

GRADATION

Gradation is a term by which we define the tonal content of a film or photographic paper. In simple terms it refers to the distinct steps of greyness that a photographic emulsion is capable of resolving, between the black of the darkest shadow and the brightness achieved on highlights. The tonal range of the film can also be controlled during processing. Short development times decrease the tonal range of the negative producing a shorter tonal range. Lengthening development times increases the steepness of the contrast curve, hence producing a negative of higher contrast. A film with short gradation compresses the tonal range therefore it can handle greater extremes of contrast. Films producing long gradation will amplify and increase the contrast of the actual subject. In order to characterise gradation scientifically the blackening effect is converted to a logarithmic system and presented in the form of a graph. The resultant curve represents the characteristic of the film and a similar graph is used to demonstrate developer characteristics. The steeper the curve is, the higher the contrast rating of the film. Since the average amateur does not have the means or the equipment to carry out 'densitometry' to evaluate his photographs, the normal gamma values are only of theoretical interest. For those interested on a practical level it is useful to photograph a shade of grey under controlled conditions. When comparing the tones on a negative to this basic grey we will gain experience, enabling us to judge whether a particular film is of suitable contrast range. An accurately produced grey card is available from such companies as Kodak and Agfa Gevaert for this very use and is often supplied together with a colour scale.

GRAIN

It can be seen that a black and white photographic emulsion when viewed under a microscope displays a speckled or grainy effect. The original silver clumps together to form an irregular pattern. The larger the original crystals were and the more energetic the film processing then the greater this clumping effect will be. The thickness of the photographic layer plays an important part in this effect. There is a relationship between the sensitivity of the silver bromide crystals and their size. In general, fast films are made up of a coarser structure than that encountered with slower materials. It should be noted that the granular structure differs considerably in films from different manufacturers. The graininess of the photographic emulsion plays an important part in the film's ability to resolve fine details. Subject contrast also plays an important role in the formation of grain. Large areas of even tone will show up granularity considerably more than areas containing a lot of fine detail. For any given film normal exposure will produce the finest grain, it is important that the film is not over exposed. Over exposure plays an important part in the production of grainy negatives. Films which come under the general heading of document film have the highest powers of resolution combined with the finest grain structure. They have an extremely low sensitivity to light and a very steep contrast gradation. However they can be used for normal photography if the appropriate processing methods are modified.

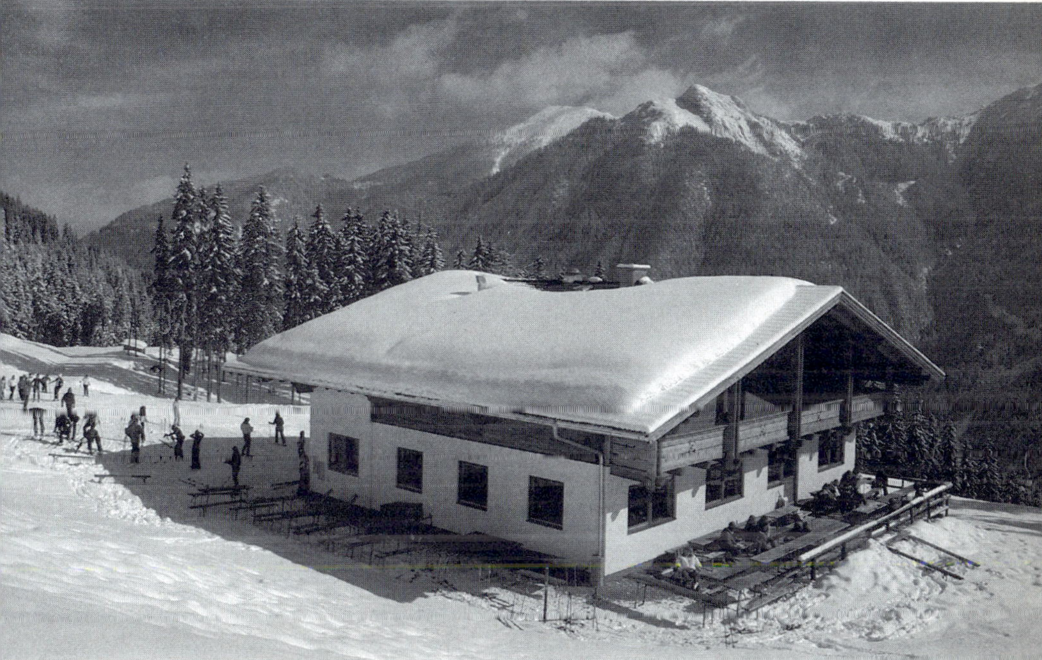

On this winter photograph no exposure correction was necessary because the background provided the balance.

HALATION AND SHARPNESS

Freedom from halation is also very important. If the original subject contains bright light sources such as windows in dimly lit interiors, spot lights etc. there can be problems. The flare caused by these subjects cannot be entirely eliminated but it can be considerably reduced. The term halation covers both diffuse and reflected halation. The term 'diffuse' refers to light dispersions within the photographic layer and can be considerably reduced when using films with very thin emulsion layers. In the second, 'reflected', case there are a series of measures which can be made to reduce halation, such as dyeing the celluloid base of the film blue, or by putting in a protective layer of dye between the emulsion and the base of the film. The correct exposure will reduce the amount of excessive light and over exposure will increase its effect. With colour films an intermediary layer has proved most effective and is disolved in a process of development.

CHOICE OF FILM

It is not particularly easy to choose from the wide variety of black and white film currently available which is best suited to the individual, since a 36 exposure length of film will be used to photograph subjects of varying contrast ranges and light intensity. It is impossible to suit the film to the subject for each exposure. For holiday journeys we should take a universally usable film of a speed ratio of 21-24 DIN which is sufficiently sensitive for landscapes and candid street scenes but can also be used for brightly lit interiors. It is not an extremely fast film nor does it have extreme resolution capabilities but it is the most useful for average use.

A question frequently asked by the amateur is "What films do professionals use?" For the busy professional, particularly those engaged in candid and reportage work the stock for many years has been relatively fast emulsions, usually around 27 DIN. The results can be astonishingly good, particularly if the full frame is utilised. Also in this type of work large enlargements are seldom required. It is essential that exposure and development times are accurate. These films are not suitable for landscapes unless a grainy effect is needed to enhance mood. The only way an individual can really find which film suits him best is by experimentation. Theory will not help. Only by comparing actual results can be decide which film best suits his needs. In order to standardise one's test procedure I feel that it is of the utmost importance when trying a film for the first time to strictly follow the film manufacturer's data sheet which is enclosed with the film, as this provides an established 'norm' upon which to experiment.

BLACK AND WHITE FILMS
HIGH SPEED FILMS

This category includes all films over 30 DIN. A new development in the field of black and white emulsions has recently been introduced by Agfa Gevaert

OPPOSITE
High speed and highly sensitive film are necessary for the short exposure time with which this photograph was taken. Summicron-R 90mm f/2. Open diaphragm, automatic timing.

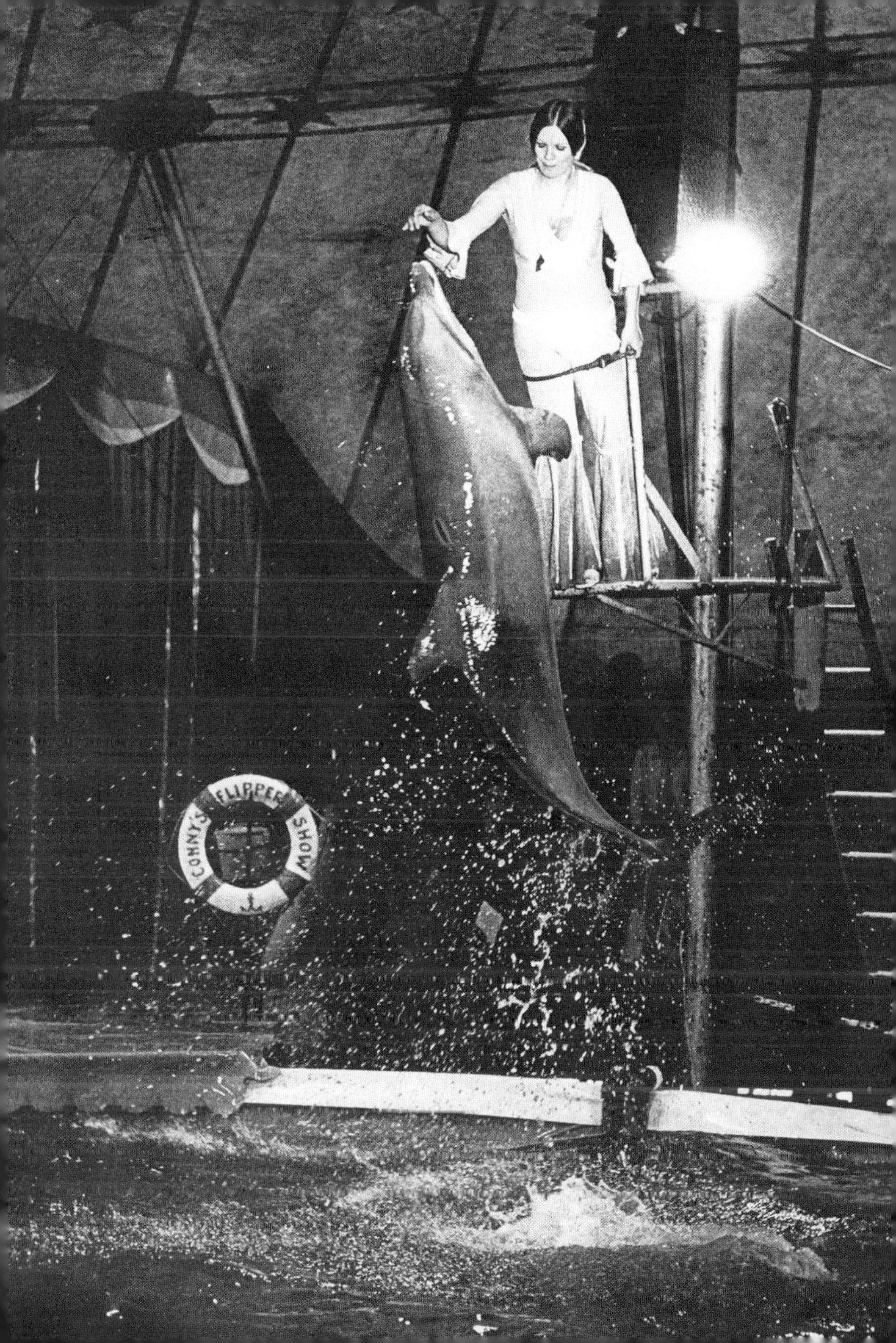
CONNY'S FLIPPER SHOW

and Ilford. The former produce Vario XL and the latter XP1. Both differ radically from standard black and white films and are processed in a different manner. The films do not use the standard silver halide emulsion but a dye based emulsion. The speed ratings can be varied enormously from such different sensitivities as 100 ASA to 1,600 ASA depending on the photographers needs. Yet correctly processed these films are capable of large degrees of enlargement exhibiting a uniquely smooth grain.

STANDARD SPEED FILMS
Films in this category are usually in the 22 to 27 DIN range of sensitivity. They allow the photographer to use a smaller aperture or higher shutter speed because of their relatively high speed and thus mean trouble free photography.

NORMAL SPEED FILMS
These films are of medium sensitivity in the range of 17 to 21 DIN. This film is the most commonly used by photographers and films within this speed range have perhaps the most favourable characteristics enabling the photographer to achieve large scale enlargements yet not restricting him to inordinantly long exposures. For normal usage the photographer will find these films perfectly acceptable for the average subject taken under normal lighting conditions. Films within this grouping have a higher resolving power and fine tonal gradation.

LOW SPEED FILMS
Films in this category are normally from 12 to 15 DIN and are capable of producing giant scale enlargements with very fine grain. The disadvantage is that the exposure times needed to produce this quality are inordinantly long for normal subjects. If the photographer uses these slow emulsions he will find it advantageous to increase the exposure time by using larger aperture and not by increasing the shutter speed. The sensitised emulsion layers of these films are extremely thin and are particularly affected by incorrect exposure. To obtain the best results exposure must be accurate and so must the processing.

BLACK AND WHITE REVERSAL FILM – PANCHROMATIC
This special film is produced for the direct production of black and white slides. A black and white transparency is produced when the film is processed. This process is unsurpassed for its tonal gradation, fine grain structure and freedom from halation. It should be noted that exact exposure times must be used as in common with colour reversal films the effect of over or under exposure is very apparent. In particular cases when a subsequent negative is required this can be produced without any difficulty by printing in contact direct onto a positive film. With films of this type the processing costs are normally included. These films are supplied by Agfa Gevaert, Kodak and Orwo. For those wishing to carry out the processing at home further information can be obtained from the publication Kisselback "Darkroom Handbook".

DOCUMENT FILMS

These films are of extraordinary high resolution capacity and extremely high contrast. There are basically two types, differing in their colour sensitivity (orthochromatic and panchromatic). The manufacturers do not state a given film speed and it is left to the individual photographer to establish the sensitivity by experimentation. However as a starting point a speed rating between 7 to 13 DIN can be used. The exposure of these emulsions is very critical so it is important that the photographer experiments using the film before undertaking an important assignment. Developers such as those of the Rodinal type will produce very good results. Application of this film is usually for the production of high quality photocopies of such items as line drawings, landscapes of extremely low contrast, and in the field of micro-photography.

INFRA RED FILMS

This is used for photographing at the extreme end of the spectrum which, although not visible to the human eye, can be recorded on the infra red emulsion. Since these films are also sensitive to some of the visible spectrum, an infra red filter should be used, in order to negate their effect. Photographing at these wavelengths of light will also effect the focusing distance and a correction must be applied.

The general application for this film is for scientific subjects, although it is becoming increasingly popular in many other fields. The Infra Red film type 8843 produced by Kodak is such that no correction is required to compensate for the focus shift normally associated with this type of film.

Good results can be obtained using an orange filter, and with this a film rating of 20 DIN is appropriate.

GENERAL TIPS FOR BLACK AND WHITE AND COLOUR PHOTOGRAPHY

With the Leica R4 camera only the standard film cartridge can be used. These are available containing the following film lengths, 12, 20, 24 and 36 exposures. Modern films always have an antihalation backing. It should be noted that films are very effected by the way in which they are stored. Always store film in a cool dry location. Special film bags are highly recommended if the film is to be used in the tropics or anywhere else where conditions may alter the characteristics.

With the standard film cartridge the film is wound on to a central spool, emulsion inwards. The cartridge itself is normally made of metal or plastic. Since the mouth of the film cartridge cannot be completely light tight neither exposed or unexposed film should be left lying around unprotected. When the last exposure has been made the film should be removed from the camera after carrying out the rewind procedure. Practise focusing on various objects in the room, meter them, try out the different effects of changing the modes, change lenses, note their effect. Time spent in this way can never be wasted. The photographer's responses will be sharpened by this practice and once out in the field photographing in demanding conditions this armchair playing will prove its worth.

OPERATING THE CAMERA

Practise using the camera. The camera can be used in many ways. For example photographs can be taken over the heads of people merely by aiming the camera. Photographs can also be taken 'firing from the hip', in order to avoid being spotted. Practise using the modes, practise evaluating the subject, wind on, focus, shoot. Keep practising until all the operating functions become second nature. The camera should be operated subconsciously. The subject is the important point of the photograph. Of course in the majority of photographs the actual practice of taking photographs is a leisure pursuit, we have time, subjects can be carefully composed in the viewfinder, contrast ranges can be judged, specific points can be highlighted. Camera angles can be moved to strengthen the composition. On the other hand sometimes the subject is seen and the opportunity passed in a fleeting moment. Familiarity with the Leica R4 will enable us to prepare ourselves, to assess the appropriate metering mode, check the exposure, focus the lens, fire the shutter, all within that fleeting moment.

At the beginning of one's relationship with the Leica R4 it is advised that these operations are practised with the camera unloaded but it is important that these operations are carried out even for practice with a loaded camera and that the negatives are carefully assessed. In order to learn swimming one must go into the water. Practice in theory is important, but the actual practice of producing negatives is, after all, the end result. One important point to practice until perfection is achieved, is the loading and unloading sequence. It is very important that this operation is carried out correctly. This operation is very simple with the Leica R4 and as it is so simple it is an operation that is easily neglected. Slap dash methods are to be avoided at all cost. The wrong exposure on one frame results in the loss of one picture, incorrect loading or unloading can result in the entire 36 exposures being ruined, or 36 exposures never having been taken in the first place. Initially it is well worth the expense of using a film to practise the sequence. The cost of the film can be recouped many times over if the wastage of it means that in future this operation is always carried out correctly. There is no need to print the practice negatives but they should be critically examined by means of a X5 magnifier, or perhaps even better is that they are projected using a slide projector. Before opening the camera back you should always check that a unrewound film is not present, this is a simple operation and should be made standard procedure. Simply press the rewind button, pull out the rewind crank and turn. If any resistance is felt then a film is still loaded. Always load the film strictly in accordance with the maker's recommendations. An important and indeed infallible indication that the film is being correctly transported through the camera is to watch the rewind knob during the wind on operation. When the film is being correctly wound the rewind knob will rotate. With the camera in the vertical position it is easier to tilt it or encounter problems of camera shake, therefore practise using the camera in this position. Photographing such items as windows and doors will soon show up any problems.

In order to check that the focusing operation is being carried out correctly and to check that at a given shutter speed no camera shake is encountered I would suggest that the photographer practises by photographing such subjects as posters, these items critically examined will soon show up any problems.

MOVING SUBJECTS WITH THE FIRST FILM

When using the first black and white practise film do not take the subjects too seriously. It is the intention to photograph objects which will indicate whether one has mastered the operating modes of the camera. It is not the intention to produce 36 masterpieces. When using this first film also experiment with varying the shutter speeds in order to judge what speed is required to stop the movement of various subjects. For example it will be found that a shutter speed of $^1/_{125}$th of a second is perfectly adequate to photograph a pedestrian walking towards the camera. However we will find with the same subject moving across diagonally a shutter speed in the order of $^1/_{250}$th is more appropriate. Judging the correct distance at which to photograph the subject is also a matter of practice. However to aid the photographer I would suggest the following procedure is adopted. It is calculated that the average height of a person is 1.75 metres, the normal variation to this height is between 1.6 and 1.9 metres therefore representing less than a 10% deviation to the norm. As we do not normally require that the figure fills the frame exactly some room must be allowed for at the top and the bottom and an allowance of 2.4 metres will cover this sufficiently. The photographer must imagine that a frame 2.4 x 3.6 metres is in front of the camera, through this imaginary frame we follow the subject. Using a standard 50mm lens the distance the frame should be imagined would be 5 metres from the camera, with a 90mm lens a distance of 9 metres and with a 135mm some 13.5 metres. It will be noticed from this set of figures that there is a simple mathematical rule applying to focal length related to subject distance. The rule is that the focal length of a lens multiplied by a factor of 100 will give the appropriate camera to subject distance.

To stop the movement of a given subject it is important to realise that the closer the subject is to the photographer the higher the shutter speed required. For example, if a 50mm lens is used to photograph a sporting subject such as a high jumper moving diagonally across the view it is doubtful if a shutter speed of $^1/_{1000}$th of a second at a distance of 5 metres would be sufficient. If the same photograph was taken with the high jumper moving towards the camera the shutter speed of $^1/_{250}$th of a second would probably be adequate. However under these circumstances the photographers position would be impracticably close. Therefore for this kind of situation the employment of longer than standard lenses is to be desired, in order that the camera to subject distance can be maintained, without decreasing the scale of the image. With longer focal length lenses it is easier to contain the depth of field and concentrate the point of focus upon the actual subject, thus providing an unobtrusive out of focus background.

TIMING THE PEAK OF ACTION

When photographing sporting events it is important that the 'peak of action' is captured. In many sporting events the cycle of activity contains a moment, normally at the height of the event, where the comparative motion of the competitor is motionless. This point will usually supply the most dramatic pictures. There is no point watching the subject through the viewfinder and pressing the release at the instant that this moment is observed, the correct moment of exposure must be anticipated. The time difference between the brain function and the finger reflex has a measurable delay. A racing car travelling diagonally across the frame at a speed of 150 m.p.h. moves some 225 feet in a second, this represents some $2\frac{1}{2}$ inches of travel during an exposure duration of $\frac{1}{1000}$th of a second. Of course in this example if it were the photographers intention to render sharply the outline of the motor car the camera would be moved in relationship to the line of travel to make good this discrepancy. Of course it is not always an advantage to totally freeze the action and a degree of blurring can often create the impression of speed better than a totally frozen subject.

With practice it will be found that 'panning' the camera will allow relatively long exposures to be made. The advantage of this is that the background is rendered in streaks of various tones or colour. Not only does this avoid a confused background to the subject but the impression of speed is enhanced. To achieve the best results the feet should be positioned firmly slightly apart, the subject should be picked up and followed in the viewfinder until the moment of exposure and as important as with most sports, the subject should then be followed through. All movement should be from the waist. The actual position in which we require the subject to be should be pre-determined and the focus pre-selected this leaves the photographer free to concentrate on the subject. See page 134 for further details of suitable lenses.

TAKING PHOTOGRAPHS ON THE MOVE

Taking photographs on the move is a technique to be advocated particularly for candid type work. To avoid camera shake make the exposure when the weight is squarely on one foot, however if possible avoid using shutter speeds under $\frac{1}{250}$th. Especially in oriental countries candid type photography must be undertaken very carefully, shooting from the hip, aiming the camera towards the subject blindly all help to obtain otherwise impossible photographs. Whilst carrying out this type of photography it is imperative that the camera controls are operated without looking down at them. The use of a lens with a wider angle than the standard will be found to help considerably in this field. Not only will the increased angle of acceptance increase the chance of framing the subject but the increase in depth of field will compensate for any marginal errors in focusing.

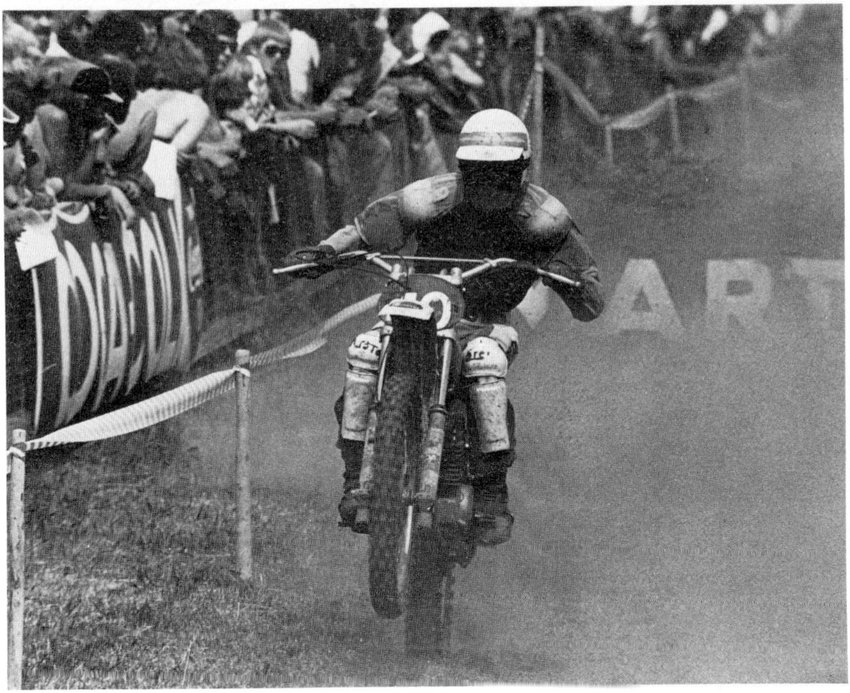

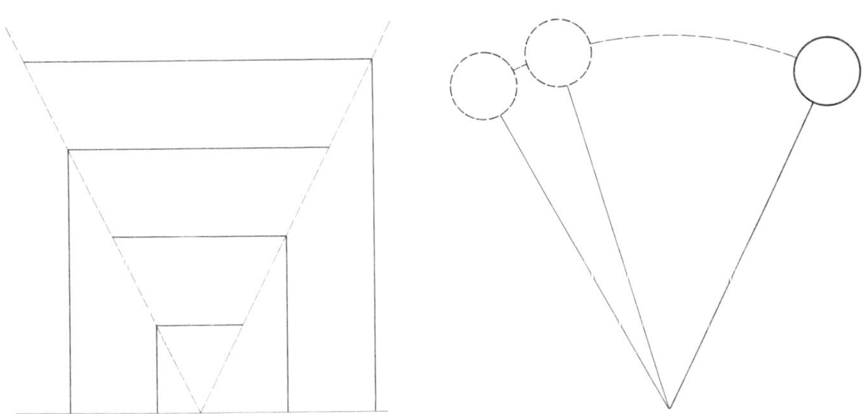

Short exposures are necessary for motor cross. This is best achieved by using the shutter speed priority mode. Set the desired shutter speed and the camera will choose the appropriate aperture. Telyt-R 350mm f/4.8. Photograph: Gunter Osterloh.

Left, The dotted lines show the angle of view for the 35mm Elmarit-R on the horizontal plane. The lines that pass through at an angle of 90° show that with this focal length the distance for the photograph and the focal length are identical.
Right. If you want to take the subject (circle) by surprise, set the camera by focusing on a subject (dotted circle) that is the same distance away. Swing the camera over towards the subject just before the photograph is taken.

THE EFFECT OF LIGHT

The most important source of light is the sun. Regardless of the wish of the photographer it describes its arc across the sky, hiding behind clouds or beaming down from a bright cloudless sky. If we are to employ photography seriously and do not wish merely to take the little family mementos we must develop a kind of sense of illumination. By means of precise observation and experience gained actually photographing subjects we will become aware that objects look different in the morning than they do in the afternoon. The bright summer sunshine can render a subject completely different to the low sun in the middle of the winter. Even the consistant lighting conditions of a bright summer day alter according to the taking position and the direction of illumination. If the sun is shining frontally on to the subject it will produce very flat details, lacking any sense of roundness. An experiment will make this effect more comprehensible. We look at a section of cobblestones, first of all with the sun at our back, then we walk slowly in a semi circle around them so that effectively the sun is now shining from the side, finally we complete our tour and observe the cobbles with the sun shining straight at us. With side lighting it will be observed that the stones achieve a sort of roundness, a feeling of depth. Only experience can educate the photographer to decide on the most appropriate direction for lighting for a given subject. It can often happen that the photographer will realise that the sun at a particular time of the day is not in the correct position to render the subject at its best. Only experience can give this sense to the photographer. If the lighting is not absolutely correct and we are on a hurried journey and the subject is important enough we should still photograph it to the best of our ability in order that at least a record can be retained. Lighting is of particular importance when undertaking architectural photography. A building can appear very dull and lacking in character without the correct lighting. Buildings can be shown to advantage with the sun at a low oblique angle, this will highlight and pick up variances in the different materials used in the construction. Ideal lighting conditions for the photographer are not those normally encountered on a bright clear day. The ideal conditions for photography are when large piles of massive white clouds are present, these act as huge reflectors lightening up the shadows and creating interest in the otherwise blank sky areas.

Even hazy sunshine provides pleasant illumination for most subjects. In the foreground the lighting should be chosen carefully, waiting for exactly the right light, for this can often result in an increase to the sense of depth. When the sun refuses to shine at all there is still no reason for leaving the Leica R4 at home. There are countless subjects which are worth our trouble even in dull weather. On completely rainy days scenes are brought to life by the myriad highlights reflected in the raindrops. Passers-by hurrying under the shelter of umbrellas provide the photographer with many subjects. But it is the foggy day which provides the photographic surprise. Subjects are seen as ghostly outlines, details of the individual subjects are lost, the scene is rendered as a composition of softly outlined shapes. Fog is the great master and simplifier of things, contrasts are softened, shapes and scale is subtley altered and transposed.

ARTIFICIAL LIGHT

Whilst during the daytime we can rarely alter the lighting conditions ourselves and our task is one of making the best of what is available, with artificial light we have the opportunity of controlling the conditions for ourselves. Normally we will commence lighting a subject with one light source, and illuminate this subject in such a way that its characteristics and features are best depicted. Clearly it is important that this main light should be positioned in such a way that even shadows are produced correctly. If it is found that a single source of light is insufficient for this task other secondary lights or reflectors can be introduced. The reflector is often found to be enough to lighten the shadow areas for our purpose and their use is much less complicated than the introduction of other light sources. The use of other secondary light sources introduces complications in that they produce secondary shadows and therefore must be used with extreme care. Lighting a subject correctly is an art in itself and is difficult to master. My advice would be to the beginner commence with the simplest type of lighting and gradually build up your experience. Only when the main light has been fully exploited can we begin to justify the introduction of more light. This second light should be used to fill in the shadow area or to add light to a restricted area of the subject. To use in this way it must be much weaker than the main light source. The second lamp can be used to add sparkle and highlights, for instance to the hair, or for independantly illuminating the background to ensure that the model stands out and that an extra sense of depth is given to the subject. It will be found that a most convenient light source for this purpose can be found by using a small slide projector. When using artificial light pay particular attention to the contrast range of the subject and ensure that it can be accommodated with the emulsion being used.

COMPOSING THE PICTURE

The best and most sophisticated camera is only a tool, its performance is determined by the photographer. Firstly we must define photographic vision, how does our eye see?

(1) The eye sees in colour, an abstraction into shades of grey as with black and white film is impossible.

(2) The eye has a limited resolution capacity, details are only recognisable over a certain range. With the camera telephoto lenses overcome the problem of distance, infra red film can cut through haze.

(3) The eye has only a small angle of vision in which it can see clearly. It adds and registers images in the brain. The camera is dependant on the lens employed and the aperture selected, it can resolve subjects over a large range, sharply and clearly.

(4) The eye only has a short 'after' image and then the image is erased, this retention is in the order of $1/30$th of a second. The photographic picture can be fixed and stored and retained permanently.

(5) The eye sees very rapid movements incompletely, it is a function of the brain to monitor and build up pictures. The shutter can expose at speeds up to $1/1000$th of a second. This can capture movements which the eye is unaware of.

(6) The eye requires a certain minimum level of light at which to see an object. The photographic exposure can be lengthened and subjects not visible to the eye depicted.

The eye and the brain are one unit, memory and feeling have a great influence, we do not see things as they are but as we are used to seeing them. On the other hand the photographic lens reproduces all subjects without emphasis. Since with a pair of eyes we see stereoscopically, in three dimensions and since our eyes always view the subject with the same focal length lens presentation is different from that depicted through the media of photography. With photography the scale of the image and the apparent perspective changes in accordance with the focal length of the lens being employed.

The adjustment of the eye to changes in lighting conditions is carried out automatically and without conscious effort. Photographically this can only be achieved with a complicated and sophisticated automatic metering system as incorporated in the Leica R4.

In the black and white picture we can translate differences in colour only into varied tones of grey. We can only depict space by means of perspective and the relationship between objects contained within the picture.

BEING CREATIVE

Being photographically creative is mostly a matter of selection, it means the ordering and arranging of subjects into a coherent entity. We live in an age where we are confronted by photographic images continually, magazines, the cinema, television. Observe the best of these examples and learn. Ask yourself the following questions, what position is best, what lighting conditions do I require, what am I trying to say in this picture? We should carefully note the change of perspective that is achieved by the merest change in viewing angle.

With close up photography it is often useful to view the subject with one eye closed, this helps us to visualise the end result.

The next refinement is getting close to the subject, filling the format; leave out any details that are not of the utmost importance. You should be able to justify every single object contained within the picture, if you cannot do this move the camera angle until you can. Since to take our photographs we employ different focal length lenses it is easy to ensure that the frame is filled. The limited ability to only be able to see a picture at the printing stage and having to resort to large scale enlargements of small areas of the negative should only be used as a last desperate means.

Basically every photograph should reflect clearly the reason we took it. A simple way of learning is to practise constantly. The tips regarding the use of the empty slide holder are to be recommended. The photographer must be aware that it is the arrangement of the subject within the frame, the ratio of scale between relevant objects, the direction of light, that prove the differences between the mundane and the outstanding. The desire to be photographically creative is a constant search, a continual goal, the decision on the correct manner in which to treat a subject should be a constant source of pleasure and enjoyment.

PRACTICAL TIPS

Very sensitive films with the speed rating of 400 ASA or higher give us the opportunity to take photographs under artificial light or in conditions of very low light. The advantage to this is that we can capture the atmosphere of this type of subject without introducing artificial light which can often destroy the very atmosphere that attracted us to the subject in the first instance. In many cases it is easier to photograph using flash but this can often result in a degree of artificiality being introduced. It is extremely difficult to judge the effect of flash. The Leica R4, with its highly sensitive metering facility ensures that accurate exposure assessment can be carried out even under the most extreme conditions. If the entire film has been used for low light subjects the subsequent processing times with black and white film can be increased by 25% to advantage. We can photograph nearly anywhere, in bright living rooms, in lecture halls, art galleries and museums all without a tripod. If it should be particularly dark then the small compact pocket tripod will be found indispensible. With it you can utilise conveniently located walls or benches to support the tripod mounted camera. If a cable release is not to hand the delayed action device can be used to operate the shutter. Family celebrations are very photogenic and in particular family weddings. Photographs in the church are seldom disturbing especially if taken from the gallery. In most cases permission must be obtained, but refusal is seldom encountered, especially if the assurance is given that no flash will be used, and that the ceremony will not be disturbed by people wandering about. The modern fast films allow us to photograph inside the church without being noticed. Before taking photographs and prior to the actual wedding it is advisable to familiarise yourself with the layout of the church and select any suitable vantage points. When undertaking interior photography including people it is advised that the largest aperture should be used in order that the fastest shutter speed can be employed. Although this restricts the depth of field this disadvantage can in part be obviated by the careful positioning of the subject. When metering the exposure take great care that bright sources of light such as windows are not included. Holiday travel requires careful planning and includes photographic planning as well as travel arrangements. Take a supply of fast film, I would advise you to take this in the form of short exposure lengths, twenty is ideal. For a visit to a low light location be it a museum or a night club the short film can be used up on that particular visit and with no wastage the photographer can resort to his normal emulsion for outdoor use.

Photographs can normally be taken in art galleries, castles, museums etc however I would strongly advise you to enquire as to the exact restriction before taking any photographs. An enquiry is only good manners and often it can result in permission being obtained to photograph in a manner not normally allowed, for instance using flash or getting special exemption to use a tripod.

In some establishments permission to take photographs is subject to a small nominal fee but particularly in churches it never does any harm to make a small donation to the church fund.

The use of modern high speed emulsion can be thoroughly recommended. In the old days the use of such film was always as a last resort, the films were extremely grainy and incapable of resolving fine detail. However today the story is somewhat different. Modern high speed emulsions properly exposed and processed are capable of producing quality of the very highest standard. Subjects containing a high content of detail and with a high contrast range are most suitable for these emulsions. Occasionally the use of high speed film will be required for sports type photography if short exposure times are required and the prevailing lighting conditions are not appropriate. They are also useful when using long focal length lenses in that they allow the photographer to employ short exposure times even with low light conditions. Also of course the reserve of emulsion speed will enable the user to use a smaller aperture thus increasing the depth of field. A further application is that of night photography in the streets of busy towns and cities. the ideal conditions for this type of photography are immediately after a shower of rain when the whole scene is transformed by a thousand highlights.

In many cases permission can be obtained to photograph at public events such as ice revues and circuses, however it is seldom allowed that flash can be used, and indeed with the Leica R4 and high speed film it is seldom necessary. The first row of seats opposite the arena is very suitable, if one has a seat further back it is possible to include part of the actual audience thus providing the advantage of adding atmosphere. Exposure times are dependent on the actual lighting but are often in the order of f2..f5.6 at $^{1}/_{250}$th of a second. The selective metering mode is very suitable for this type of photography as it enables individual acts and performers to be metered. High speed black and white films do not become unusable if stored for prolonged periods however the speed rating can decrease therefore never use outdated film for important events.

DOCUMENT FILM

These films have a capacity for resolving extremely fine detail with very fine grain although the contrast is very high. By using the appropriate developer the disadvantage of the high contrast can be somewhat controlled. Their performance when used for subjects such as landscapes is amazing. Especially for photographing in dull light conditions the performance of document film is unsurpassed. For the photographer fanatically interested in sharpness and fine grain these films will provide a most useful tool. The only non controllable disadvantage with these films is their low sensitivity. Most manufacturers of document film decline to give or indicate a speed rating for these emulsions therefore I would recommend that you consult the information previously given in this book.

The Orthochromatic type of document film used in conjunction with a green filter is strongly advocated for use with suitable landscape subjects. For the beginner it is recommended that the exposure times should be bracketed in order that the correct film speed rating can be established. Not all photographic shops stock document film therefore to avoid disappointment these films should be ordered.

Document film is very suitable for the production of exceedingly high quality technical photographs. Pictures of engineering detail, fine china, electrical components etc. The combination of fine grain and outstanding resolution enables the miniature format photographer to produce the sort of quality normally associated with large format cameras. To summarise, this film correctly processed and used with great care is capable of producing outstanding results in particular photographic fields.

PEOPLE IN FRONT OF THE CAMERA

You will not be instructed in this chapter on how the busy professional works, but how the average amateur goes about providing 'snaps' for the family album. If you are looking for a traditional model then many examples can be found in the art galleries. Most of these portraits depict the head in half profile with the left ear visible, exactly as was required for passport photographs a few years ago. We can use the same technique even with babies. They should be photographed in a room sitting close to a window, in this sort of location the light will not be too bright for the young child and this will avoid the usual squinting normally associated with photographs of small children, particularly those taken out of doors in bright sunlight.

In a room the light from one window can produce too much contrast, a large white cloth at a distance of about two metres from the subject produces enough extra light to illuminate the shadow areas. Projection screens can also be used for this purpose and they have the added advantage that they have their own stand. The exposure time depends of course on the amount of light that is coming in through the window, the curtains should be drawn right back in order to let in as much light as possible. An exception to this is if the sun is shining straight through then the curtains can be used as a diffuser.

Also when photographing children it is a decided advantage if an assistant can be present who can occupy the baby's attention. The camera position should never be higher than the head. It is no extravagance to take a dozen photographs and select the best three. Film is cheap, so ensure that you cover the subject fully. High speed film is suitable for this type of photography and the selective metering mode should be used. During the winter it is often too dark for this type of photography and we must resort to artificial light. If this supplementary lighting is by electronic flash the same basic procedures are recommended. The light should come from one side. The other side should be provided with a suitable reflector, or a smaller fill-in flash. The following method is suitable for photographing children or similasr subjects in the open air. Many of our modern homes have light external walls, the children should be allowed to play at a distance from this wall of between five and seven meters. It will be found that in bright sunlight the wall will act as a large reflector hence filling in the shadow areas and reducing the contrast of the subject to an acceptable level.

Open air portraiture can be ruined if the subject is made to look straight into bright sunlight. Therefore ensure that the person to be photographed is placed in such a position that they can be comfortable in their pose.

There are unfortunately no one hard set of rules to cover all photographic problems since the situations vary so much. Usually if the photographer stops and thinks about it he will realise that the problem is not insurmountable and that the versatility of the Leica R4 enables the most complicated problems to be resolved. One of the most difficult photographs for the family album is presented when the 'family group' is to be photographed. In the early days of photography one did not hesitate to take the trouble of arranging a large group of people in the most complicated setting. Although predating photography perhaps a good example of this is to be found in Rembrant's painting 'The Night Watch'. Today this type of photography tends to be executed in a more informal and personal manner. The best form of lighting for these large complicated groups is in the open under a bright cloudy sky. The overall bright diffused light will avoid any lighting difficulties. For photographing groups of people indoors we should use artificial light bounced off or reflected back by walls and ceilings in order to achieve the same overall effect as diffused sunlight. If we do not want to use a tripod we can still take hand held photographs with highly sensitive film, the exposure meter of the R4 will advise you reliably and accurately.

THE MOVING SUBJECT

This chapter is mainly concerned with the more difficult subjects in photography, such as sport where the Leica R4 is particularly easy to use. Because of its handiness, the varied focal lengths of its lenses and the high speed films which can be used, the R4 is ideal in difficult situations. What is a moving subject? It can be a snail which slides slowly through the grass, it can be a pedestrian who covers five kilometres in an hour or a racing car which shoots past at 180 miles an hour. What effect does speed have photographically? It is important whether the object moves sideways or comes towards us. Photographically the scale at which you are taking the photograph is important because the movement is noticeable as lack of sharpness on the film. A movement of 100 miles an hour can also be calculated at 150ft. per second. If we expose at $^1/_{1000}$th of a second then the actual movement is reduced to 2.4in. and it should be an easy matter to photograph. In reality the difficulty is more that of releasing the shutter at the right moment. Since we react with a certain hesitation we will require a certain amount of thinking time in order to release at the right moment. The Leica R4 has a time delay of about 25 milliseconds as, when we press down the release button, the mirror must first swing out of the way, at the same time the diaphragm is closed and the shutter operates. In practice these things must become a feeling in the finger tips, it is typical of a beginner that he releases too soon. In the chapter 'The way to manual dexterity' you will find many tips to help you improve that fingertip feeling.

Family groups become more difficult as more people have to be included on the photograph. An indoor shot is always preferable as expressions are more relaxed. If flash has to be used try to bounce it from the ceiling rather than use it directly.

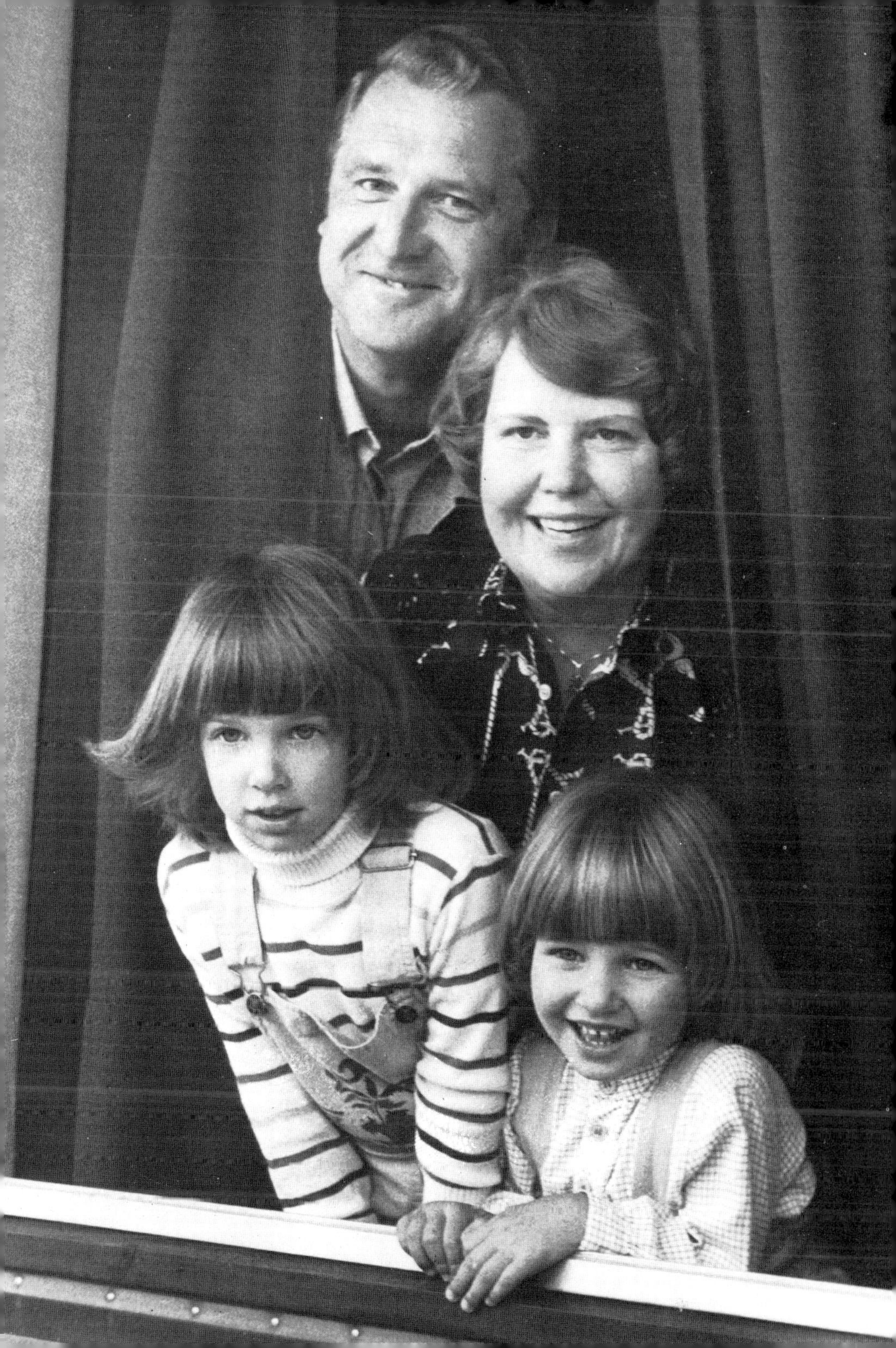

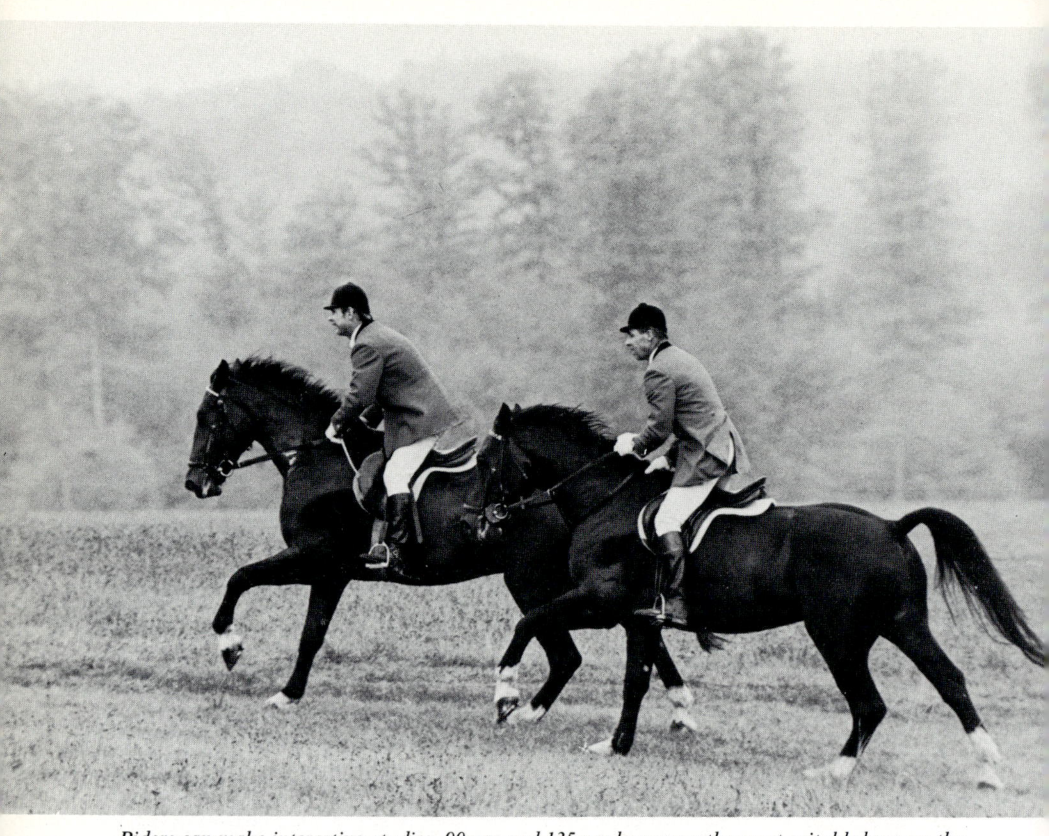

Riders can make interesting studies. 90mm and 135mm lenses are the most suitable because the relationship of the rider and the landscape is made more picturesque due to the background being out of focus. Photograph: Günter Kisselbach.

PANNING

If rapid forward movements are followed in the viewfinder then one automatically goes with the movement trying for a more or less format filling image. The focal length effects the scale, therefore the use of somewhat longer focal lengths are more appropriate for following a subject (i.e. panning). With a 135mm focal length lens the distance is 2.6 times larger than with a 50mm lens. However the depth of field is noticeably less with the longer focal lengths. It is less well known that this has a different effect in practice. When the scale of the image is the same the depth of field also remains the same. If I set a distance of 5m with a 50mm lens with a diaphragm of f8 I would obtain a depth field from 3.8 to 7.5m, that is a depth of field covering 3.7m. Correspondingly on a 135mm lens achieving the same image scale at 13.5m, with the same aperture a depth of field from 12.2 to 15.9m is obtained, that is once again a range of 3.7m. In this case the narrow angle of vision and the transition between sharp and unsharp gives a more three dimensional effect.

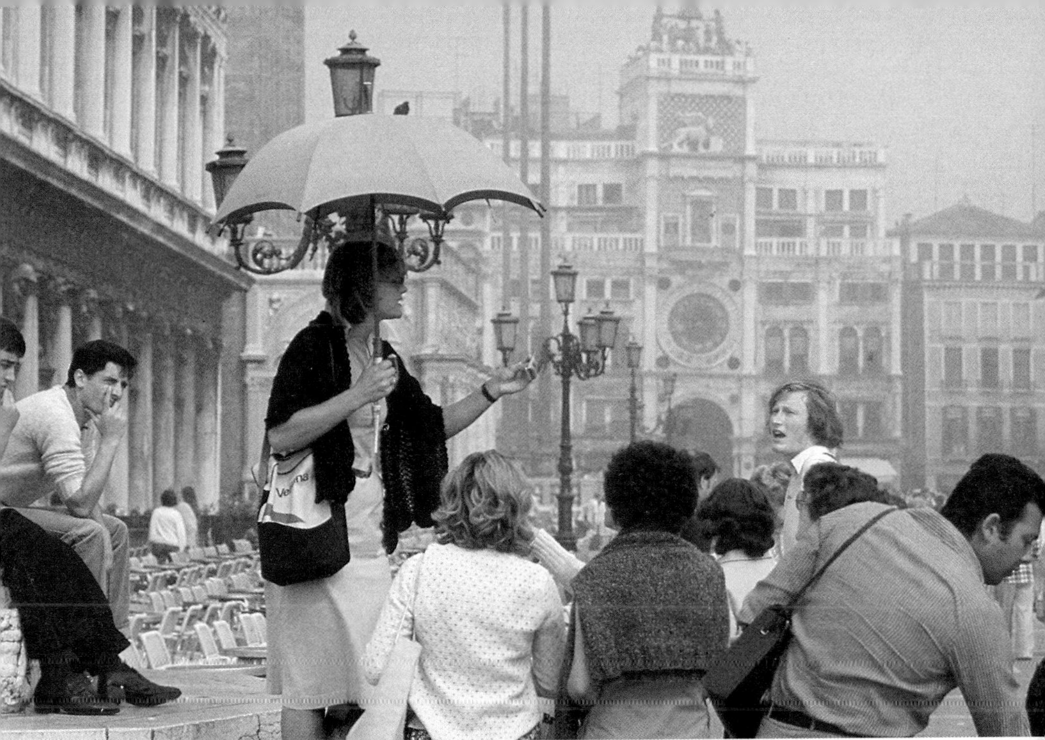

Who has not themselves eavesdropped a little when a charming courier has been telling her group details about the place we are visiting?

SNAPSHOTS

It is not always possible to select your position freely. If there is no chance of standing in the front row of an audience then often the longer focal length lenses will help. A slightly higher position is advantageous in order to achieve a free view for the shot. There is no sense in being thrifty with film. If one considers the total outlay in going on an excursion the film consumption is the smallest expense, ensure that you have enough film with you. It is also advisable to take a supply of highly sensitive film as a reserve in case the lighting conditions should deteriorate. Despite the necessity of filling the format one should not forget that a few overall photographs with a wide angle lens are useful for a general impression.

THE SNAPSHOT TECHNIQUE

Speed is not magic for a good snapshot technique. We should carry the Leica R4 slung round our neck and we should be prepared. It is assumed that the photographer will have set the metering mode that he feels appropriate. The lens should also be set to a average distance setting. With 35 and 50mm lenses in most cases, one can estimate this distance, however with longer focal lengths it is more reliable to set the range precisely. If we wish to obtain the maximum surprise we should focus using the triangle method previously described. It is advisable to use a faster shutter speed and open up the lens in order that subject movement and camera shake are avoided. A snapshot is

135

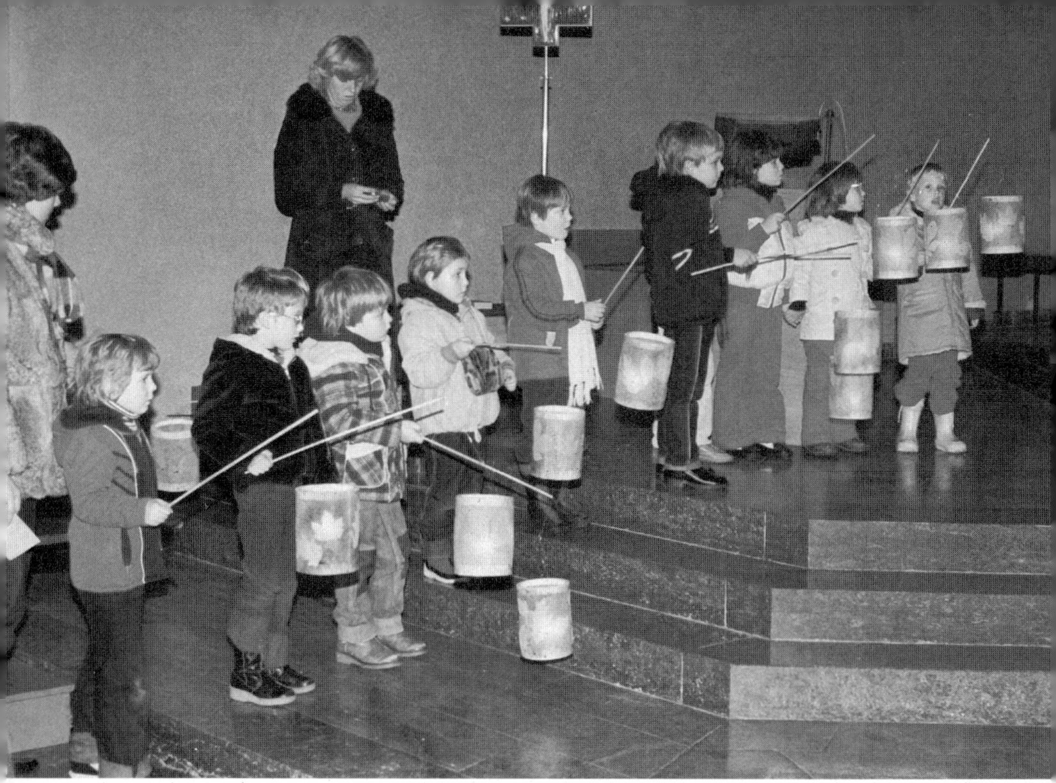

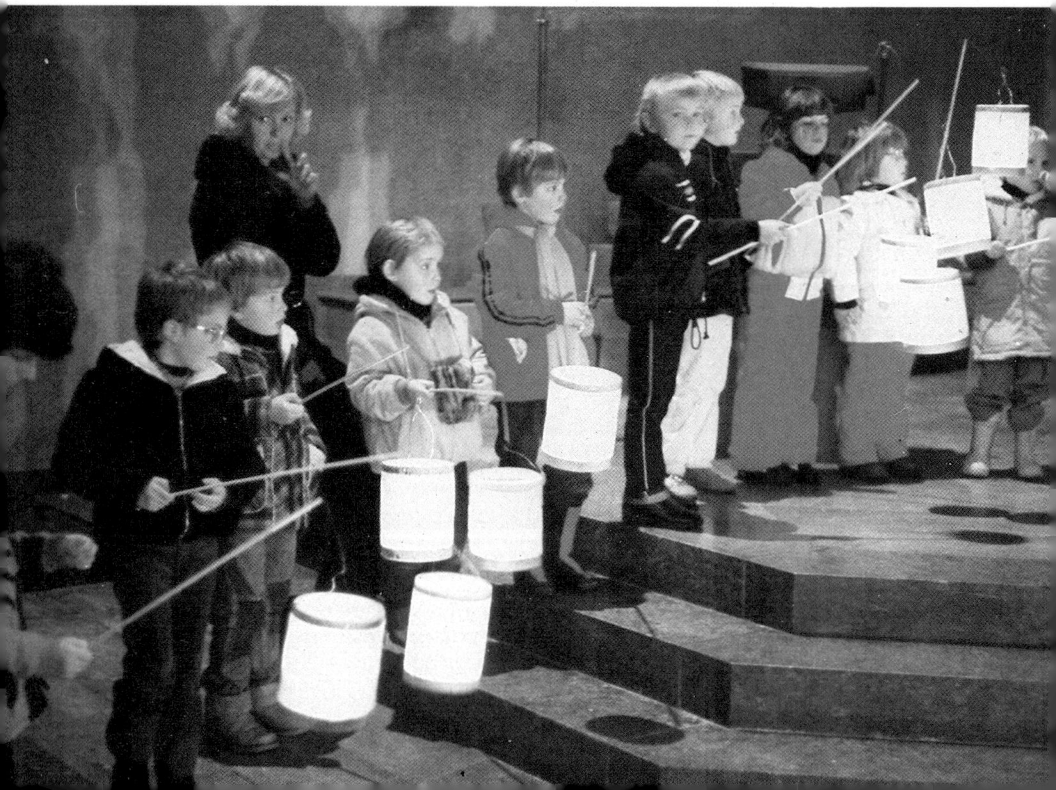

not always concerned with photographs of rapid movements, it is more important that the total situation is typical of the event. People often like to look at snapshots which capture the comedy of a situation. Not only must the Leica R4 be always ready but we too must develop an instinct for times when snapshots are possible. A crowded square affords many opportunities for observing human behaviour, whilst street scenes interest us little at home, we find the hustle and bustle in exotic countries fascinating. Photography is not always looked upon kindly, it is then a question of tact whether we do without the photograph or whether we secretly point the camera and expose.

FLASH LIGHT PHOTOGRAPHY

The effect of other sources of artificial light can be determined beforehand but the length of illumination of a flash bulb is so short that we cannot judge the effect. There are two different types of flash equipment, bulbs which only fire once and electronic flash units which can fire again and again. The type we choose depends on several factors. Those who take very few flash photographs will not be worried by the slightly higher cost of individual flash bulbs. They have the advantage that the equipment needed for firing the flash is much smaller and cheaper. On the other hand those who want to use flash more frequently will be better off with an electronic flash. It is more expensive to buy but then the individual flashes cost very little.

FLASH BULBS

We require a small piece of equipment to fire flash bulbs, this is the flash gun. Newer models are very small and only suitable for flash lamps with glass mounting. With these lamps a glass bulb is used which contains inflammable metal and oxygen. Such a bulb can only be used once since it burns out once and for all. According to the size and manufacture of the bulb there are certain times (on average $1/60$th of a second) between ignition and the full brightness. Flash bulbs are therefore used with a fairly long exposure time (mainly $1/30$th of a second). The brightness of the individual flash bulb is reliably constant. For colour photographs blue tinted flash bulbs are necessary. Flash cubes which each contain four flash bulbs in one unit can be used to take a quick sequence of photographs. After releasing the first flash the cube is turned by 90° and the second flash is then ready to be used. The third and fourth follow in the same way.

ELECTRONIC FLASH EQUIPMENT

While the flash bulb only lights up once, the flash tube is an electronic piece of flash equipment which can be ignited again and again. It is filled with a gas which is made to illuminate electrically by a supply of high voltage current. The illumination time is very short, between $1/500$th and $1/30\,000$th of a second.

These photographs show the difference in atmosphere when flash is used (top picture) or when the lens is used with a large aperture and the longest possible exposure time for hand held photography $1/15$th using available light (bottom picture).

There are various models from small, light amateur equipment up to the heavy professional equipment with correspondingly higher light output and more rapid recharging cycles. The performance of the equipment depends on the capacity of the electrolight condenser to store the electrical energy. Electronic flash equipment takes this energy from a storage battery which can be recharged or from dry batteries. The figures given by the manufacturer for the battery performance is only obtainable under favourable conditions. It is useful to keep a supply of fresh batteries in reserve for important occasions. For the care of accumulators the following is recommended. When they are not being used, turn the equipment on every three to four weeks until the lamp lights up but do not release the flash. After two or three months charge the storage batteries, then check the acid content with lead batteries, if necessary top up with water. Even when we use the equipment we should not release the last flash. Leave it in the condenser but switch off the equipment itself. A particular type of electronic flash equipment works with an automatic flash according to type at certain distance. The flash energy is automatically reduced if we use the flash from shorter distances, the process is as follows. The apparatus has a built in light sensitive sensor. The flash intensity is measured during the flash from its reflection. If there is enough light available it is switched off. The unused energy on the newer models remains in storage for the next flash. Here is a practical example. At a distance of 5m flash equipment is used to its full capacity, the illumination time of the flash is $1/500$th of a second. If we reduce the distance to 2.5m it is not necessary to make any adjustment to the diaphragm of the camera. The flash will automtically but down its output by one quarter by means of adjusting the flash duration to $1/2000$th of a second.

TECHNIQUE FOR TAKING FLASH PHOTOGRAPHS

The majority of flash equipment is built in such a way that we can use it directly on the camera. This is of course very convenient and sufficient for casual photographs. Unfortunately direct frontal lighting leads to a very flat illumination. The decrease in light, that is the light in the foreground is much more intense than on the background, has a very unpleasant effect. In the case of flash photographs of people on colour film the back of the eyes light up red from the effect of the light reflected by the retina.

If we remove the flash unit from the camera we need a connecting cable. We must however be able to hold the camera with the right hand and to press the shutter release. If we have an extension cable 1m in length then we can use flash illumination relatively freely. In normal living rooms it is very effective to reflect the flash off the ceiling. Then we obtain a very diffuse reflection similar to that with normal internal lighting. This however absorbs light which causes a noticeable reduction in the guide number by up to approximately one half, but it has so many advantages that I always recommend it if there is no danger of underexposure. Flash equipment with swing reflectors also allow for indirect flash if they are connected to the camera. If they have a computerised automatic flash then this is fully effective when the built-in sensor is directed to the main subject. Since there are various manufacturers one should follow the maker's instructions.

FLASH AND DAYLIGHT COMBINED

There are many situations in which flash and daylight combined can bring outstanding results. We can brighten up shadows which are too dark or we can brighten the subject under dull conditions. At short distances the flash can be brighter than sunlight. In order to obtain the correct exposure first consider the flash illumination. The additional daylight reading can be obtained from the exposure meter. Since in many cases the shutter time remains fixed, with flash photographs we must take the corresponding brightness value for the daylight into account by stopping down the lens. If we use flash in the open then we lose about half a stop.

GUIDE NUMBER

As a practical measurement for the brightness of the flash the guide number was introduced. The following calculations can be used for its application.
Guide number divided by distance = aperture.
Guide number multiplied by aperture = distance.
The guide number assumes the following; light decreases by the distance squared and the light intensity of the subject reduces by the aperture number square. Since both values alter by the square they can be interchanged. However the usual guide number shows deviation from this because reflected light is calculated. The guide number therefore only gives an average value for photographs in normal rooms and for medium distances where the light is reflected from walls and ceilings. In small and bright rooms the guide number can be somewhat higher. Large rooms with dark walls or photographs taken in the open reduce it. Also with photographs taken at very short distances the guide number is reduced if the proportion of reflected light is low. Guide numbers therefore change and their use is dependant upon the speed of the film. If a particular guide number is given for colour film then it can be used for black and white film of the same sensitivity. The guide number calculation is almost completely unnecessary with a computer flash device, only the film sensitivity needs to be set beforehand.

CLOSE UP PHOTOGRAPHS

It is not just the big things that are exciting. Normally one does not come across the new impressions, which tend to happen on world tours. However it is possible to go on a captivating voyage of discovery without leaving an area of a few square metres. With a magnifying glass in our hands we can enter a completely new photographic area, 'the close-up'. Precisely where this begins is not clear. Many miniature cameras can only be focused down to 1m with a standard lens, everything closer counts as a close-up. Since we can photograph the same subject field with several focal lengths and from different distances, it is not always the distance of the photograph but the scale of the image which is important. What is the scale of the image? Our format is 24 x 36mm, the subject is 120 x 180mm which is calculated as 1:5, that is reduced to $^1/_5$th of its original size. The proportion of the image is 1:5 also written as $^1/_5$th = 0.2. The decimal figure has the advantage that it makes it easier to calculate the increased exposure time required. If 5:1 is given this means that

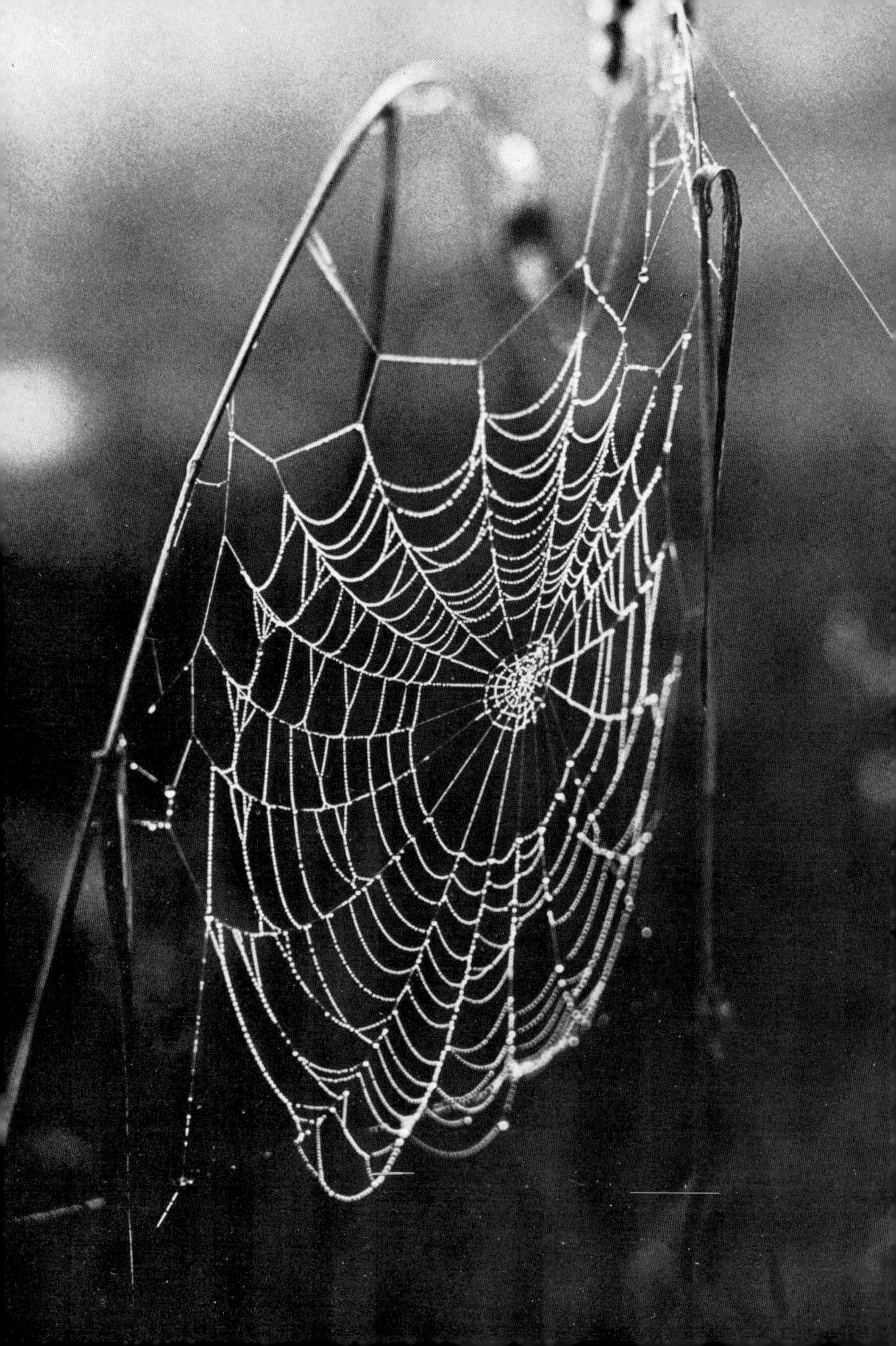

the subject was photographed 5 times less than its original size, it is 4.8 x 7.2mm large. The proportion of the image is therefore the relative size on our film because it is from this that the increased exposure factor is calculated. These factors however only play a role if we use a simple exposure meter. With the Leica R4 all factors are automatically catered for by the metering system.

How do we achieve sharp reproduction in the close up area? We focus our lens and set it at 2m. This is not a particularly exaggerated close-up. To do this we have had to extend the lens. Therefore the question now is how much do we have to extend the lens to achieve real close-ups. Generally speaking it corresponds to the proportion of the image. If we go back to the previous example, with a scale of 1:5 the extension is $^1/_5$th of the focal length. Used with a 100mm lens an extension of 20mm is necessary and on a 50mm lens 10mm. The Macro-Elmar-R 100mm has a focusing movement of 30mm and so no additional part is necessary in order to focus the photograph. On the other hand the Summicron 50mm has a focusing movement of only 5mm. The 5mm which is lacking can be added by means of an additional intermediary ring but this would be difficult. A different solution is used, by additional optics it is possible to obtain a sharp reproduction in the close up area. The Elpro close-up attachments alter the optical powers of refraction in such a way that it even produces a better reproductive performance than when an extension of the lens only is used.

How large is the depth of field? If we look at a focusing table then we can immediately establish that depth of field decreases more and more in the close-up area. With a scale of 1:10 and an aperture of f/8 we have about 60mm depth of field, with the same aperture but a scale of 1:1 we have a depth of field of about 1mm. These values are obtained from the table and they are calculated to give a circle of confusion of $^1/_{30}$th of a millimetre. In practice one should not be put off from taking photographs even when according to the table it is doubtful if the depth of field is adequate. However in most cases we will operate with small aperture diaphragms f/8, f/11 or even f/16 are usually employed. Exposure metering for close-ups are made in the same way as for normal photographs with the Leica R4. Selective metering is recommended, since the measuring area is small there are no difficulties in finding an appropriate position. On a few close-up devices metering must be carried out at the working aperture, further instructions come with each piece of equipment. The increased exposure factors which result from extreme close-ups are automatically catered for by the R4. If the intensity of illumination with a stopped down lens is not adequate then it is possible to meter with an open aperture and convert this to the working setting.

OPPOSITE
The wonderful construction of a spiders web can only be photographed successfully if it is against a black background. Because the threads are so fine it is best to photograph in the early morning when there is a dew on the web. A longer focal length will help to throw the background out of focus. Photograph: Günter Kisselbach.

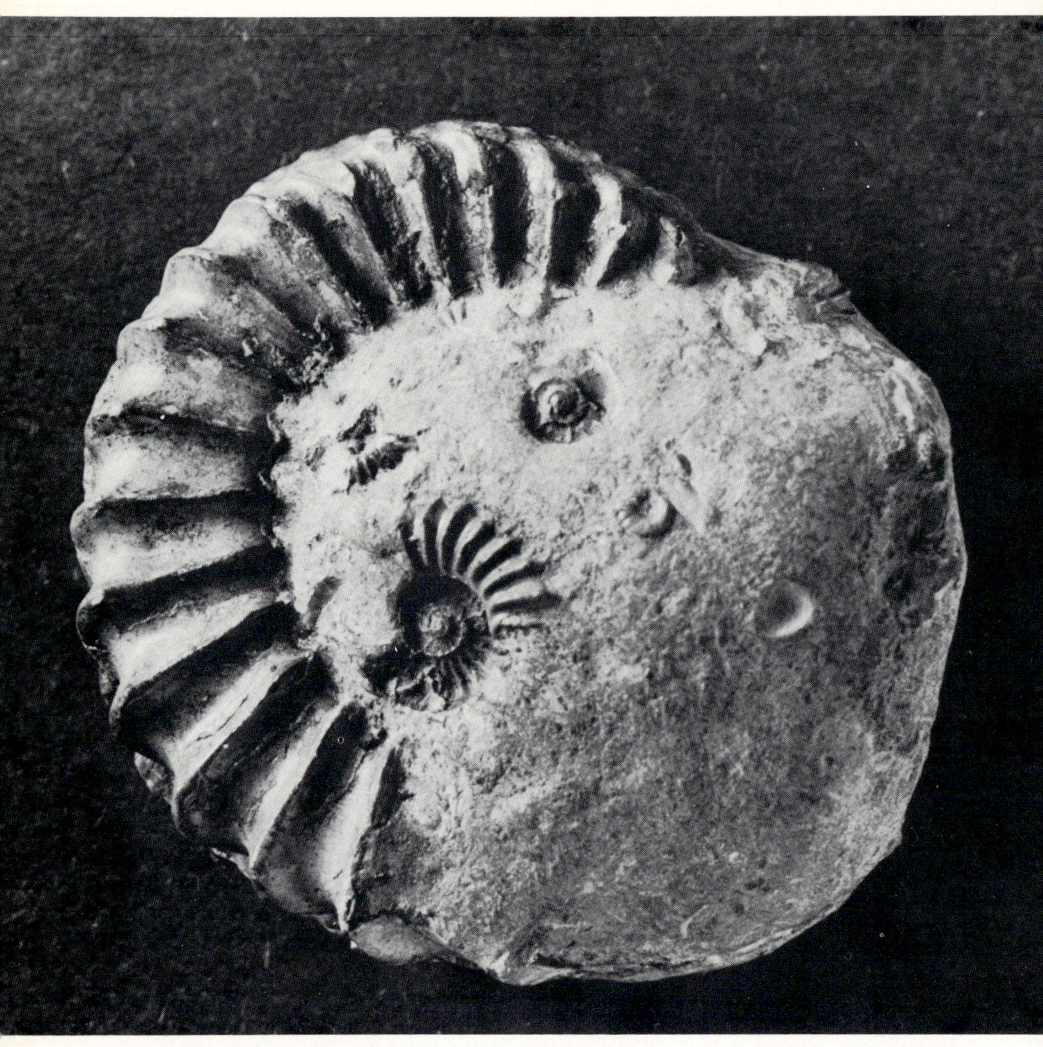

Ammonite (Arietities) from the Liocene period, approximately 190 million years old. Reduction on the negative 1:3, positive enlargement x6. Enlargement x2 on the page.

ILLUMINATION

With smaller subjects the illumination technique has a decisive role to play. The general illumination should be mixed with direct light if possible in a similar way to that in which sunlight is combined with general illumination from the sky. the rays of light from a small picture projector are particularly suitable. We can direct this light by attaching a mirror in such a way in front of its lens with a piece of wire so that we can point the light in the right direction. Never illuminate too harshly but always balance it out with an appropriate deflector or diffusion screen. Always check the effect of the light with one eye.

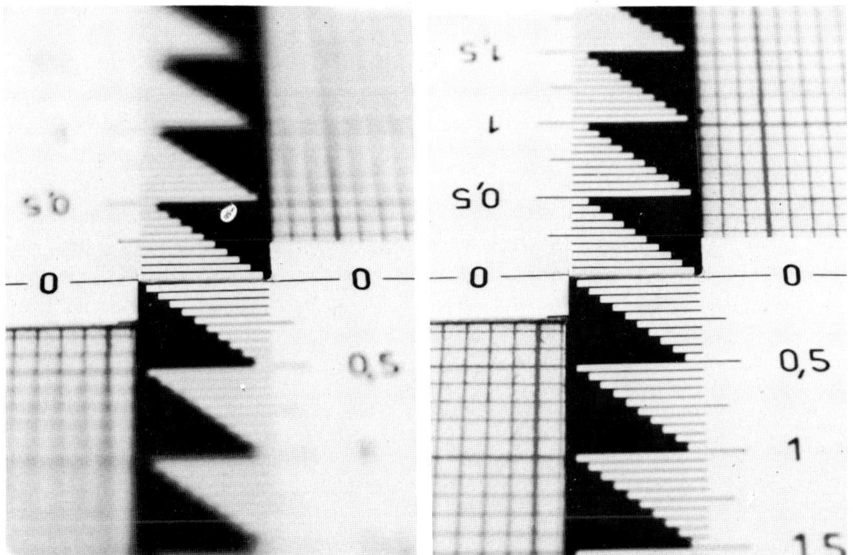

Photographs in order to make the increase of depth of field clear when stopping down in the close up field. On the left f/4 on the right f/16. Scale 1:1. The photograph shows 1mm graph paper which was photographed at an angle of 45°, showing the sharp middle area. Every millimeter on a diagonal corresponds to a difference of 0.7mm 10mm in the photograph corresponding to a depth of field of 7mm. In practice depth of focus in the close-up field is larger than that shown in the table.

Full sunlight is often too rich in contrast for close-up photographs. Whether the contrast is reduced by means of reflector screens or made softer by diffusion screens depends on the circumstances. Mirrors and tinfoil provide even more reflection than light boxes at short distances. For against the light photographs it is possible to look through an opening in a white box. The aid of a tripod can scarcely be dispensed with for close-up work. Only in this way can the picture be positioned down to the last millimeter.

FLASH LIGHTS IN THE CLOSE-UP FIELD

For electronic flash the useful synchronisation time of $1/100$th of a second on the Leica R4 is very handy. It is however completely up to us if we want to increase the proportion of daylight by synchronising at $1/30$th of a second. The intensity of flash light in the close-up area is excessive even on a low powered unit, being greater than the power of the sun. Therefore it is possible to take photographs with small apertures in order that the maximum depth of field can be utilised. By taking a series of experimental pictures it is possible to get an idea of the exposure factors. If developing at home then a black and white film can be used. If you know how its exposure values correspond to those of the colour film which would normally be used. Otherwise it is easier to do the test straight away with colour reversal film. The test is carried out in such a way that a subject of medium brightness is constructed at a distance of 70cm in front of the flash lamp. The reflector screen should stand in such a way that the path of the flash light via the reflector to the subject is about 1m. The smallest aperture should be selected. If the guide number is 22 then we begin with a guide number of 22 and we open up by half an aperture for each photograph until we have reached f/11. The intensity of the flash will be doubled if we reduce the distance between the flash lamp and the subject to 50cm on the other hand it will be halved if we increase the distance to 2m. The flash is not used directly on the R4 but slightly to the side and above, as can be seen from the sketch below.

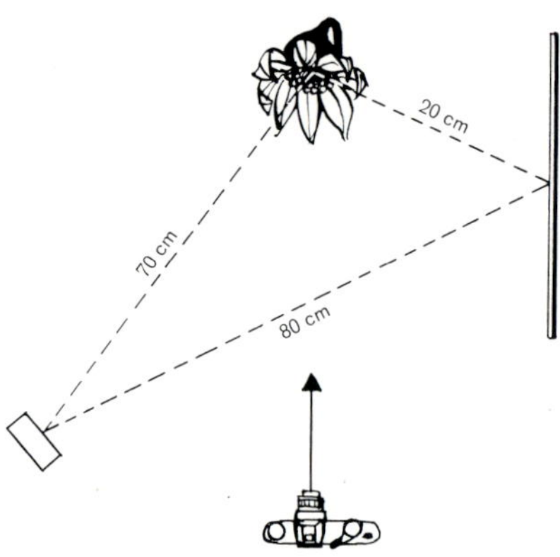

The guide number provided by the manufacturer is not accurate in the close-up field. Aperture and distance can be determined by means of the test series described above.

The use of the reflecting screen means that there is no danger that the contrast will be too high and the plasticity of the picture is much better. The increased exposure factors on close-up photographs are not taken into account when flash light is used. The following table gives a point of reference in case lengthening factors play a role.

Scale	1:5	1:4	1:2.5	1:2	1:1.4	1:1	2:1	3:1
Increased exposure factor	1.5	1.6	2	2.3	3	4	9	16

It is not easy to determine the correct aperture for the best exposure time if daylight is combined with flash light. With close-ups the flash will always provide the main light source, the daylight has only a lightening effect. The aperture is determined according to the guide number and then one should consider how much the aperture should be opened up if the reflection of the surroundings is slight, or whether the aperture should be closed down because of the brightness of the sun.

REPRODUCTIONS

If writing and pictures are to be reproduced at the same time then work according to the half tone method. Normally such photographs are taken with a simple copying stand. The Leitz Repro stand saves a great deal of time and is more precise. It has a base board of 46 x 50cm and a column with guide rails 80cm high. The camera arm has a clamp for rough adjustments and a large turning button for fine adjustments. The Leica R4 can be arranged so that it is precisely perpendicular. If we want to photograph from above the best focal length depends on the size of the subject. From a distance of 80cm with the Summicron 50mm f/2 an area 32 x 48cm can be reproduced. For smaller subjects the Macro Elmarit 60mm f/2.8 can be used. The next requirement is even illumination With artificial light use identical lights on the left and right. The distance of the light should not be too small so that the angle of illumination of the light is not steeper than 45°. If the illumination is made steeper then the shadows can become a problem. In daylight it is possible to work close to a window, keep a distance of between 1 to 1¹/₂m according to the height of the windows so that reflections can be avoided. The reduction of light from one side to the other side of a subject can be balanced out by using a white sheet some distance away from the subject on the side away from the window, this will reflect the light. The subject should be arranged in such a way that in books the slight curve of the page does not produce any shadows. When measuring the exposure pay attention to the various measuring angles of the Leica R4 programmes in order to obtain the correct exposure time. Do not meter the subject itself but a white surface. The value obtained is then still not the exposure time but it must be corrected according to the brightness of the subject. This appears to be rather involved to begin with but it has the advantage that we obtain precise values. This is because the exact exposure time is dependant upon the reproduction of the white above all. It is unimportant whether the proportion of black lines is large or small. Exposure meters react to the relationship between brightness and darkness as an average value. The exposure which is measured on white paper is doubled for linear reproductions and tripled for half tone reproductions. It is not unusual to make exposure corrections with the lens stop since for most purposes an aperture of f/11 is most convenient. Some of the most difficult subjects are dark shining objects such as pictures under glass or oil paintings. These subjects can prove difficult because of reflections. With smaller subjects it can be helpful to photograph through a hole in a black box. If coloured subjects are to be reproduced on black and white film then the colour sensitivity of the film and the colour of the filter play an important part. Less sensitive black and white films are used for half tone reproductions and they are usually panchromatic. Document films are particularly important in the reproductive field. They are specially designed for reproducing the finest of lines and therefore they have a high resolution capacity. Since they have a steep tonal gradation they should be developed with great care (further information can be found in Kisselbach 'The Darkroom Handbook'). According to the method of development they can be adapted for use for either line or half tone photographs. The exposure range is very small and it is

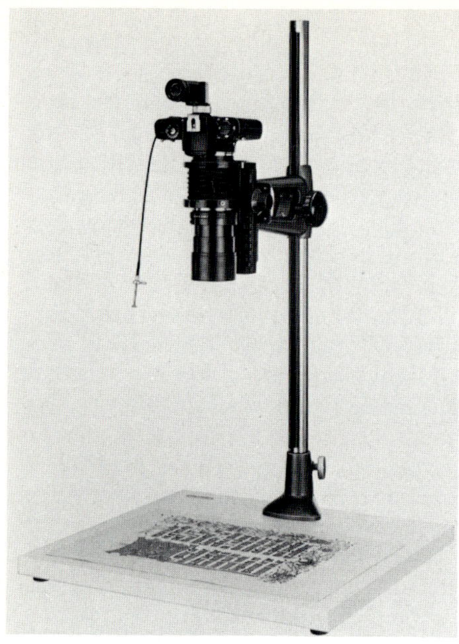

absolutely necessary to begin with to experiment by means of a test with graded exposure times to obtain the correct exposure.

When reproducing coloured subjects one must consider whether daylight or artificial light film should be used. In most cases there will be a daylight colour film in the camera, direct sunlight or diffused light is suitable for this. According to the angle of illumination there can be reflections therefore the document should not be laid on the floor but should be attached to something vertically so that the edges run parallel. The camera should be at right angles and the lens must be central in relation to the middle of the document. The exposure time is again measured with white paper. The lengthening factor for photographs in the open air is 4x and with dark subjects 5x. Electronic flash is also suitable and after a certain amount of practise is equally useful as a source of light. Its guide number for the close-up area must be tested, but for reproduction two sources of light are better as this ensures eveness. With flash this can be achieved by illumination from the left and then from the right

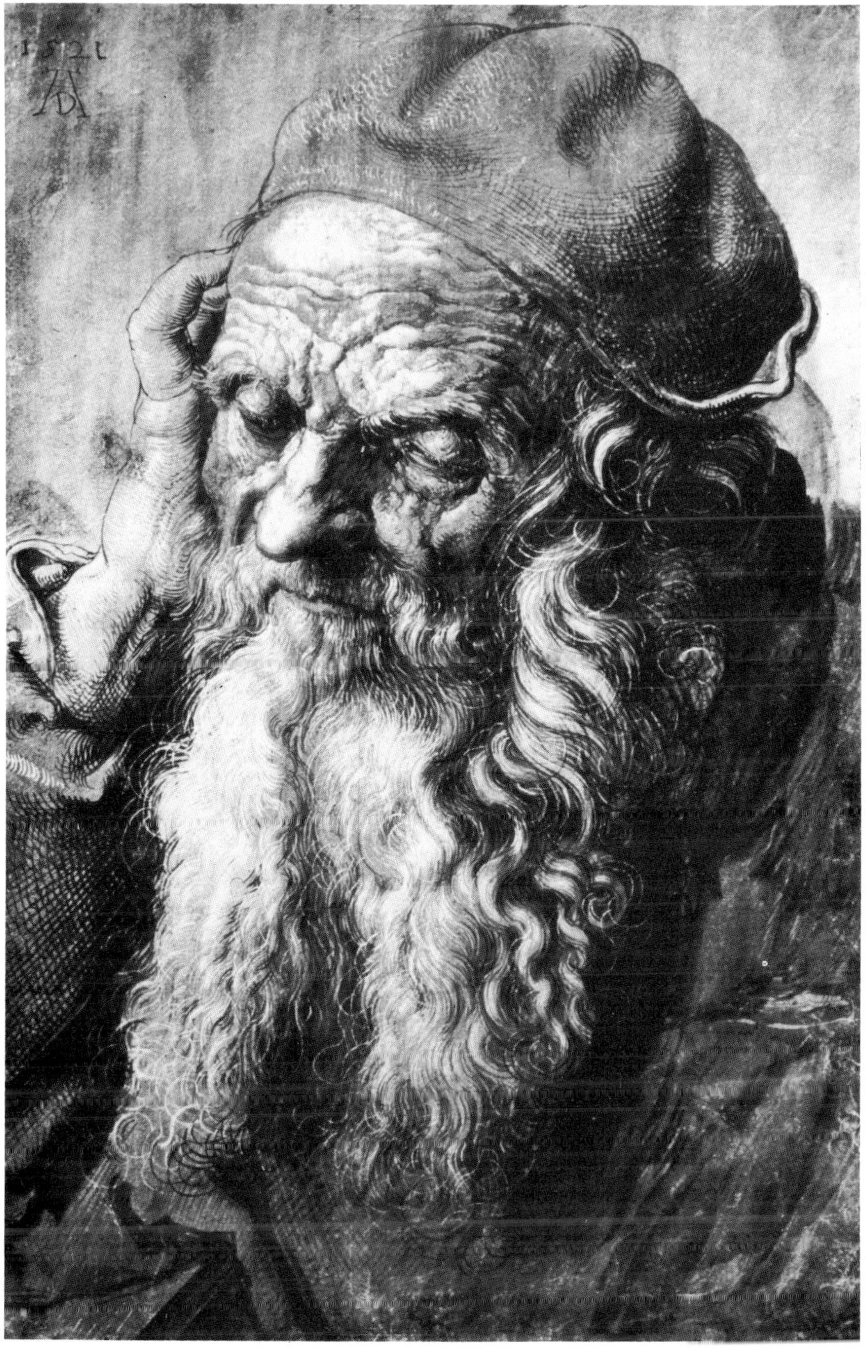

consecutively. Of course two flash units are more convenient giving simultaneous illumination from the synchronised contact of the R4. The first method it will be necessary to set the camera shutter in a nearly completely blacked out room and fire the flash by hand. Beware! The method of using the flash on the camera cannot be used because of the danger of reflection.

PHOTOGRAPHIC DOCUMENTATION

In this book we have often talked about practice photographs which will increase our photographic capabilities in the most varied areas. A really useful series would be a photographic documentation or record of the valuable items in our household. A collection of carpets, pictures, antiques or other interesting valuables. If these items were stolen, lost or destroyed by fire it is often difficult for those involved to describe the objects precisely or to prove their existence. By means of good photographs you can aid the police and simplify insurance documentation. The knowledge which we will gain in taking these photographs can be used on journeys. If for example we want to take photographs in museums the experience gained will come in very useful.

PHOTOGRAPHING INTERIORS

In many cases we need a wide angle lens, distance is limited because of the size of the room. A stable tripod is another necessity for then we can establish our position in peace and take time exposures under the normal illumination of the room. Since we meter through the lens the low lighting level will not always allow the correct exposure to be indicated. In these conditions we

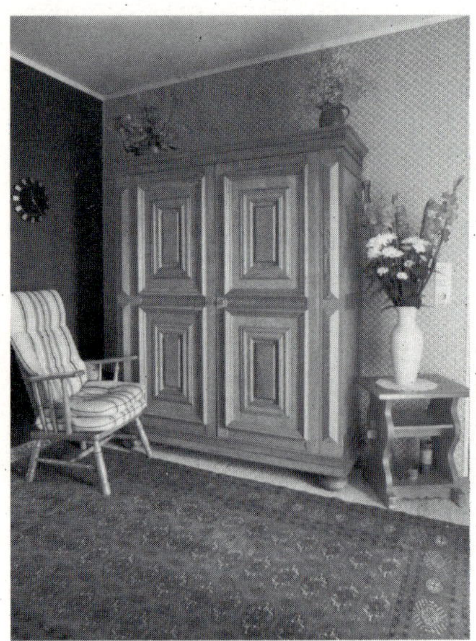
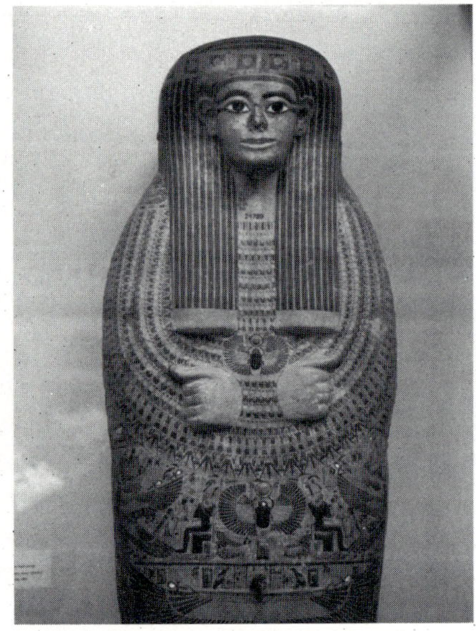

Photographs in museums are often permitted and the tips contained within the text of this book should be noted.

should meter with the lens wide open, and calculate the value for the working aperture. At f/11 the exposure is 16x longer than f/2.8. If times of several seconds are produced then because of reciprocity we must expose for double or even treble the time. First of all we look at the piece of furniture to be photographed from all angles in order to decide on its characteristic features. The standpoint from which we take the photograph is decisive. The back of the camera must be vertical otherwise we will obtain converging verticals. Since we are using artificial light the subject can be illuminated from the side by a second person holding a hand light (100 to 200 watts). With longer exposure times it is a good idea to move the light so that the effect is softened and more balanced. The light of this lamp must not fall directly onto the lens otherwise flare will result. If we have inadequate daylight illumination then we can lighten this additionally with flash light. With time exposures it is possible to use flash without it being connected to the camera, for example to illuminate a bright wall or a white ceiling by using the hand release on the flash while the camera shutter is open. Highly sensitive films shorten the exposure time and this can be very important with museum photographs because we are taking the photographs hand held. With a tripod this does not matter and the longer exposure times of a medium sensitive film is no hinderance. Paintings are more difficult to photograph as their surfaces may cause obstrusive reflections. Pictures under glass are the most difficult. Here the reflections disappear if a large dark surface is ranged opposite the picture made up of black cloth. This cloth should be larger than the painting. If an opening is to be made in the middle for the lens then the screen can be made of two cloths overlapping slightly and leaving room for the lens. For important photographs on colour negative film photograph a colour scale together with the picture. This can be sent to the copying firm in order to make their colour control easier.

PROJECTION

There are a large number of Leica enthusiasts who take photographs in colour on colour reversal film. Not only is this cheaper, but by projection we can obtain the most impressive reproduction of pictures. All the fine shades of colour can be produced without loss as a positive slide. They can display a larger range of brightnesses than a print, for the positive slide has light passed through it. The size is influential on the plasticity of the picture. Our eyes have a stronger effect if the picture is larger. The distance from which it is seen also plays a role. A picture of 1 x 1.5m on the screen has a completely different effect to the 9 x 13cm print in the family. What is shown is important. It is not the quantity of the pictures but a well arranged selection which creates the effect. If we want to show them to a large audience everything should be well prepared. Our show must be well organised. Of course it is much easier to speak in conjunction with slides, because one picture follows another we can see our cues on the screen. The number of pictures should not exceed the receptive capacity of the audience. Quality is better than quantity. The more pictures we show the less time we have to explain them. We must not speak without stopping, many pictures require a period of silence to create their effect. By using a magazine unit slides once arranged are immediately ready for a show, they also remain free of finger prints since they are not handled for projection. Those who want to have a particularly effective show will arrange taped slide shows of their journeys or other themes. There are control devices which can make an appropriate change of picture automatically. Sound can be provided by means of a tape recorder. Those who wish can even use the fade over technique which no longer causes technical difficulties. By fading over, a harmonious transition from one picture to another is achieved. By using two projectors the first picture disappears whilst the other one appears. The fluid transition can be quick or slow. All the necessary equipment for this can be obtained from Leitz, who have a strong tradition and great experience in this field. Leitz projectors are known the world over because of their brightness, their optical quality and the comfort afforded to the projectionist. There is a large selection. All equipment for projection is called Pradovit. Additional letters or numbers denote the different models.

THE PRADOVIT PROJECTORS

The Pradovit C is a top quality model with a slide change of $^1/_5$th of a second. There are no ugly dark phases between pictures. The Pradovit R is the simple model with a slide change taking 1.4 seconds. All models with automatic focusing have the letter 'A' designated. The following numbers give information about performance. All Pradovit R models have 24 volt 150 watt bulbs. the pradovit C (250 watts) comes without autofocus all other models have autofocus. There are special models with built in facilities for plugging in connections for the various fade-over control devices. The 24 volt/250 watt Halogen lamp is about 40° brighter than the 150 watt lamp. This increase in brightness is only noticeable over a certain picture size (2m and larger) or with an inadequate black out.

Lenses are obtainable with focal lengths from 35mm to 300mm. For home projectors 90mm lenses are normal. Since vertical and horizontal formats are used for the photographs the projector screen should be square. The picture surface on slides is 23 x 35mm. With the Pradovit C or CA projectors the short focal lengths produce a very interesting projection of square format photographs. A good projection surface of at least 2 x 3m is needed for this. Projection is carried out from a distance of 4.5m with a 50mm lerns (3m with a 35mm lens). Slides which are not too dense and a good blackout are needed for the best results. With landscape photographs one has the feeling that one is standing in the middle of the picture. So that the magazine unit does not cross the rays of light under projection it should only be filled with 36 slides when a 50mm lens is being used (30 with a 35mm lens).

Prado Universal. With this projector the slide changes are carried out in the old way by means of a manual change. Picture strips of 24 x 36mm can also be projected with a special attachment. It is equipped with a Halogen bulb of 24 volts/250 watts. It can be fitted with projection lenses from 35 to 300mm. It is built by modular construction and can be converted with a few alterations and the appropriate parts to take slides of 5 x 5cm, 6 x 6cm and 7 x 7cm. It is at the top of its class in its high level of brightness. It is suitable for large lecture halls and its versatility ensures its suitability for schools and universities.

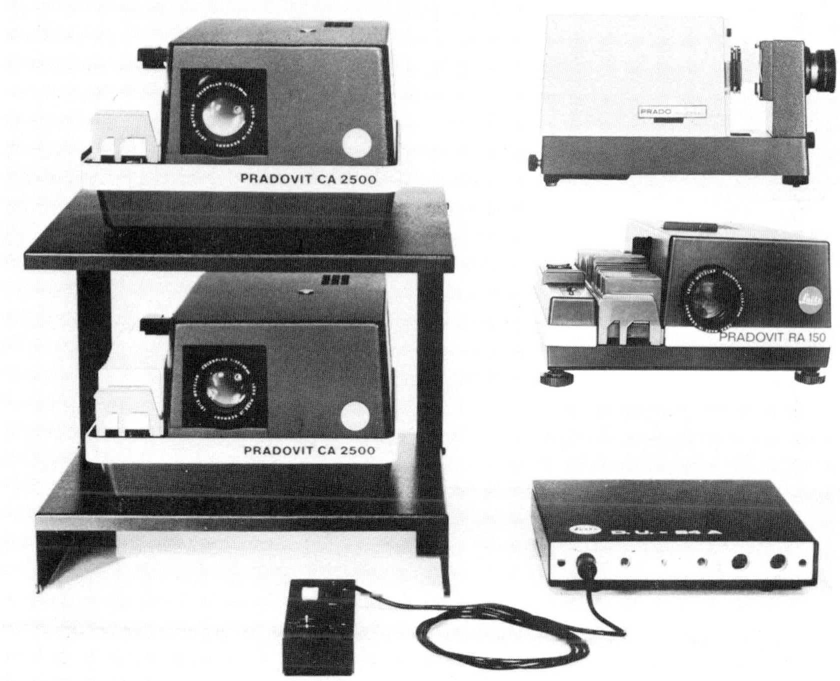

The Pradovit CA 2,500 with the control device for auto fade projection. Pradovit R 150, Prado Universal.

THE AUTOFOCUS

This allows the Pradovit projectors to automatically adjust the focus. Normal lenses cannot balance out the curve of unglazed slides, this is only possible with a new Colour Plan CF, the CF standing for 'Curved field'. The 90mm model is already available and other focal lengths are in preparation.

THE INTERNATIONAL LEICA PASS

With the Leica R4 every purchaser receives an international Leica Pass. The booklet is postcard size (A6) and has 18 pages. It is useful for many purposes. All important information such as camera and lens numbers can be preserved. This can be important for journeys abroad and for insurance documentation. In addition the pamphlet gives information about the rules of the International Leitz Guarantee and Leitz representatives in Germany and abroad. Your name and address should be written on page 15 in large letters. The first frame of every film should be of this page taken from a short distance (50cm) then one is indisputably recognised as the owner in case the envelope or package containing the film is damaged in the post. The laboratory or post office can then establish without any difficulty to whom

151

the film belongs. A detachable answering card between pages 6 and 7 addressed to the Leitz Information Service assures the Leica owner that he will be regularly informed about Leitz products.

CUSTOMER SERVICE

If repairs are necessary then Leitz equipment should only be dealt with by authorised contract repair shops. Abroad these can be discovered from the relative representative or direct from Leitz at E. Leitz GMBH, Technical Service, Post Box 2027, D 6330 Wetzlar. The Leitz information service is a special source of information on Leicas. It can be reached by telephone (06441) 292436 Monday-Friday 08.00 to 12.00 and 13.00 to 16.00. Written enquiries to Leitz Information Service, Post Box 2020, D 6330 Wetzlar. Telex 0483849. Telegrams Leitz Wetzlar.

Developing and enlarging were not discussed in this book. My own 'Darkroom Handbook' discusses black and white techniques and Rudolph Seck in his book 'Home Laboratory Practice in Colour' discusses the developing and enlarging in the colour sector. Both books are published by Heering Verlag, Munich.